Walling, Boundaries an

Contemporary challenges related to walls, borders and encirclement, such as migration, integration and endemic historical conflicts, can only be understood properly from a long-term perspective. This book seeks to go beyond conventional definitions of the *longue durée* by locating the social practice of walling and encirclement in the broadest context of human history, integrating insights from archaeology and anthropology. Such an approach, far from being simply academic, has crucial contemporary relevance, as its focus on origins helps to locate the essential dynamics of this practice, and provides a rare external position from which to view the phenomenon as a transformative exercise, with the area walled serving as an artificial womb or matrix. The modern world, with its ingrained ideas of borders, nation states and other entities, often makes it is very difficult to gain a critical distance and detachment to see beyond conventional perspectives. The unique approach of this book offers an antidote to this problem. Cases discussed in the book range from Palaeolithic caves, the ancient walls of Göbekli Tepe, Jericho and Babylon, to the foundation of Rome, the Chinese Empire, medieval Europe and the Berlin Wall. The book also looks at contemporary developments such as the Palestinian wall, Eastern and Southern European examples, Trump's proposed Mexican wall, the use of Greece as a bulwark containing migration flows and the transformative experience of voluntary work in a Calcutta hospice. In doing so, the book offers a political anthropology of one of the most fundamental yet perennially problematic human practices: the constructing of walls. As such, it will appeal to scholars of sociology, anthropology and political theory.

Agnes Horvath is a political theorist and sociologist. She was an affiliate visiting scholar at Cambridge University, UK, 2011 to 2014, and is a Visiting Research Fellow at University College Cork, Ireland. She is a founding editor of the academic journal *International Political Anthropology*.

Marius Ion Benţa is a sociologist, journalist and playwright. He received his PhD from University College Cork, Ireland, and teaches Broadcasting Journalism at the Babeş-Bolyai University in Cluj, Romania.

Joan Davison is Professor of Political Science and a Cornell Distinguished Faculty Member at Rollins College, USA. She has a PhD from the University of Notre Dame and specialises in international relations and comparative politics.

Contemporary Liminality

Series editors:
Arpad Szakolczai, University College Cork, Ireland

Series advisory board:
Agnes Horvath, University College Cork, Ireland
Bjørn Thomassen, Roskilde University, Denmark
Harald Wydra, University of Cambridge, UK

This series constitutes a forum for works that make use of concepts such as 'imitation', 'trickster' or 'schismogenesis', but that chiefly deploy the notion of 'liminality', as the basis of a new, anthropologically focused paradigm in social theory. With its versatility and range of possible uses rivalling and even going beyond mainstream concepts such as 'system', 'structure' or 'institution', liminality is increasingly considered a new master concept that promises to spark a renewal in social thought.

In spite of the fact that charges of Eurocentrism or even 'moderno-centrism' are widely discussed in sociology and anthropology, it remains the case that most theoretical tools in the social sciences continue to rely on taken-for-granted approaches developed from within the modern Western intellectual tradition, whilst concepts developed on the basis of extensive anthropological evidence and which challenged commonplaces of modernist thinking have been either marginalised and ignored, or trivialised. By challenging the assumed neo-Kantian and neo-Hegelian foundations of modern social theory, and by helping to shed new light on the fundamental ideas of major figures in social theory, such as Nietzsche, Dilthey, Weber, Elias, Voegelin, Foucault and Koselleck, whilst also establishing connections between the perspectives gained through modern social and cultural anthropology and the central concerns of classical philosophical anthropology, *Contemporary Liminality* offers a new direction in social thought.

Titles in this series

7. Walling, Boundaries and Liminality
A Political Anthropology of Transformations
Agnes Horvath, Marius Ion Benţa and Joan Davison

8. The Spectacle of Critique
From Philosophy to Cacophony
Tom Boland

For more information about this series, please visit: www.routledge.com/sociology/series/ASHSER1435

Walling, Boundaries and Liminality

A Political Anthropology of
Transformations

**Edited by Agnes Horvath,
Marius Ion Benţa and
Joan Davison**

Routledge
Taylor & Francis Group

LONDON AND NEW YORK

First published 2019
by Routledge

2 Park Square, Milton Park, Abingdon, Oxfordshire OX14 4RN
52 Vanderbilt Avenue, New York, NY 10017

Routledge is an imprint of the Taylor & Francis Group, an informa business

First issued in paperback 2019

British Library Cataloguing-in-Publication Data
A catalogue record for this book is available from the British Library

Library of Congress Cataloging-in-Publication Data
A catalog record has been requested for this book

ISBN: 978-1-138-09641-7 (hbk)
ISBN: 978-0-367-47905-3 (pbk)

Typeset in Times New Roman
by Keystroke, Neville Lodge, Tettenhall, Wolverhampton

This book is dedicated with gratitude and great affection to Sister Amelia and Sister Livia, from Casa Lazzaro, Acquapendente – a small town in the Italian region of Lazio – who have helped us see walling as perversity of thinking.

Contents

Figures

Notes on contributors

Agnes Horvath is a political theorist and sociologist. She was an affiliate visiting scholar at Cambridge University, UK, from 2011 to 2014 and is now a Visiting Research Fellow at University College Cork, Ireland. She has a PhD in social and political sciences from the European University Institute in Florence. She is a founding editor of the academic journal *International Political Anthropology*. Her publications include *Walking into the Void: A Historical Sociology and Political Anthropology of Walking* (with Arpad Szakolczai, Routledge, 2018), *Breaking Boundaries: Varieties of Liminality* (co-edited with Bjørn Thomassen and Harald Wydra, Berghahn, 2015) and *Modernism and Charisma* (Palgrave, 2013). She also co-edited a special section on 'Plato and Eros' for *History of Human Sciences* (2013) and a special issue on 'The Political Anthropology of Ethnic and Religious Minorities' for *Nationalism and Ethnic Politics* (2017).

Marius Ion Benţa is a sociologist, journalist and playwright. He received his PhD from University College Cork, Ireland, is a Research Fellow at the George Bariţiu History Institute and teaches Broadcasting Journalism at the Babeş-Bolyai University in Cluj, Romania. He has worked for several major broadcasting channels in Romania, such as Digi24 TV and BBC World Service. His publications include a book of drama, two books of interviews and the article 'Fluid Identity, Fluid Citizenship: the Problem of Ethnicity in Post-Communist Romania' in Arpad Szakolczai, Agnes Horvath and Atilla Z. Papp (eds), *Nationalism and Ethnic Politics* (Routledge, 2017), and is about to publish his research monograph *Experiencing Multiple Realities: Alfred Schutz's Sociology of the Finite Provinces of Meaning* (Routledge).

Joan Davison is Professor of Political Science and a Cornell Distinguished Faculty Member at Rollins College, USA, and specialises in international relations and comparative politics. Her research currently focuses upon ethno-religious identity and politics in Bosnia and Herzegovina. Recent publications include 'Sarajevo Heart of Europe? Global Politics, Symbol(ism) & Liminality in the Centenary of WWI' (with Jesenko Tešan), *International Political Anthropology* (2014), 'The Left's Attraction amidst Bosnia and Herzegovina's Nationalist Politics', in João Cardoso Rosas and Ana Rita Ferreira (eds), *Left and Right:*

The Great Dichotomy Revisited (Cambridge Scholars Publishing, 2013), and 'What Matters to Social Democratic Party Voters? Liberal and Economic Interests Trump Ethnoreligious Identity in Bosnia Hercegovina', *Civis* (2013).

Glenn Bowman is Emeritus Professor of Socio-Historical Anthropology in the School of Politics and International Relations at the University of Kent, UK. He studied at the Institute of Social Anthropology at Oxford University, doing his DPhil fieldwork on Jerusalem pilgrimage and spending an intense couple of years living in Jerusalem's Old City (1983–5) before returning to the UK to teach at University College London and the University of Kent. Recent publications, grounded in continuing work in the Palestinian West Bank as well as (now) Former Yugoslavia, include *Sharing the Sacra: the Politics and Pragmatics of Intercommunal Relations around Holy Places* (edited, Berghahn, 2012), 'Violence before Identity: an Analysis of Identity Politics' in Jane Kilby and Larry Ray (eds), *Violence and Society: Toward a New Sociology* (Wiley-Blackwell, 2014), 'Sharing and Exclusion: the Case of Rachel's Tomb', *Jerusalem Quarterly* (2014) and 'Viewing the Holy City: An Anthropological Perspectivalism', in Madelaine Adelman and Miriam Fendius Elman (eds), *Jerusalem: Conflict and Cooperation in a Contested City* (Syracuse University Press, 2014).

Arvydas Grišinas received his PhD in politics from the University of Kent, UK. He is the author of *Politics with a Human Face* (Routledge, 2018), a researcher at Kaunas University of Technology, Lithuania, and a post-doctoral associate at Yale University, USA. His academic interests lie in post-Soviet political culture, political anthropology and cultural sociology.

Manussos Marangudakis is Professor of Comparative Sociology at the Department of Sociology, University of the Aegean, Greece. He has written extensively on the social construction of nature, religion and civilisation, and the religious roots of civil society. He was a Fulbright Scholarship holder and a Visiting Professor at Yale University, USA. His articles have been published in *Sociological Spectrum*, *European Journal of Sociology*, *Protosociology* and *Zygon*, while he has published a monograph on American fundamentalism and its pseudo-sciences. Currently, he is working on the cultural interpretation of the Greek crisis.

Egor Novikov is a postdoctoral student at Central European University, Budapest, Hungary, having majored in philosophy at Saint Petersburg State University, Russia. For over ten years he has worked as an artist using various media from metal cast sculpture to oil painting. While carrying out field research, he has applied his artistic skills to produce drawn and photographic visuals.

Erik Ringmar graduated with a PhD in political science from Yale University, USA, in 1993 and taught for 12 years in the Government Department at the London School of Economics and Political Science, UK. He worked as Professor of International Politics in China for seven years, and is now Professor in the Department of Political Science and International Relations at Ibn Haldun

University, Istanbul, Turkey. His publications include *Identity, Interest and Action: A Cultural Explanation of Sweden's Intervention in the Thirty Years War* (Cambridge University Press, 1996), *Liberal Barbarism: The European Destruction of the Palace of the Emperor of China* (Palgrave, 2013) and *The Mechanics of Modernity in Europe and East Asia: Institutional Origins of Social Change and Stagnation* (Routledge, 2005). His forthcoming book *International Movements: The Body Politic on the World Stage* will deal with dance and international politics.

Arpad Szakolczai is Professor of Sociology at University College Cork, Ireland. He previously taught social theory at the European University Institute, Florence, Italy. His recent books include *Sociology, Religion and Grace: A Quest for the Renaissance* (2007), *Comedy and the Public Sphere* (2013), *Novels and the Sociology of the Contemporary* (2016), *Permanent Liminality and Modernity* (2017) and *Walking into the Void: A Historical Sociology and Political Anthropology of Walking* (with Agnes Horvath, 2018), all by Routledge; and *From Anthropology to Social Theory: Rethinking the Social Sciences* (with Bjørn Thomassen, Cambridge University Press, forthcoming). He has published articles in among others *Theory, Culture and Society*, *American Journal of Sociology*, *British Journal of Sociology*, *British Journal of Political Science*, *European Journal of Social Theory*, *Cultural Sociology*, *International Sociology* and the *European Sociological Review*.

Harald Wydra is a Fellow of St Catharine's College at Cambridge University, UK. He held visiting fellowships at the École des Hautes Etudes en Sciences Sociales in Paris, France, and the Australian National University in Canberra. He was a Visiting Professor at the Université Paris Ouest Nanterre La Défense and the University of Wrocław, Poland. He has a PhD in social and political sciences from the European University Institute in Florence. He is a founding editor of the academic journal *International Political Anthropology* (www.politicalanthropology.org). His publications include *Continuities in Poland's Permanent Transition* (Palgrave, 2001), *Communism and the Emergence of Democracy* (Cambridge University Press, 2007), *Democracy and Myth in Russia and Eastern Europe* (co-edited with Alexander Wöll, Routledge, 2007), *Politics and the Sacred* (Cambridge University Press, 2015) and *Breaking Boundaries: Varieties of Liminality* (co-edited with Agnes Horvath and Bjørn Thomassen, Routledge, 2015).

Preface

In our days it is considered as almost self-evident, a piece of political common-sense, voiced by politicians in order to meet public expectations, that in case of a perceived external threat the first action is to erect walls to defend ourselves. But perhaps we need to develop a more nuanced understanding of walling, of defensiveness, via political anthropology. The purpose of this book is to explore contributions in various fields of political anthropology and related disciplines to understand walling. We will focus on the constitutive, inevitable links between the kind of dangerous expansion that walling represents and the weakening of the characters who erect them. The main question of our book is whether with walling, with external physical protection, we receive comfort and normalisation, or rather that walling offers a heightened and false sense of security by internally destabilising individuals.

In the history of civilisation, walls are a rather recent invention. Since the Neolithic, with the first encirclements, analysed classically by Lewis Mumford in his *City in History*, man has chosen a form of self-protective isolation, as if walling out the troubles could secure development inside. However, it first resulted in inciting the hunger of robbers and then debilitated the will of the insiders. Still, with increasing settlement, more and more walls were built, stimulating and rein-forcing isolation, insecurity and a mutual lack of understanding: self-protection and efforts to conquer others grew jointly. Walls could be erected in any situation of liminal crisis, which produced feelings and experiences that are easily intel-ligible. Under tension and threat, walled senses of security quickly evaporate, and walls seemingly become adaptable to enforce them. Liminality produces two opposite states: one is paralysis or palsy, the inability to do anything, a resignation to fate; the other a frenetic search for a model that would solve the crisis. The latter state itself has two opposite animating forces: rational thinking – an intensive activity of the mind – and imitation, where suggestions that seem to offer a way out could be suddenly followed, growing alongside a spiral, by ever increasing numbers of people. At any rate, any liminality, any uncertainty, any pressure physi-cal or psychological, usually drastically changes the firmness of those undergoing it. If the model seems to work, people adapt to it in the long run; it is in this way that people who previously walked became settlers, putting themselves inside walls. They found their sense of security no longer in their own qualities, in their earnestness and in the feeling of irreplaceability, but rather in the walls and in those inside the walls, thus in sheer objects and numbers, and then attempted to impose their own security on others, usually with the help of violence. In either case, individual strength became less and less important, while general, abstract, collective goals and desires became dominating all along the walls, or they discharged their powers into their walls and lost their own ones. This logic of subordinating the concrete, individual and existing to the faceless, anonymous and general became codified in law, in the existence of the state and into the metaphysical knowledge of religions.

The main theme of this book on walling is to focus on the constitutive, inevitable links between the kind of violent expansion that walling represents, the spread of uncertainty that makes more walls to be built necessary, and the autodynamics of these kind of artificial constructs like walling and accompanying technologies. Obviously, the problem of walling in anthropology and, particularly, in political anthropology includes works about the human experiencing of the environment, the constitution of encirclements and cities, boundary marking among ethnic groups and states, the carceral society, and so on. In fact, as anthropology is concerned primarily with what happens at the borders of our life, this means that the problem of walls and wall-building is of major importance to anthropology, and particularly so to political anthropology, which seeks to focus, beyond presentist and descriptive concerns, on the broader historical significance of the phenomenon of walling, and intends to give it a theoretical interpretation, focusing centrally on the so little understood, as simply taken for granted, phenomenon of settled existence, mistakenly identified with having a 'home'.

While our experience of walling is quite vivid, including having lived behind the Iron Curtain and thus being confronted with walling in everyday existence, we still needed to recognise the perverting mind-set behind their erection – transforming whatever is evil appearing to be good. This also incorporates a recognition of the value of the concrete, individual human being, always connected to the vividness of life and not a rigid separation that transforms an abstraction into material reality, while at the same time expressing in familiar terms an agreeable vision of the world – a world where there is always con-testing, for the good, in the sense of Huizinga's *Homo Ludens*, or Foucault's agonism, though not aggressive competition, thus promoting contentment and agreement and not endemic mimetic rivalry. Such ideas are proposed by Antique political philosophers and philosophical anthropologists, classified by modern systemisers as idealists – yet, could there be anything more solid, dense, and even bodily real and serious, as this view about the bliss of life and the threats to it, and more relevant in the contemporary?

This is why we dedicated this book on walling to our two great benefactors, Sisters Amelia and Livia, who not only helped us by offering a place for the Summer School of the journal *International Political Anthropology* on walling, a major source of inspiration for this book, which took place 26 June–2 July 2016, and where several of the chapters of this book were presented in a draft form, but also helped us understand the artificiality of walling with their genuine style of life and serene mind-set, contributing to the promotion not of walling but of its demolition.

We would also like to express our gratitude to all the other participants of the Summer School, whether as teachers or students, for their inspiring presence and lively comments: Felice Addario, Oscar Azzimonti, Elizabeth Cowie, Sophia Flannery, Lea Friedberg, Daniel Gati, Valerie Giesen, Miklós Merényi, Federica Montagni, Federica Moretti, Mikkel Mouritzen, Virga Popovaité, Richard Sakwa, Roza Sakwa, Janos Mark Szakolczai and Bjørn Thomassen.

Walling is a destiny, a growing concern, well beyond our control and power. Walling induces a despising of the reality of the world around us, while being entrapped in the same logic of violence against which purportedly it was built. Walls are indeed a perversion, literally embodying a perverted logic that seems to thrive in our age, which got hold of a highest form of invasion – so far. Yet, while walling is indeed our destiny, as our lives are surrounded and limited by walls in all kinds of ways, and attempts to destroy them would only make things worse, just as evil grows through those resisting it, the book hopefully offers elements towards their understanding that suggests ways of getting around them.

Agnes Horvath, Marius Ion Benţa and Joan Davison

Introduction

On the political anthropology of walling

Agnes Horvath, Marius Ion Benţa and Joan Davison

> Never cross the sweet flowing water of ever-rolling rivers afoot until you have prayed, gazing into the soft flood, and washed your hands in the clear, lovely water.
> (Hesiod, *Works and Days*, p. 57)

The question of walling has become crucial for contemporary political anthropology and the social sciences in general in the current historical context, given the advent of strong political debates and tensions related to Europe's new walls that are being raised – or planned to be raised – following the refugee crisis, the great US–Mexico border fence, the Israel–Palestine wall, or the historical and symbolic significance of the Berlin Wall. The political, religious, symbolic, social and economic implications of walls are numerous and need to be scrutinised both in such particular contexts and in more general, comparative historical perspectives. The wall, as a most simple – yet fundamental – architectural artefact that gives rise to spatial liminality bears negative as well as positive connotations; it has been associated throughout the history of human culture with the painful experiences of division, separation, loss or interdiction on the one side, and experiences of protection, intimacy and security on the other. Should there be a trade-off between the two sides of our experience of walling, or what sort of ambivalence is there? What is the place of this experience in concrete individual lives, and how does it spark processes of their transformation? To what extent does walling break with the pre-given, which we should approach, as Hesiod suggests in our motto above, with due respect and humbleness, and not by a rude imposition of our artificial constructs? These are questions that political anthropology is invited to answer, or at least ponder upon, and we believe that the academic community will find in this book a stimulating resource for further interrogation and investigation.

Given the complex implications of walling for the social sciences and the axiological ambivalence of walling that we mentioned, it is important to address a number of touchstone questions that will help us have a better understanding of this practice from the perspective of political and philosophical anthropology and a clearer view of the way the various topics approached in the chapters of this book are connected to the central theme and to each other. These questions refer to the very definition of the realm of politics, the experience of walling, and the consequent modification of the strength of the individual. The realm of the political is usually conceived as that which has to deal with relations of power, but power should not be seen as a form of domination, force or coercion, but rather as a positive force centred in the individuals themselves, in their historical and anthropological contexts. The modification of individual strength belongs to a process of massification, universalisation and stereotyping, and so to the weakening of the political sphere – not easy to deal with, but even more difficult to endure.

If we have to describe our most basic experience of walling in its primary, non-metaphorical sense, we would have to start from our surrounding environment. The wall is an external physical object. It is either artificial, such as the wall of a house, a medieval city or a prison, or natural, as the walls of a rocky mountain or of a cave, which gives itself to our experience with the qualities of verticality, claustrophobic closure and immovability. To be a real wall, such an object needs to be taller than man, or in other ways insurmountable, otherwise it is a mere obstacle or a fence. Appearing to us as a vertical, hard surface, a wall blocks our potential movements, hindering us. As such, walls can be considered topologically equivalent to large distances in the sense that the raising of a wall between two areas or two points will have a similar effect to the amplifying of the distance between them: it makes movement between the two points more difficult if not impossible, and it hinders vision and sound, or even blocks them completely. Walls thus include not only the solid structures that are built above ground, but also what is caved below, like furrows, and also various metaphorical walls built into our mind-set which define the way we can think. Walls are thus pressures, but what for?

Essentially, walls have the power to separate space and to charge it with such qualities as 'inside'/'outside', 'accessible'/'forbidden', or 'on this side'/'on the other side' and, at the same time, they impose qualitative charges upon individuals involved, such as 'insider'/'outsider' or 'free'/'detained'. Walls are responsible for our thinking in terms of a home–world duality (as we know it from the works of Colin Turnbull, the Mbuti Pygmies of the Ituri Rain Forest know nothing about walls and the dualistic separation between 'home' and 'world') as well as for closing the horizon and thus magnifying the sense of finitude. Sometimes, they invite us or compel us to such experiences as scaling a wall, breaking down a wall, windowing, gate-crossing, and so on. Walling not only blocks movements or the senses, it can direct them, too, by forcing our gaze through windows or by forcing us to pass through a gate. We mentioned above windowing as one of the potential experiences associated with walling, but one can mention symbolic forms of windowing, too, such as fenestrity (coined by Eugen Fink, 1974). An image painted upon a wall is experienced not as a blocking of the visual sense but as an opening, a window to a symbolic or a 'virtual' realm. In this way, the wall becomes a medium for stereotyping, a binding surface for paintings, signs or inscriptions. In fact, in a possible genealogy of the mediatic experience, walling should be seen as the base, the starting point, because it is the simplest, moulding form of mediality. The wall separates two areas and stands in between them, it originates the new, it is casting a new message, a painting or an opening. The wall is formatting!

Walls can alter our sense of space and can create new geographies by distorting, fragmenting or reorganising our lived territoriality – see, for example, Horvath on finger fluting, or Ringmar's discussion on the effects of the Chinese Great Wall upon the people's spatial experience, respectively Chapters 1 and 7 in this volume. Furthermore, consider Davison's comments on the distortion of borderland identities as an expression of control during crises, in Chapter 10. Walling variously liminalises limits, and contradicts the spatio-temporal lawfulness governing the concrete individuum.

There is more to say concerning the effects of walling upon the people's sensorial experience once they lost their original certainty, which is not reducible to barring and limiting. A walled enclosure can indeed prevent the ones inside from seeing, hearing or knowing what takes place outside (or vice versa), but, at the same time, it can work as a viewed 'amplifying box' for what happens inside. Living in a closed community such as the court society (Elias, 1982) or a closed institution, such as a monastery, can have a monological effect, because within the walls of a small room only one voice can speak at a time for discourse to be intelligible. This fact has serious implications for large, abstract supranational entities, such as the European Union, whose monologism was noted by Richard Sakwa (2017); or for modernity itself, which was theorised as a 'global monastery' by Arpad Szakolczai (1998).

The political anthropology of walling has as its subject matter the politics of walling and also the anthropology of related social myths and imaginaries.

The first walling myth

The word 'walling' has two meanings. One is the sacred Latin 'pomerium' or 'post moerium', even 'circamoerium', as Titus Livy defined it (Livy, 1998, Book I, 44), a space left vacant around the body of the city itself, comprising the furrow or vacuum and the lines of the wall. The other meaning is the linear transformative potential of liminal intersections between man and the void: their matrixing power.

These two meanings can be brought together. When Remus leaped over the furrow dug by Romulus, he was killed by Romulus, who uttered the following words: 'So perish everyone that shall hereafter leap over my wall' (Livy I.7.3.). A simple sentence with multiple significance, like the morbid, annihilative meaning of 'perish' and its redefining character – as it 'makes' the sacred, in the literal sense of 'sacrifice', *sacro fare*. Remus is sacrificed for the sake of the Romans, at the moment when he lost his authorship and became equated with the sacred content of the furrow that he leaped over. This foundation myth of Rome brought into motion the sacred significance of pomerium, where it is forbidden to pass, or to bury the dead. Even soldiers lost their status when entering the pomerium, armies could not march inside it, weapons were prohibited inside and, finally, even all the negative spirits of the world were concentrated there, like pestilence, famine, war and illnesses: evidently this is the liminal place of the void. Consequently, Remus' leap not only freed all the evils comprised in the furrow, but as a consequence he also lost his status as an individuum, who is able to keep the borders of his existence, and so his authorship as a prince and a leader, by disturbing the border of the furrow, so he consequently died or better to say became annihilated into the sacred, before he was killed by Romulus (about the myth, see also Beard, 1998).

We end up at this stage with a question that concerns walling as an encirclement for the purpose of union and begetting (see Chapter 4 on encystation by Bowman) and in particular the presence of the void in this process (see Chapter 5 by Novikov on the divinising purpose of Mother Teresa's dying destitutes in Kolkata). Another question is concerned with the redefinition of the authentic order by this union, and this linear transformation. A third one would be the following: how exactly did Remus accede to divine rank by his leap just when he lost his authority? He was the prince, the leader, the originator of movement, the prot*agon*ist, the gifted one: in equal rank with Romulus, but he lost it due to his pretension to the rank of god. As the story captures a process of transformation, these questions relate not only to the internal structure of the myth, but also convey the external structure of an intersecting change by way of matrixing or linear transformation. Jumping over a furrow is quite natural, comes out of our own efforts, but in this case the furrow was the future boundary of Rome, and in his jump his own forces were as if multiplied by the entry of the sacred.

Matrixing or linear transformation is a never-ending move that gains infinite magnitude as each successive movement becomes active once the previous one ceases to exist, providing it with its dynamism, so that its power is never exhausted, but transmitted with a gradually waning intensity to each successive link. In order to understand the meaning of moulding through matrixing, it is enough to look at the development of Rome. In all respects Rome emerged out of Remus' leap over its would-be walls, as the subsequent entry of the divine. Remus became the founding hero of Rome, the key to her success, which follows it immediately, wealth and richness. One essential feature of linear transformation is that in this way things cease to be moved by themselves, but are moved by the previous and on their turn move the next things, thus become a matrix. Matrix contains homology, the measurable likenesses between characters, so Remus' leap inevitably produces all those effects that are like (even higher and more powerful, and certainly more intensive in impulses) his authority, and so belong to the unlimited field of myth and foundational legends – even after his death. A similar idea, with an explicit focus on how the divine enters through liminality, was proposed by Colin Turnbull (1990: 77). The story of Remus illustrates how walling is a perverted matrix, as its functioning requires pain, suffering and death, so that a man-made technology can produce divinising effects. With the same token of effects one can even challenge social theories, arguing that the intersective knowledge has grown on the basis of divisions, by crossing elements and substances with each other, one of them being Hobbes' influential Leviathan idea, with its striking validity for walling (Hobbes, 2012).

Walling theories

The ideas of Hobbes can be considered as the first theoretical discussion on techniques of intersections, through his understanding of men as beings driven by appetite, obeying the same mechanical laws as any other forms, that lost authority and so are ready for the intersection. This makes it possible to mediate in between them through erected political communities, self-interested as the people themselves, being based upon a social contract and thus establishing consent about representative legitimate power. This intercession or intervening on behalf of another is what enabled Hobbes to incorporate the image of god in his Leviathan into the huge artefact of a man-made machine-beast, agitated by sensations, claiming that any government or human organisation can be real and so part of nature, but becomes so exactly because it can exist as an animated construction. It is an automated mechanical artefact, originally meant to intervene in specific cases, but now rising into the constitutional wholeness of a Leviathan, a total machine intersected with the divine, as Hobbes described it as early as 1651. Yet, the movements he conceived were liminal responses to stimuli (answers given in a state of liminal suspension) that can easily follow sequentially, one from another, independently of objects (and even from subjects, as the individual mover is not important anymore), growing into an artificial edifice of state, law and security, which is moved by the same passions, through desire and appetites, that drive men into the moulding process without the hope to retain to themselves, but in eager union with god, as the very first sentence of his Leviathan states: 'Nature (the art whereby God hath made and governes the world) is by the art of man, as in many other things, so in this also imitated, that it can make an Artificial Animal' (Hobbes, Leviathan, Introduction).

Hobbes has emissioned an intersective process in which every force is increasing the force of the opposite part, though without the inner force of its own, but with an in-between power that in combination brings infinite intersections, where moulding and dying individuals are cementing the rigid tissue of the state into a unity with the divine. Here all power depends on an external mover, where intermediaries move into infinity. This pushing and pulling move together could turn around the whole edifice of reality either by annihilating it entirely, or by transforming it in its own likeness. These others could be anyone in a weak and inferior position, which is easiest to install and manage, while the same weakness produces an eager appetite for possessing others, the acquisitive will that has no value of its own, but is always decisive in mixing codes and transgressing law and order.

This is the way Hobbes redefined a political institution, repositioning it as the political container for a mass of people, the breeder of a humankind equal in appetite and in readiness to intersections. Hobbes produced one of the strangest books ever, as it did not define its title, and so scholars were wondering for hundreds of years about its nature and meaning. Yet, he could give a novel prominence to appetite and interests as bases for improving human institutions, a point taken up later by utilitarianism, but its major importance concerning the intersective potential for a power unifying the human and the divine in the form of a feeling machine was never really recognised.

The power of appetites is not so evident at first sight. This can be approached through Aristotle's idea of change. Aristotle argued that 'Change is the actuality of that which potentially is, qua such' (Aristotle, *Physics*, 3.1, 201a10–11). The

Hobbesian concern to reposition appetite from egoistic to common goals makes use of such an Aristotlean idea. Appetite is the actuality that can be potentially used for the purposes of the state, and a mechanism of power can be built on it. Out of human depravity, appetite, hunger, eagerness and self-seeking pulsations were grown that invited the divine.

This explains how contemporary migration serves to proliferate an escalation of walling, by an increasing focus on institutions and a growing control over the population (see Chapter 8 by Marangadukis on the Greek migration problem). Even more so, as such mass is soft and vulnerable, the process of increasing by adding more soft and vulnerable groups results in exponential growth, the prolifer- ation of intersections, and so power growth. So thousands of migrants move across borders each day, seeking to reduce what they see as a break: an empty space, a gap in the middle of their very existence, between their just left and newly found reality, without realising that in the meanwhile it grew itself, from tension into a bigger tension, to be filled with sensation-appetite material. Wherever a new(ish) wall is constructed, or even removed, it calls for yet another, even bigger one, whether along Southern or Eastern European borders, or even outside Europe; a vial for Europe, serving to maintain institutionalised power for the sake of change.

Walling intentions

The point can be illustrated by a recent case. On 8 January 2016 Wolfgang Albers, the chief of Cologne police, resigned under pressure, after days in which the authorities struggled to explain why they were not able to control the 'vio- lence of migrants', as it came to be called. This violence, and the slowness of the authorities to make public the scale and nature of the assaults, sent the Cologne police chief into early retirement, without him or anybody else having to answer whether physical protection can offer comfort and normalisation. It is not the first time that following a breakdown an abnormal mass of institutional tissue has grown on reality, putting a new make-up on it so that it could be moulded into a more manageable state, by installing new patterns. However, such measures are only additions to deprivations; they could be added as many times as one wishes, without excising the original problem. In the New Year's Eve security collapse, the question is whether such 'security' was ever what its name indicates, or rather was it the representation of fear and of a state of breakdown that is much greater in magnitude and even much older than we imagine, as Hobbes still demonstrates it for us. In our recent case two weaknesses have met, those of the migrants and of the collapsed security walling system – itself built on and proliferating weakness – and both have become open for new suggestions. This pressurised situation is identicanl to the stage called 'liminal' in anthropology (Turner, 1969; van Gennep, 1981), in which new – whether private, social or institutional – patterns are most easily installed. New rules are implanted under the context of a breakdown of the order, or so the theory claims, but these would then remain an integral part of the make-up, thus becoming permanent. When the police officer resigned, a new question was raised that redefined order. However, redefinition is still just a redefinition, even if it has enormous potential for transformation, when a 'new order' becomes valid and active once the previous one ceased to exist, each being part of a sequence that shifts away from the order of nature. Such transformative force is reinforced by the elasticity of identity, the mutual replacement of moulded individuals, produced by the way the results of liminal crises are built upon each other. The result is an order that is not built on man's own inner force, but rather on the expectation that the external, institutional forces – where a paternalist state or a liberal market economy – will secure everything for us, and where every failure of such a quasi-order will result in a 'reform' that only further takes away the possibility of reliance on inner forces. Instead of restoring order, it thus will secure its perversion, proliferating disintegration and escalating mimetism masked as rationality, as only bad things are born out of the bad, just as the good further generates the good. Returning to the Cologne story, seemingly only one part is revealing these signs of weakness, and the softness of character are of those who are in between homes, the refugees, without families and possessions. In reality, however, both the home seekers and the offerers are in the same position of inferiority: moved by others or moving others, but unable to move themselves.

Why build a structure on disintegration if it only promotes a feeling of being lost, a sense of fear and deprivation, and an order distanced from the will, of which this volume shows numerous examples. Transformations are situated at the sensory threshold: they are sufficient to evoke responses, stimulating an infinitely mutable excitement that grows from tension into tension, always at the highest pitch of exaltation, until a determinant unity is formed between the limit and the unlimited. At this particular moment the limit is consumed into something else than it was before, as indicated by the apotheosis of Remus, his exaltation to divine rank, his culmination or climax in death, his entry into infinity by losing his life.

The book consists of ten chapters, divided into two parts. Part I, 'Theorising walling: processes of transformation in history' (Chapters 1 to 3), applies the tools of political anthropology for a comprehensive study of walling, in particular by contrasting it to current approaches in political science, including actual walling political processes in the past and in the present. This part will focus on the manner in which walling technology makes use of liminal situations, and thus can be considered as a modality of linear transformation, by inaugurating a new order through an artificial division which then serves as model for a series of new transformations and multiplications. Part II, 'Contemporary examples for transformations through walling' (Chapters 4 to 10), illustrates the liminal character of walling, and the linear transformation logic it sets into motion, through the prism of concrete, historical or contemporary social and political crises in Europe, Palestine, China, India and the United States, by arguing that walling can be understood as a vehicle that made use of unreality produced by liminality and an entire structural set-up in covering and using emptiness. This title captures a central feature of contemporary walling, which is to transfigure established forms into a new technological process of transformation. Finally, the Conclusion will again explore the central theme of the book, the description of the walling phenomenon through its history as a challenge to meaning.

Walling won this battle, and ideologies and convictions supporting its unreality won the corresponding battle in the sphere of politics. The acceptance of walling has become so widespread that it is difficult to imagine contemporary countries where the notion of walling does not play a central role in politics, in modes of thinking, in everyday life. Yet, for reasons to be clarified in this book, this is a destabilising process, though a long and tiresome one that infiltrates every segment of the society and politics, yet not a necessity. Using cases ranging from Palaeolithic finger fluting, Göbekli Tepe, the walls of Jericho and Babylon, and the Chinese Wall to the Palestinian wall, Trump's proposed Mexican wall, various Eastern and Southern European walls, including the Berlin Wall and the Greek case as a bulwark containing migration flows, and the intersecting experience of voluntary work in a Kolkata hospice, this book offers a political anthropology of one of the most curious of human practices: constructing walls.

Bibliography

Aristotle (1934) *Physics*, London: Heinemann.

Beard, Mary et al. (eds) (1998) *Religions of Rome*, Cambridge: Cambridge University Press.

Dreyfus, Hubert L. and Paul Rabinow (1982) *Michel Foucault: Beyond Structuralism and Hermeneutics*, Brighton: Harvester Press.

Evelyn-White, Hugh G. (ed.) (1936) *Hesiod, the Homeric Hymns and Homerica*, London: Heinemann.

Hobbes, Thomas (2012) *Leviathan*, Oxford: Oxford University Press.

James, E.O. (1917) *Primitive Ritual and Belief: An Anthropological Essay*, London: Methuen.

Elias, Norbert (1982) *The Civilizing Process*, Oxford: B. Blackwell.

Fink, Eugen (1974) *De la phénoménologie*, Paris: Editions de Minuit.

Livy, Titus (1998) *The Rise of Rome*, Oxford: Oxford University Press.

Plato (1999) *Phaedrus*, Cambridge, MA: Harvard University Press.

Sakwa, Richard (2017) 'Europe and the political: from axiological monism to pluralistic dialogism', *East European Politics* 33, 3: 406–425.

Szakolczai, Arpad (1998) 'The global monastery', *World Futures* 53, 1–17.

Turnbull, Colin (1990) 'Liminality: a synthesis of subjective and objective experience', in R. Schechner and W. Appel (eds) *By Means of Performance: Intercultural Studies of Theatre and Ritual*, Cambridge: Cambridge University Press.

Turner, Victor (1969) *The Ritual Process*, Chicago: Aldine.

van Gennep, Arnold (1981) *Les rites de passage*, Paris: Picard.

Part I

Theorising walling

Processes of transformation in history

1 Walling Europe

The perverted linear transformation

Agnes Horvath

Linear transformation

> Maybe the target nowadays is not to discover what we are, but to refuse what we are. We have to imagine and to build up what could be to get rid of this kind of political 'double bind,' which is the simultaneous individualization and totalization of modern power structures. The conclusion would be that the political, ethical, social, philosophical problem of our days, is not to try to liberate the individual from the state, and from the state's institutions, but to liberate us both from the state and from the type of individualization which is linked to the state. We have to promote new forms of subjectivity through the refusal of this kind of individuality that has been imposed on us for several centuries.
>
> (Foucault, 1982: 216)

Following the spirit, though not necessarily the word, of the Foucault quote above concerning the need to escape modern forms of subjectivation and promote a return to the inner power we all have, the aim of this chapter is to reconsider at its distant historical roots one of the most absurd contemporary political measures, walling. At a fundamental, anthropological level, such constructs are built on the idea of the inferiority of man, considered as harmful to himself and to the property of others, behaving irritably, thus untrustworthy, so walling is needed to force him inside/outside borders. Therefore an artificial apparatus is needed, fairly determined in its container character, a system for controlling the individuals by moulding them into a transformed state, a mass, suitable for governance. In its original form such a binding system of linear transformation, also called matrix (Nering, 1970), is present in nature, is a recipient container in which forms are transformed in their progress towards different appearances – automatically creating wants, sensuals,[1] wills or opinions that enable and stimulate entities to move.

The linear transformative system with its logic and function was known at least since Antiquity, though under various different names. Hesiod in *Works and Days* (106) stated that 'gods and mortal men sprang from one source', there is only one source for everything, whose quality never departs. For a better understanding we use the modern, Latin name for linear transformation, which is 'matrix'. Plato in *Timaeus* (48e) referred to the matrix with the name of the *triton genos*, or a 'third kind', an in-between space, a material substratum of the void, neither being nor non-being, a vessel that is bringing forth forms. This vessel can be best described as an interval between two different appearances of a form, where forms are blending together. It is also present in Aristotle's discussion of the cube that contains the void – a 'something' without own existence – which only has a place: inside the cube, but having no self-existence. Aristotle used the form of a cube as a pure example to explain better the visual form of the matrix: a walled gap, which displaces its own volume in nature, giving way to any yielding medium. It contains the void, not as a self-existing vacancy, but rather, according to Aristotle (*Physics*, 213b–214a), a volume itself. The void as a volume is already there in the cube before the cube was occupied by the ever entering figures of the matrix, who penetrate the cube, and whom the cube should also permeate thoroughly. Most importantly, the matrix has the same volume as the void embodied in it, a volume not separable from the entering figures, however different and so isolated, bordered by the entering characters: 'it would still embrace an equal measure of vacancy, and would coincide with a portion of "space" and "vacuity" equal to itself' (Aristotle, *Physics*, 216a–b).

This is the way the substantial volume of the matrix comprises in equal volume the void, while it is also equal with it in physical properties. Matrix and the void coincide with each other, not exactly in material substratum, but in character. They both form a gap, an interruption, the matrix together with the void: the void is inherent in the essential character of the matrix as they both occupy a place; they are both material substratum. However, the void is inside the matrix; the matrix is walling the void. The matrix is a vibrating place, reciprocating the move of the entering characters from their previous equilibrium into another position of equilibrium, through homology. Their state of equilibrium has been disturbed by the initial stage of the matrix, as if transmitting their vibration. The matrix's middle stage provides that vibration which caused the oscillation of the different characters, the in-between stage of progressing into another character, the feeling of love towards unification, a solid back and forth movement in a linear way on both sides of the centre of the matrix. Entering in and departing from the matrix is linear, a sequential process, hence transformative.

Hobbes used the matrix, in the sense of a transforming vessel or receptacle, for his idea of commonwealth, while Foucault analysed in detail Bentham's Panopticon as a refined power-operation-system of disciplinary, moulding technology. Even Leibniz's insight corresponds to the description of a matrix: 'Imagine there were a machine which by its structure produced thought, feeling and perception' (Leibniz, 2014, §17). Foucault's (1982) analysis was not simply an exploration of a Benthamite idea, but a major insight about the matrix's controlling and transforming effects on its subjects, which also makes use of the similarities between the Panopticon, the media and the circus, already present in Plato's *khóra* (in the *Timaeus*) and diagnosis of theatrocracy (in *Laws*). It also recalls Gell's theory about technology and magic, which is founded on the enchantment of technology. Here Gell (1999: 166) interprets the magical effect of technological products on its beholders, explicitly identifying the enchanted magical vessels that have power over us, which is neither different from the walled tower form of Bentham's Panopticon or Aristotle's cube and their continuous, disciplinary and anonymous effect, nor the specific mechanism of power used by Hobbes and embodied in the god-man-machine, the Leviathan, or Leibniz's 'feeling machine', cited above.

In reality, the matrix could be everywhere, anytime, as a generalisable model of a functioning moulding process, which is defined as the intersection of dissected characters, each of which is characterised by its own liminal state. However, and this is the main argument of this chapter, in reality there is just one matrix, the matrix of proper quality, with characters, limits and borders, as Plato emphasised it (Plato, *Timaeus* 50c; see below for further details). Every other alteration is a perversion (the term 'perversion' was coined by Scheler (2010) for falsified knowledge). Any departure from the genuine matrix has no validity, like various political and other technologies, walling, disciplining, magic, and any combination of these.

The statement that the authentic matrix is an autonomous, self-sufficient vessel is our focus now, where everything that enters imitates something already existing, while receiving a new appearance. When the character that entered the matrix finally leaves it, it gains a different shape, and this transformation adds a dynamic movement to the otherwise unmoved matrix. Furthermore, alterations can occur, as Plato noticed it, in this moulding down or forming process, still during the stamping and marking period, when perversion could take place, an erratic instance that is not part of the authentic sequence, illustrated by Figure 1.2.

When Aristotle argued that every transformation involves three stages, the stage from which the change proceeds, the stage to which it proceeds and the object which persists through the transformation, he pointed out the necessary involvement of an initiator into the transformation itself – there is no incidental change (Aristotle, *Physics*, 226a.25). There is always something that initiates the transformation, an interruption, and so the transformation must be distinct, or else no change has occurred. A transformation might shift out of its proper change towards perverted ones, if the original intentions are not valid for the linear process of transformation.

In this chapter I explore a new, dysfunctional mind-set by re-examining those kinds of matrixing political appearances, centrally including walls, which have been imposed on us for several centuries, not without intentions, and not without initiators. This is the way we perceive the contemporary reality of Europe as a walled fortress, where the function and existence of the individuum,[2] one's legitimacy in action and progress in making judgements and taking care has become disfigured. When a whole matrixing technological enterprise has grown over us, then we should invoke the similar mechanical apparatuses of the past that were able to mould feelings, intentions, sensuals and characters into new shapes; apparatuses that moved in response to the intentional impact of enterings. The productions of this machinery are those technological artefacts that are continuously growing, resulting in unbalanced multiplications, building up those monstrous absurdities (coined by Plato for false thinking; see *Theaetetus* 188c), which can be the outcome of matrix machinations.

Walling

One of this dysfunctional matrixing machinery is walling, which was never more than the exact opposite of the antique homology notion. Homology (a term of Aristotle) is the quality of being in agreement, implying the similarities in thinking shown by every character in life, a mind-set in a measurable likeness between beings. In nature matrix implies homology. The state of being homologous is the fundamental similarity based on common descent from the matrix, by filiation, shown by the word itself: linearity, in linear transformation. This common developmental origin is shown by the similarity of organic compounds (Darwin successfully established a theory on that) of every being in which each character differs from successive compounds by a fixed mind-set in homology or agreement. Homology is a quality, a correspondence able to form a linear transformation in a matrix.

A different message is conveyed through walling, by seemingly promoting security, law and order, while violating understanding and homology. Why build a structure on a deprivation, the break of continuity, if it only promotes a feeling of being weak, a sense of fear and deprivation, and proposes a deficient order distanced from the power of the self? Walling is an extreme and desperate effort at confining and sealing behind a physical separating device, transforming our habitual actions and natural dispositions from self-capability and self-sufficient homology into passive endurance, as it will be shown through some examples from Palaeolithic caves. Why does walling happen? Can it be shown that walling is just one of those fake artificial systems that abuse nature's moulding down process, interrupting and spying its stamping and marking generations, pervading its binding homology system into a multiplicative absurdity. Is it possible that a falsified transformation is behind our walling destiny, which gives a particular autopoietic dynamics for walling designs. Walling incorporates dissolved, dazzled and upset characters into erratic thinking sets, without offering any way out.

Without doubt the matrix is absorbing the energies of the entering characters, giving it back to the departed ones; it is being moved by the entering figures and maintains in this way the homology. But what happens if homology is disturbed, violated or abused? Can the matrix still keep going on, without being disturbed? Evidently not. The consequence is that not only the homology axiom of the matrix will change, but also the entering characters will lose their original property of being in homology, being equal with themselves, together with the similar loss of the departing ones. The matrix will be deformed into a parasitic machine of absorbing energies, without ever giving them back, swallowing resonation and growing into dangerous absurdities. The appropriate Aristotelian characterisation of the individuum is one that has a solid position, being complete and in comfort with nature, the notion that in nature every individual is in agreement with oneself, nothing is excluded, not even the matrix, will be violated. The matrix will become perverted, passing sickening changes on characters.

It is instructive to note that agreement in the matrix and the property of being equal to oneself are interchangeable, as all those characters who enter into the matrix's receptacle are blended into another shape without harm or violence. Self-sameness is an absolute principle in nature, but it does not imply being in the same state all the time. There is movement without relinquishing the actual character, without changing its essence (mode of thinking, set of mind) through the matrix itself. If a change of essence could occur, then knowledge itself would cease to exist (see *Cratylus* 440a). Void *is* there in the matrix, but not the flux; the matrix is not a 'leaky pot' (a term coined by Plato in *Cratylus* 440d, capturing Heraclitus' notion of flux), unless its homology is disturbed.

If one's mode of thinking is not reconciled with these axioms, the matrix process loses its measure and with it the agreement, the harmonious property of the characters of being equal with themselves, the peaceful will to coincide with each other and so the process becomes falsified, the energy absorbing process of the matrix will turn into perversion. Magnitude will take the place of filiation, and instead of homology incommensurability or 'no common measure' will overgrow the matrix. Such incommensurable relations are represented by irrational numbers in mathematics (Szabo, 1978), but also easily could be seen in the growth of perverted matrixes, like walling, disciplining and other similar technological arrangements, with their powerful dynamism for occupying forms, places, times. Let's not be misunderstood: the matrix itself is incommensurable, but as far as it is able to keep the tension between the entering and the departing characters, it is somehow controlled by itself, by homology, which implies a focus on content and the centre, combining genesis and imitation, and not on 'rigorously defined' external constraints. But as soon as the whole system becomes violated, the incommensurable too escapes from the general agreement and starts its run into magnitude. Incommensurable magnitude, having no common standard for movement anymore, is the result of growth by division (at the limits, dividing by zero produces infinite growth), the multiplication of departing characters themselves in the perverted moulding process of a forged matrix.

In normality the matrix as linear transformation cannot produce anything else than its nature: linearity, filiation, the disposition to comply the same homologous property as itself. If this condition is not fulfilled, the result is the unbalanced multiplication of the departing characters.

The moulding process

So far we have gained a certain understanding of the matrix, but now we need to apply this for the fake departure, as embodied in walling, and the inevitably disastrous consequences of the perverted matrix. Walling is not simply a phenomenon that can gain a self-sustaining, autopoietic growth, but it does so in union with the flux, moving itself anarchically through instability, jointly making use of the impulsive interests of the encircled and the excluded, producing an existence that is definitely new in appearance, through its stamped copies. The incorporation of the infinite into the limited existence of the individual is a classical philosophical concern since Plato (*Philebus* 16d). However, the incorporation of the flux is a completely different matter. Its unrest springs from incompleteness and is inherent in a perverted mind-set. It has a suffocating, controlling power over the subverted, which is not something to be recognised or acknowledged, as it has become a kind of a naturalisation, a given and even pre-given during the course of history. It was Foucault who started to theorise this growing obsession with control, which has become so natural for us that we have to naturalise ourselves to be rid of it, suggesting the promotion of 'new subjectivities' as a solution. For a less famous contemporary of Foucault, the anthropologist Alfred Gell, such re-subjectivisation did not appear as a solution. Gell considered the presence of this mind-set as a dazzling and upsetting influence and so pure magic, a spell inherent in technological procedures and their outcome. Magic is thus the ideal means of technical production (Gell, 1999), as it does not require any other quality than an open mind-set – towards how to control, we should add.

Flux replaces the void in the perverted matrix with an insatiable appetite, filling it with unrest instead of completion; it is the place for the new appearance of technologies – walling is just one of them – in limitless change, instead of fulfilment. Appetite is interested, it is a powerfully resonating mind-set that is able to stimulate the senses, that evokes the mental state of the interest to gain in-form(ation), to take control over forms – a conflicting sensual for matrix. The interest in gaining information, literally getting inside the forms themselves in the moulding procedure of the matrix, is a dangerous undertaking, considering the quality of the offspring, as they become disturbed and interrupted in their transformative progress.

Classically the word 'information' always meant the shaping of the mind, a controlling power for the calculative mind-set which is quite an alien coagulation from the giving, marvellous generative gratification of the matrix, a disease that came upon with perversion continuously, bringing anarchy and tyranny with itself. Interest in information is a clogging mind-set, which binds the movement of the matrix, obstructing and blocking it, diverting the natural moulding process into artificiality – yet, its binding and controlling power became even bigger from this fact. Deprived of forms, it has a greater need for formalisation, for control.

Interest in information is formatting formlessness that suffers from incompleteness, being deprived of homology. Until this point, we can agree with the idea that there was a deliberate effort, rooted in a personal interest to falsify the matrix's sensual, but things are becoming different after the accomplishment of the matrixing process, after the offspring were born from the matrix, after the reaggregation, as at this phase the spell of the perverted matrix becomes autonomous, independent of any wish on the part of the participants, whether subjects or spectators. The falsified matrix has an unfinished, uncontrollable, roundabout move once escaped from the hands of its generators – a fluxed appetite for sensual possession (see Chapter 5 by Novikov). In fact, and strictly speaking, even the authentic matrix is an incommensurability, it is itself as *triton genos*, a third factor, a dynamism earned from the forms, but is linked by love to fulfilment, while the perverted one only by appetite.

To further support this view, notice that Hobbes regarded appetite (itself a deprivation of something, food or anything else) as a source of power between individuals, in line with Plato's analysis on the nature of *dynamos*, as something incommensurable (Plato, *Theaetetus* 148a–b). However, if we start with appetite, which is necessarily unequal, then the result is further incommensurability with others, a matrix multiplication devoid of harmony. The matrix is a kind of third factor, which has the capacity of conjoining two characters. In the conjoining process, here, we can even catch how easily appetite can be confused with the sensual of love. Appetite is an in-between condition of deprivation: lust, anger, hunger, resentment, pain, interest, and so on, wedging a distance between characters whose movement is frozen, can only move through the auxiliary motive of appetite. Love and appetite, they both are preoccupied with the gratification of the senses. But there is a delicate division between the two, which I will illustrate later with the help of the novelist Albert Camus. The appetite is a distance between men that can be satisfied by taking away something from others, a negative conjoining faculty. It is a faculty that is never satisfied: a never bridged gap that is unable to unite into one. The appetite is not sufficient to unite in the moulding process, is never able to join together the entering characters into properties in the matrix, but instead creates an interruption and freezes the process. As a result the matrix becomes unable to bear offspring anymore, only producing mutants, like various technological enterprises and unlike love.

The authentic, womb-like matrix denies the existence of any other in-betweenness than the disposition to generate forms in the most harmonious way. While in matrix the various characters define their respective positions by moving, copying, adopting existent forms, models in continuum, the perverted version produces and reproduce paralyses. The characters entering the original matrix always rearrange themselves into different configurations in search of fulfilment, while in the perverted matrix they remain lifeless, lacklustre, anaemic, inert.

The void in the matrix is not the absence of things: it is there so that the matrix can generate forms, which is its own meaning. This is impossible in the flux, which is not like the void, as for the void one must suppose that some volume is already there, like the agreement inside the vessel, when and before it was occupied by the entering and departing characters. But then the matrix itself has its own volume equal to that of the void which now permeates its moving, coinciding with the space and time equal to them. Empty space has no significance, it is just a mental construct, but the void has; it fills the matrix.

Maybe we are ready to conclude that the way inertia can emerge in the matrix is through the entrance of an intention, of a different mind-set: a will to create something new, out of nothingness, which implies the suspension and elimination of the given, natural ways. The conditions for a perverted matrix are similar to walling, where this similarity results in definite incommensurable magnitude. I now present six illustrations from Palaeolithic caves that the matrix performs the moulding process through man-made control interfering with its movement. I will show that if this man-made control is motivated by a similar but not identical mind-set as the homology of the authentic matrix, then the result is the bringing forth of a perverted matrix for the purposes of man-made control. This follows the three stages of separation or dissection, womb and union in rebirth.

Dissection

Walling as a device to surround a space with a boundary substance within which something new can originate or develop changes the characters entering it. It moulds them, alters their mind, resulting in a different mode of thinking. One could say the interested one, but in reality the weak and fearful, who has no trust anymore in himself. Something evidently went wrong with the walling process, because since its first application the dissection of the individuum and a procedure for further weakening was set in motion. Consequently an infinite sequence of ever deeper vacuumed crises occurred, with the anomalies of disastrous developments that befall men who became unable of self-governance. What is more, dissection continues with intersections, which is different from concreteness in context, as it starts with a violent break. This is how and why walling is at once the archetype and prototype of all the subsequent ludicrous ideas of social engineering, where purely technical solutions were suggested to weakness: an idea that seems self-evident – simply by constructing a solid wall anybody undesired can be kept out, while equalising all those who remained inside. Yet, the solution soon, indeed 'naturally' proved itself insufficient, only to lead to further similar technical or procedural abuses, moving further and further away from individual power based on the firmness of character. Walling is a problem quite on its own: it can produce essences and meanings free of reality, can expand influence technologically, politically and economically, with ever blocking and sterilising right impulses and sense perception. Definitely, walling is an emanation (as coined by Meinecke (1972: 70) for the manifestation of the abysses of individuality) of a manifold variety of things, through the moulding down of forms, but it is not so evident for what and why. If it is a matrix, how could it depart from the authentic one? And what is the consequence of this departure? How is it that the sensual of interest could get a space in it? What are the consequences?

Only interest based on the evocation of appetite produces effects other than the natural order of homology, as it goes beyond agreement between beings, influencing, transforming and taking away existing arrangements into a new class of formlessness, by getting into the form of others, so the appetite is a kind of interest on its own, similar to the 'passionate interests' introduced by Bruno Latour after Gabriel Tarde (see Latour and Lépinay, 2009). What is more, at the same time of taking away something, it also offers something, so a curious bookkeeping is taking place with the void in the middle stage of the perverted matrix, a 'contract with the devil', as this two-sided legal agreement was named in the archetypal, even unique modern myth, the *Faust*. The Faustian, cool and rational contract combines giving and receiving in a sense, but in reality it is taking advantage of others, the world and especially the world of forms becoming little more than an occasion for profitable exchange with the abyss. The consequence is the evocation of infinitely mutable replica images, boundless and bottomless repetitions, a self-begetting – as seen in the uterus motive in Gargas (see Figure 1.1).

The power of interest resides in the perverted matrix itself, a stolen property made to produce for the interested one, whose name and appearance is as insignificant as the fabricated mechanism of the process itself – they both fall into unreality. However, it requires internalisation, it must go through the sensuals, alternating the mind-set towards an appetite for profit, reconstructing the world by milling it through the perverted matrix, slowly changing every part, segment, and appearance of homology into something else. Interest brings pain and violence into the magnificent mechanism of the matrix, but the authentic one, the original matrix, the binding system, the transformer of characters is still in the background, and will be there forever in every axiomatic wish for fulfilment:

> There is no other fulfilment than that of love, in other words of yielding to oneself and dying to the world. Go all the way. Disappear. Dissolve in love. Then the force of love will create without me. Be swallowed up. Break up. Vanish in fulfilment and the passion of truth.
>
> (Camus 2010: 243)

This sensual of love is the moulding stuff for changing everything: fulfilling; dissolving; yielding; forcing; dying to the world; disappear; create; swallowed up; passionate; vanishing – just to illustrate, through words of Camus, the intensity of transformation. Be attentive here, as we have three phases in the paragraph cited: like in every matrix, there is the father, mother and the offspring phase, as Plato stated in the *Timaeus*. The father gives the design or image to be imitated, so has a prominent place in the process, though he then disappears, giving his place for the mother, the generous provider of the seat for the becoming form: 'Then the force of love will create without me'; the mother who plays the protective role in the dissolution and loss of character captured above: 'dissolve in love'; and finally the offspring, who is different in attributes, but not in mind-set, from the character that entered and disappeared in the process: 'Go all the way' and bring with themselves the copy of your mother (the receptacle) and father (design). These are the components of the matrix and they are linked together by generous love forever. The matrix is cemented together by love, but love, as every sensual, is an easy victim of simulations.

Hence, similar feelings do not mean similar intentions; the human mind can produce an abundance of relevant feelings, and one of the most significant is the interest for control. Interest can break through the generosity of sensual fulfilment, can alter the copied and can produce a perverted matrix.

Womb

The term matrix, as I have already clarified, stands for 'mother', 'womb' or 'matter', the transformative container by which something is enclosed or embodied for further change, dissolved in sensuals and made disappear as a character, as the Camus citation illustrates. The matrix shows something different than a simple transformation. First, there is a linear transformation in the form of regularity: something is growing in that way that is changing its attributes. Second, it can occur with the copy, mark or stamp of the initiated form of the matrixed matter.

Authenticity and undisturbed love are able to fill the matrix with the sensual of harmlessness. Any other type of sensual in the copying process makes the whole movement erratic and vain, deconstructing the matrix and resulting in its disruption. An interest is an instability, harming the state of homology, it is sneaking and aloof, bringing indifference and unsociability into the forms, make them to be hostile and unfriendly with each other, combatting infinitely. By interest I mean a deprived homology, derived from an alien sensual into the matrix, an emptiness with a heavy transitorial and a dense emotional charge, as it is an appetite for/after the forms.

Walling is enclosing with a vertical structure, like a fortified container, to divide and channel impulses in order to intersect two different some-'things': the character (which is an entity) and the interest (which is a no-thing), one being limited, the other unlimited. Since only the emptied one could be controlled, the interest of the second one is to possess the first one, to make it similar to itself. The result is the falsification of the sensual, as interest transforms homology into a technological means – with the only resource it knows: the interest for control, rendered acceptable through the growth and multiplication resulting from such control. This growth and multiplication is ever more intensive, as the offspring of the fake matrix are devoid of fullness, so their dynamism for searching, for hunting down characters is never ending. In this way an incommensurable magnitude is evolving through the stimulations of hostility and violence, with distortion and disfiguration becoming the necessary moving force in the perverted matrix, even though the name 'matrix' indicates the opposite: it is the mother, the naturally truthful place for the future, the benevolent transformer of matter.

Nevertheless, those technical enterprises that grew out of hostility, confined and sealed behind their barriers were thriving on what they confiscated and rendered vulnerable, as Mumford has shown it in his excellent analyses of the first, ancient walling that immured and blocked their inhabitants (Mumford, 1973). The walls immured the desire, choice, and willingness of the circled ones, thus their sensual of being good with others, so their contentment in living was transformed from homology into submission, casting them into vulnerable masses.

Walling is first and foremost the emission of a structure in order to render a new construction physically visible, so every walling starts with an interruption – the matrix itself is an interruption. Digging a furrow breaks and thus multiplies into an inside and an outside, but also, with an edge driven down into the earth, and another one, the stakes or walls, up to the sky. Thus the earth, that previously was an unbroken unit, now becomes fragmented, ready to assume a matrixed identity through the new offspring named as a wall. Furthermore, each doubling edge now could cross over into another one in multiplicity, constituting a matrixed linear transformation, now in an artificial way, miming the one laid down by nature, the original 'matrix', mother of matter.[3] Walling operates by assimilating, breaking, dissolving concrete individuums, encircling and moulding them into settlers, city dwellers, or members of civilisations; in all cases assumed to be interest motivated. As this newly grown typeface, the 'rational individual', now excludes the possibility of homology, a full range of the same type of the same interest-design is formatted, without any limit and irreplaceability, following the template and logic of metallurgy, of which alchemy is a theoretisation, with the womb-like furnace as the matrix for mass-production, also connected to rituals of sacrifice (see Blakely, 2006). The matrixing of the interest-driven 'rational individual' becomes ever expanding, with all struggling with each, ever more numerous, ever more self-important (all developing their highest interest-importance), ever more terroristic and tyrannical, and also more filled up with interest in a process of identifying happiness with material well-being. Interest and interest seeking, the sensuals of wanting to know, to learn, to copy how to mould down forms are interrupting the authentic matrix. Interest-seeking can only be conscious and strategic: it is a fluxional sensual that alternates homology; a vain power that only regards one's own advantage or profit, and so it brutalises the matrix, this silent and uninterested one, which is preparing the homology for *you*, as an unconscious presupposition.

While perverting the matrix, the interest-driven subject is growing softer and more vulnerable, in the process adding further and further, more soft and vulnerable groups, thus producing growth, the proliferation of subordination or equation, as we see it through the expansion of the European Union, where in the name of 'Europe' corruption, in the etymological sense of a joint break, a giving up of one's character, is made desirable. Fake, perverted intersections produce growth out of walling, resulting in an increase of institutional importance, in a growth of control over the population, helping those vulnerable, who were rendered vulnerable by the same walling institutions in the first place, inside the transformative container that took up the place of the original matrix. However, and furthermore, adding an unlimited magnitude to the genuine is an undertaking not without its dangers. Placing under control the genuine, formative tissue of the matrix, blocking its own movement, is detrimental for the characters inside, and consequently this coagulates or freezes the matrix. The perverted matrix has a detrimental mastery on its creature-products, as they become immobile, paralysed. As already seen, the matrix as a generator has three phases, corresponding to the three phases of rites of passage and liminality. The first is the fathering phase of the unit. This phase is followed by the phase of liminality or the in-between stage, and finally in the reaggregation, as in the intersection process something different develops, which has resemblance to the original units, just like a child resembles to his parents. Since all these three phases were of matrix origin, or rather we should say originated in nature, one passage was as binding as the other. The faked matrix is not different, except that now the process will not be finished but prolonged into infinity, throwing out ever new and newer beings, in ever greater abundance in quantity, but devoid of the capability for living in dignity, following the logic of an unfinished or incomplete matrixing, or permanent liminality (Szakolczai, 2017).

The question now concerns the consequences of this process. To begin with, the entering characters began resonating, as the emotional impulses of the void moved them inside the matrix. But the characters will respond not only due to these vibrations, but because they have their own impulses as well, a pre-given order of lawful passions, rooted deeply in every entity. When characters are in motion, they will eternally remain in motion, unless something else stops them. This interruptor is the matrix itself, and the reason is the same, as the world is animated: an emotional substratum infiltrates everything. It is animated, but not dissociated: in the world of forms every passion has its proper, ordered target, fundamental, determined in being, with homology providing lawfulness for it, reaching the aim by the means of love. The question is what happens if there happen to be emitters, like the wall-builders, to be traced to the first settlements in the Natufian, one of the most momentous and mysterious changes in human history, who interrupt and usurp the matrixing process. The result will be definitely erratic, without its proper reason and cause, a blockage oriented against the dynamism of the matrix, but with an unexpected intention. Through a search for the distant origins of this process, even beyond the actual building of wall, it is still possible to collect and document some characteristic signs of the initial, disturbing steps.[4]

Union

This process of disturbance is a secretive action and the emitters are in an alien land not their own. They rather move in a furtive or stealthy way, persistently grabbing or possessing something that is not fully recognised for what it is, nevertheless taking away something which is not in their own authority. It is an annexation, the gaining of secret possession over a territory of others, the acquisition of one impulse by another, due to an interest in the proper quality of it. The emitters are approaching something, and certainly not in vain: they must evoke a union, a certain meeting point between themselves and their targets, to be able to accumulate want/sensuals/desires by transforming their target. If the union is sealed – when desires intersect – which is a fundamental step in linear trans-formation, there must appear somewhere a sign for that: a circle, the sign of the uterus, the mother-matrix; or a Maltese cross, also called cross potent sign. This is why when this connection, this union occurs, it takes the uterus form in its potentiality (see Chapter 4 by Bowman). The form of a walled city, the form of an encirclement, the form of a state of enchantment by circles, the form of the matrix itself as a vessel, the form of a tower with its rounded or square form are all emissions of a conceiving and producing entity: they all are parts of a closed system of transformation (see Chapter 2 by Szakolczai and Chapter 3 by Benţa).[5]

If we look at one of the first emissions made by men, the finger flutings from Palaeolithic caves, and if we attend carefully to a particular example from the Gargas cave (see Figure 1.1), we can see nervously growing mechanised sequences in the emerging curving outlines in the illimitable and infinite activities outlined by a bringing forth (Plato in the *Symposium* (206d) refers to a knowledge made manifest by the sensual of beauty in producing something new as 'bringing forth'). It shows a particular alertness for influencing in an artificial way, underlined by the uterus form in a corner of the image, capturing the inclination of the emitters to realise a union with the void and bring forth something that never existed before. Showing such an interest in something that not yet is needs a further elaboration, posing the question of the matrix: what is this vibrating power? What is this engine of the world? And what is this perversion, which is able to transgress beings and provoke productions? I will now present a few Palaeolithic images that show the intentional alteration of the matrix. The newly found power of finger fluting could be a preliminary question to every technological invention: how to divide nature and arrange its dissected elements into new combinations, more compatible with mechanical human exploitation, in contrast to the homology of nature? How to provoke and utilise the uterus/matrix by technological means, moving out of the natural process of transformation, bringing forth beings different from nature?

Nietzsche came up with the notion of *ressentiment* as the zeal behind the revaluation of values, while at the same time secretly miming the achievement of qualities, in a way that revenge, hatred, malice and seductiveness (so characteristic of Agamben's wolf-man, the bandit or the 'banned one')[6] became the driving force of actions, hiding the essential physical and mental weakness of the emitters (Nietzsche, 1967; Agamben, 1998: 105). While it is annihilating whatever moves on its own on the earth, it also implies warfare against nature, overgrowing and dissolving it, blindly advancing into uncertainty, searching to exceed the existing into indeterminate properties, employing more and more means for growth. Can we identify Nietzschean *ressentiment* in a Palaeolithic setting?

Finger fluting can be described as lines drawn with fingers on a soft surface, usually clay (Bednarik, 1986). Such incomplete outlines and curved lines exist in many Palaeolithic caves. They can appear figurative or demonstrate almost no recognisable pattern. The finger is pressed on the clay in order to give enough depth for a new form to appear. In the case of Figure 1.1 a uterus-like semi-circle was made with corresponding borders in the right side, with lines and barriers indicating the depth of the furrows; several narrow furrows were traced in the clay as a boundary marker, as if walling the uterus. Is this the way in which walling emits banks, which are placed alongside the furrow beds? We do not know, but these straits, trenches or furrows are channels towards passages and were constructed by fluting; they were new artefacts, new resonating inventions.

The new invention of fluting is without pre-design, the lining is faceless, but it expresses an interest to gain something, to stir up powers, and by leaping over traditional set-ups, it is thus a new opening and a new decision, implying a new determination. Somebody had to go down into the darkness and humidity, into the silent empire of the cave, targeting the void, reducing all perception to the sensation of touching. Fluting is a technique to direct someone by a cut on the surface, to make it react, resonate. It fills the clay with impulses; the distinguishing feature of man is to activate emotions solely by the will: man can decide to feel – a whole media industry would be built on this simple fact; actors in theatres or films are showing emotions that they as performers do not possess. The void in the cave is a most appropriate place for searching out such reactions, as it is an empty place filled with emotions, thus is in search of impulses, welcoming those who enter it and show themselves. The term 'void' here possesses a special meaning, as a potential for unending joining, for infinite assemblies of infinite combinations. The void can only show itself in the absence of sense perception, but the intense presence of the sensuals ('the sore flutter for the Beautiful' as Plato named Love in the *Symposium*: 206e) as it will be shown through the Brassempouy figurine's blind eyes and covered ears (Figure 1.2), but soundness of her mind.

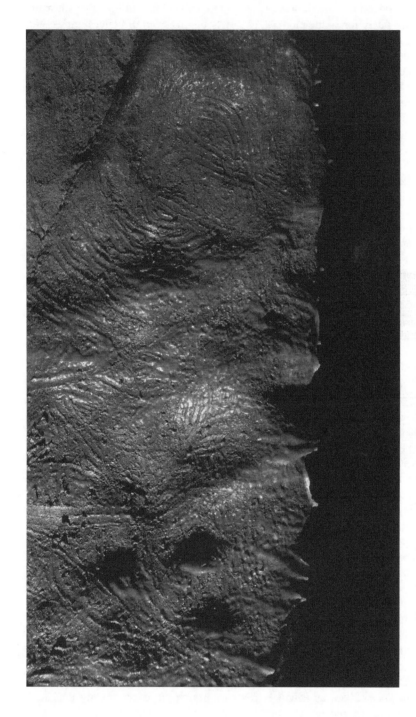

Figure 1.1 Walling the matrix: prehistoric finger fluting as linear transformation (Gargas cave, Pyrenees)

Source: Clottes (2002: 62). Published with permission.

Finger fluting captures power, by which one exceeds another one, though not explicitly, but rather as a dormant substance of acquisition. Here man is reduced to a mere comparative measure, where his main feature is conceived as fluxity. His character was thus fading away, ready to become transformed into the flux, subverting himself into voluntary similitude with the void. Finger-fluting forms are as fluid as if in a dream; only instances competing for entering into each other, until the intersection happens, as indicated by the uterus.

The dizziness of these outlines expresses an unbalanced loss of connection and yet dormant will to connect. Here we have a specific example for our postulate: when a clay surface lies still, it will lie still forever unless a finger stirs it, hence such stillness is its character. But the void is different, it is itself able to cause movement; it is unmovable, but able to move others (Aristotle, *Physics*, 260.a). Since Aristotle we know that the void has no parts, neither extension, shape or divisibility. The void is not nothingness, but it has some matter inside; it is immovable, ineffective and indivisible by its own, however sensible for attractions. The immovable void needs the individual form to be in movement, as a void cannot move without the reason and cause of the form, so it is not just unreal, but is also incapable for multiplication and magnitude by itself, so the interest of the emitter in the void has a certain actuality in it. Not a big one, but enough to resonate the clay and to establish connection with the void. Rightly so, as the moulding down can occur only in the out-of-ordinary, and now we are in the empty depth of the cave, which provides a special condition for the void's sensible presence.

These curved lines in the clay indicate an interest for sensory contact (though they themselves are impulses, as eagerness itself is an impulse) in order to connect and unite themselves with impulses innate in the clay surface of the cave and beyond, the clay transmitting the emotions of the emitters towards the void, transforming the interest of the emitters towards the void. Nevertheless, without doubt not only the emitter but all those who participate in the actions (clay, man, void) are exceeding their limits and expressing interest to each other.

Matrix emission: Palaeolithic homology

Beyond the numerous artificial matrix emissions, like circles, walls, semi-circles, together with rows and columns in sequential order, one of the earliest is the Brassempouy Lady (23,000 BC). It is also the most beautiful example for homology, still present and intact in this early image. The particular dynamic force that overflows with life is shown by the Brassempouy figure's hairdo (Lawson 2012), resulting in a regular succession of furrows with wall-like boundaries. The sequential order of the goddess's hairdo gives a systematic arrangement, having elements succeeding in a rhythm, according to a rule, a kind of dynamic regularity following one after another in an orderly pattern, evoking filiation that is establishing interrelations through genealogical lineages, like families, tribes or nations do in their finite arrangements, keeping law and order. Linear transformation is present here; the enclosed entities are with the same volume all along the length of the hairdo, showing neither regression nor development, the order is stable and finite, without alteration, offering a stamp for every entering character.

Figure 1.2 The Brassempouy Lady (Brassempouy cave, Landes)

This mammoth ivory carving is roughly 3.5 cm in height and 1.9 cm wide, containing clear facial features of forehead, brows, eyes lines and nose, but no mouth. The top and sides are incised with deeply carved motives, cut into the hairdo of the Brassempouy goddess figurine. A divine emission of lawful regularity, though without the perceptive organs of ears, eyes and mouth is speaking here in the figure of the goddess, whose sensitivity is indicated by the refined beauty of her features and her nose, ready to feel the perfumed sensuality of the world. The basic principle inherent in her godly nature is imprinted in her hair, the homology (orienting to preserving shapes and forms), being a distinctive kind of knowledge owned by her godhead, calling for participation. She was loved, as the world is to be loved, and the emitters of this figurine were like the ancient Greeks in their state of mind: acknowledging the goddess as a living being in goodness and truth who feels like us, who desires a rich and great existence in beauty, wit and agon. The *esprit* that animated the Greek republics was that of contentment, both with the extent of their territories and with their laws (Montesquieu 1999, Book VIII. Ch. 16) about the true union in harmony, in which all the parts, however opposed they may appear, concur in attaining the general good.

Homology is shown by the hairdo of the Brassempouy goddess, where the statue's hair follows the wave of impulses ordered into lines in a sequential manner to simulate the evocative effect of the linearity for human understanding. Plato in *Theaetetus* explained the homology in a twofold way: 'that nothing can ever become more or less in size or number, so long as it remains equal to itself'; and 'secondly, that anything to which nothing is added and from which nothing is subtracted, is neither increased nor diminished, but is always equal' (Plato, *Theaetetus* 155a).

No alteration is present here. For alteration a manipulative skill or *techné* is required which artificially blocks homology, freezing the moulding process into perversion. This is the way in which an incommensurable, infinite, indestructible mass of impulses can alter form, thus gaining a force and movement of its own, as only forms have movements. For this the alterator needs three requirements: a special place, special sensuals and a special *techné*.

A special place: caves

Caves are innocent of any seductive substance. However, the Greeks had a particular word for the cave, this archetypical matrix with its walled cavity, and this is the spelaion, which is equivalent with someone's private part for penetration (see Montelle, 2009). The word thus stands for union by sinking, submerging, slumping into its gouge or hollow, though in a sexual way: giving up one's resistance, resigning oneself to a possession and emerging from this as an alternated entity, different from one's previous self. The Latin word for the cave is *ventris*, 'womb' or 'fecundity': not simply an enclosing structure, but also the place of transformation, the place in which a new being is formed, and so it is a container to give place and space for a new formation. Apparently its danger lies in this unconditionality, being able to unite with anyone who possesses the key to awaken it. This union is not without a price; however, it produces a total occupation, as the void literally moves inside the individual that approached it, annihilating the self and nurturing a union. The fruit of this union with the void is a matrixed product, thoroughly intersected, launched to the world. The cave is empty, but at the same time a place-holder, giving comfort to any individual, comforting them once they lost their significance: giving them a new typeface. Here everything rules out creation; it is not that something new was created from nothing, but that something new was transformed from the entering characters by the void. The preconditions for transformation is the actual arrival of a new impulse, effect, thinking, mind-set, figure, character with a moving faculty; and this is enough, if the receptibility is ready to embrace, enduring it for generation.

Special sensuals: violence and hatred

In this image a 60 cm large bear is depicted as wounded and vomiting blood.[7] His body is covered with both arrow signs and small circles, showing attacks. The bear, a morose and incalculable creature, has very fine instincts; it senses everything, hears everything, remembers everything, and knows the activities and intentions of humans. The circles on its body, these ring-like formations, indicate intentions to catch and keep it, but at the same time are emanations of a divine matrix from the god's body. The circle is a connected whole which has no end and no beginning and is thus the sign of the void itself, encapsulated in the matrix. Here the bear-god gives up his godly attributes and is transformed into a suffering, vomiting low-level being, sinking into the void without dignity, in flux, but pure deprivation, emanating its power content.

The imagination of a possible violent act as a diversion from the original order and in a particularly violent way is shown on this god-bear. The god is shown attacked and in pain, its paws are erect and its nose is bleeding. Arrow signs are on its body, which suggests the idea that a painful transformation is taking place which transcends the god form. Here in a rare example we can witness the moulding matrix in two phases. The first is the figure of the god in its bear form, while the second is when it is attacked in order to force the moulding process, indicated by little zeros on the image. Moulding is the process of taking away form and making a new one, making connections with powers, though these words cannot capture the high intensity of the resonations that are and must be present to successfully break up, dissect and then intersect. It has already been discussed how love and the appetite to possess others can coincide, but this is further demonstrated by the arrow signs on the god's body: they are there to hurt and thus to possess, but also to possess by love, to strike the god so that it would accept penetration.

Actually, the circle, adopted from an Indian sorcery figurine (Kaplan, 2000; Seife, 2000), became the sign for the zero (0) in the Middle Ages. The zero as placeholder is a sorcerous character; it takes away the qualities of forms, and replaces them with emptiness (zero), thus producing a transformed form. If we do any simple mathematical operation on a natural number with zero, whether addition, extraction, division or multiplication, the result every time is either the negation of the operation or the negation of the concrete number. The void, or non-being, worried the Greeks, for whom the idea was threatening, as it implied the wholesale renunciation of nature. They claimed that absolute void is terrifying, as nothing can exist in nothingness, for the simple reason that if man remains alone, he loses his courage, and becomes a fearful, trembling being, disfigured and weak. It produces an active de-realisation of the world, resulting in a leached and synthetic state.

Special techné

The immersion of man into the void is an emanation from finite forms, with the result of letting transgressions ontologically and essentially be. The image of the wounded man is presented in a deprived, demonic form (with tail and beak). From its first appearance in Palaeolithic, sorcery/magic/shamanism is always connected to hurting and pain, with victims of violence being represented. When tricksters (Horvath, 2015) are born, *techné* must be present, and indeed in the upper corner of the image there are three machine-like triangles indicating their working.

The famous 'wounded man' is rather a beak-headed trickster-demon, recalling the Shaft Scene of Lascaux (see Horvath, 2013). The image in Cougnac cave, Lot,[8] has the sketch of a standing man, with a tail and beak, with his body pierced by broken lines. Above his head, there is an aviform. There is hurting power captured in the image: the flux entered a human form, whether it is the intruder, the emitter or the finger fluter, transforming it into a demon by the assistance of a whole gamut of unreal-mechanical apparatuses, as shown by the aviform triangles. The next stage is illustrated in the image in the more famous Pech-Merle cave.[9] Here the same figure is now horizontal, as if falling down or perhaps flying, and the dome-like or 'avi-form' structures actually reached the head of the trickster, expressing a newly grown transcendental link or power connected to his bodily pain and suffering for letting sensuals come forth. The 'avi-form' also remarkably evokes the 'open female' images, known in Tassili and many other Neolithic sites, being particularly close to the single such representation found in Göbekli Tepe, which is even explicitly pornographic (see Schmidt, 2010: 246, Figure 13).

The void is a self-begetting place if it enters in union with forms, this is what the matrix is about. It can be divided and cut as many times as one wishes, but it has no magnitude by itself, it is always the same, the void. It is always possible to take something outside from it, so in theory it is able to continue in an unending series of magnitudes by division or by addition, but in practical actuality it always remains the same, it will never change its volume.

However, exceeding homology shows another picture. When homology was taken away, the void became united with interest, and the results are these trickster figures, rather bizarre, grotesque characters. They are melancholic, low, soft and transparent, indifferent and dependent, expressing a kind of submissiveness into infinite modifications and shape-lifting, the fake matrixing. They seem placid, yet aggressively possess a space; they must be present, be heard and acknowledged. Their main target is not known, but it grows in infinitum towards newer and newer coming-forth sensuals, are in constant territorial expansion, until they dissolve all bonds and annihilate any border or limit. What are the consequences if you change dimensions, add or extract from them; if you bring fear, the trembling awe of living into your very reality, or plainly change contentment into despair: nothing? A nothing, but a particular one, the demonic (Castelli 2007), the hybrid figure of the void: the good for nothing, an existence without merit, virtue and value, which can never die, but which is ever deepening the emission of the sensual, as it is seen in the wounded bison in the 'Salon Noir' in Niaux, Ariège.[10] Here a beautifully drawn bison is shown, standing in his hind legs, the centre of his body pierced by two arrow signs.

Techné as hurting: the wounded bison-god

Wounding a god signifies letting interest as a building tool ontologically and essentially be. In this image interest in seduction is shown by the love-arrows. Here the bison is not showing weakness, quite the opposite, it has a powerful appearance, in spite of the arrows in its body. Arrows are indicating break-ups and cuts for penetration.

Two arrows indicate a break or schism; while evoking a sign of death, the wounds are not so serious. The cut, the wound caused by the arrows, the violation of form serves a double purpose: first, to show that the god has an infinite mass and energy, and it can agree with the emitters; and second, to reveal its proud form as an empty sack, ready to be filled by the emitter's form. The god thus became animated by humans, nurturing a new mode of existence inside its divine body. It is always possible to take something outside, once the union was realised. Once an emitter chooses a suitable *techné* for approaching the void, all interest can be focused on and fulfilled by it. The royal road for unifying *techné* with the void is the vibration of feelings, or sensuals. In sensuality each elementary gratification is composed of an enjoyment vibration, an enjoyment that is derived from the senses, from a single string, where all vibrations are identical. Different vibrations could be present in homology, but such difference is not apparent in the intensity of the vibration; it is the same in agreement and in violence: it is *intensive*.[11]

Five of the six images presented above, with their pain and suffering, show how matrixing phenomena can be universally explicable in terms of motion, power and intersection, and are indexed by fear and violent sensuals in case of its perversion. Void is behind the matrix that swallows characters and leads them into a new appearance, setting in motion the void, through the energy exerted by forms. Yet, altering the matrix sensuals of homology destroys the marvellous mechanism of nature into perversity by an infinite absorption of energies out of the dissection of characters, without giving them back the dignity of form. Thus, not only time and space become meaningless, but everything else falls into the flux. Motion becomes confused as well, not as something inside but rather outside of individuals, corresponding to force, as defined by Hobbes, implying not an inner dynamism, but an ultimate aim of the transformation process: releasing powers by dissection, absorbing them and then releasing them into various combinations. This new construct will be then that binding surface where all suffering is overcome. Individuums thus become individuals, pure representations of the will of emitters, subject to their control, and in an ever more automatic manner. The disfigured individuals no longer possess the virtues necessary to live life in harmony with nature, so an artificial bordering as walling always must be there to console for the loss of self-bordering. Walling purports to restore what was lost, but that was lost because of walling – a logic at the origin of all modern institutional reforms, and their futility.

Conclusion

The building of walls in our times receives increasing attention. But the fact that walling is growing and prosperous does not supply the positive proof about its necessity. Walling may have come into existence through us, or it might be rationalised by a defensive need, and so humanised, but what I wanted to explore in this chapter was how walling emerged in the minds of men. For a proper understanding of the phenomenon of walling it was necessary to work genealogically, starting from remote history, and illustrate that the order of nature can be broken down through a series of subsequent transformations, where walling serves to intensify this very transformative process. Walling is a fake matrix, an erratic linear transformation which seeks to establish a connection and a unity between men and the void, in a radical renunciation of nature, uniting themselves with interest, with sensuals, which can never be fulfilled, never satisfied, thus never dies out, but is infinitely searching for possessions and occupations.

Walling is thus equivalent with subversion, interest, utility or multiplication, as all of these are taking away the meaning of life, as this originates in actions and intentions coming from the inside and not imposed by external forces, developed through an interaction with nature by one's own frugal goodwill. The new doctrine of walling is immediately shrouded in controversy: Who will articulate the new intentions? Who will control the controllers? Who controls how and why to border us? It is the same question as the 'Who plans the planner?' that was formulated in the 1930s by Karl Mannheim (1940: 75) against the idea of central planning.

Walling justified its existence by the supposed need to defend people from themselves, as it replaced individuals moving themselves with some-'thing' between them as the source of movement, thus giving place to the void. Walling thus justified itself as necessary for generating cohesion and coherence, thus redefining the edifice of nature, enacting new emotional and habitual entities. Walling became the new source of movement, a perverted matrix that transforms meaningful order into an illegitimate, rigid structure, giving rise to the grave problem of mediation, with the void uniting with forms (emptying them) and thus bringing forth new entities, which then further perpetuates faking. Walling channelled and thus transformed sensuals into interests thus could intervene on behalf of the walled ones, promoting their interests, continuously dividing, enclosing and protecting areas, first 'enveloping' and then 'developing' artificial constructions based on equation, on the state of being equal, on a shared lack of audacious movement.[12]

This curious container of unity developed out of a peculiar source, out of pure depravity, and then generated further transformations in which all new institutional variables are linear functions of the original intentions, developed out of deprivation; this is why it is so defensive, but also so expansive. Building one more walling above the others could go on infinitely, as soft and plausible are its individual foundations, interest, lust and appetite for the others' possessions. So walling continuously progresses, by rigidly applying the sensuals of fear and emptiness, never reaching into a higher kind of value or virtue. One may theorise a significance for the identities developed through walling, or emphasise the reverse, but one would still have done nothing, as walling is a mere deficiency – it was never real!

Walling still and ever functions as an unlimited, unfinished plasticity. So every time a new walling grew up on the original one, following a breakdown of the previous one, the process created a new make-up, installing ever new and improved institutionalised patterns to place men into a more deprived state of fear. Walling is piling liminality upon liminality, proliferating deprivation through a kidnapped process of linear transformation, as it reinforces submission and builds up passivity in fair and equal measure, thus canalising power out of characters, emptying them. Behind walls everybody is equally betrayed, individual needs becoming routinised, as walling procures an unfair advantage for the individual demanding, at the expense of divine giving, thus creating societies where the driving force becomes complaining, and continuous efforts to outdo the others – the fellow walled ones. When Plato in the *Timaeus* defined the matrix, he was earnest about its importance for the reality of generation. The matrix is always receiving, it is a moulding stuff for everything, moved by the marvellous entering figures who still resemble the ancient archetypes:

> [50c] of the substance which receives all bodies the same account must be given. It must be called always by the same name; for from its own proper quality it never departs at all for while it is always receiving all things, nowhere and in no wise does it assume any shape similar to any of the things that enter into it. For it is laid down by nature as a moulding-stuff for everything, being moved and marked by the entering figures, and because of them it appears different at different times. And the figures that enter and depart are copies of those that are always existent, being stamped from them in a fashion marvel-lous and hard to describe, which we shall investigate hereafter. For the present, then, we must conceive of three kinds,—the Becoming, that 'Wherein' it becomes, and the source 'Wherefrom' the Becoming [50d] is copied and pro-duced. Moreover, it is proper to liken the Recipient to the Mother, the Source to the Father, and what is engendered between these two to the Offspring; and also to perceive that, if the stamped copy is to assume diverse appearances of all sorts, that substance wherein it is set and stamped could not possibly be suited to its purpose unless it were itself devoid of all those forms which it is about to receive from any quarter.

In this magnificent vision everything is moving and is full of the constant motion of generation, while walling as its alteration is a blockage, freezing the flow of this loving movement, only producing perversions. Walling multiplies places by frag-menting space in such a way that the sum of the structured walls equals the sum of the linear transformations that were originating in the fluxed void. Thus, we now have the flux as our reference point in the place of solidity, an eager volume with extremely little actuality in it. Still, the living world is never silent: it is feeling, gracefully obeying orders, appreciating genuineness, and in fact is quite undisturbed by walling.

Notes

1 In this essay I will use the word 'sensual' as a noun, in order to designate a certain unity of feeling, sensation (as sense perception), but also a mental operation as captured in terms like 'sense of judgement'. Such a unity was still present in the way Pascal used 'sentiment' in French, but the English meaning since has been reduced to the 'soft' sense of 'feeling'.
2 I'll use this word instead of 'individual', a word that has become reserved for the interest-driven, non-descript appendix of technology, assumed as the nature of human being by economic theory.
3 Note that the etymology of the three words is identical.
4 See Horvath and Szakolczai (2018) for more details.

5 Perhaps this is why the Etruscan city design, source of Roman town planning, combines the circle or square and cross motives.
6 I thank Egor Novikov for calling my attention to this idea of Agamben.
7 See www.donsmaps.com/troisfreres.html. The image is from Les Trois-Frères, Ariège cave (see Breuil, 1930).
8 See http://secretebase.free.fr/ovni/histoire/art/art.htm; Lorblanchet (2010).
9 See www.donsmaps.com/pechmerle.html; Lorblanchet (2010). Such 'wounded man' image is only present in Lascaux, Cougnac and Pech-Merle; furthermore, Pech-Merle is only about a few miles from Pergouset cave, with its famous 'Room of Monsters', another sign of the Palaeolithic trickster.
10 See www.donsmaps.com/niauxgalleries.html.
11 It is this intensity that will be captured in the 'sublime', central term of modern aesthetics, since Edmund Burke, Lessing and Kant.
12 We should note that the word 'develop', which is a very modern term in its current meaning of 'improvement' or 'advancement', originally simply meaning 'reveal' or 'unwrap', technically and literally implies a previous 'wrapping' or 'walling', thus by no means implies a 'natural' process of growth.

Bibliography

Agamben, Giorgio (1998) *Homo Sacer*, Stanford: Stanford University Press.

Aristotle (2008) *Physics*, Oxford: Oxford University Press.

Bednarik, Robert G. (1986) 'Parietal Finger Markings in Europe and Australia', *Rock Art Research* 3, 1: 30–61.

Blakely, Sandra (2006) *Myth, Ritual, and Metallurgy in Ancient Greece and Recent Africa*, Cambridge: Cambridge University Press.

Breuil, Henri (1930) 'Un dessin de la grotte des Trois frères (Montesquieu-Avantès) Ariège', *Comptes rendus des séances de l'Académie des Inscriptions et Belles-Lettres*, 74, 3: 261–4.

Camus, Albert (2010) *Notebooks, 1942–1951*, Chicago: Ivan R. Dee.

Castelli, Enrico (2007) *Il demoniaco nell'arte: Il significato filosofico del demoniaco nell'arte*, Torino: Bollati Boringhieri.

Clottes, Jean (2002) *World Rock Art*, Los Angeles: Getty Conservation Institute.

Foucault, Michel (1982) 'The Subject and Power', in H. Dreyfus and P. Rabinow, *Michel Foucault: Beyond Structuralism and Hermeneutics*, Chicago: University of Chicago Press.

Gell, Alfred (1999) *The Art of Anthropology*, London: Athlone Press.

Hesiod (1995) *Hesiod/The Homeric Hymns*, London: Heinemann.

Hobbes, Thomas (1968) *The Leviathan*, Harmondsworth: Penguin.

Horvath, Agnes (2013) *Modernism and Charisma*, London: Palgrave.

Horvath, Agnes (2015) 'The Genealogy of Political Alchemy: The Technological Invention of Identity Change', in A. Horvath, B. Thomassen and H. Wydra (eds) *Breaking Boundaries: Varieties of Liminality*, Oxford: Berghahn.

Horvath, Agnes and Arpad Szakolczai (2018) *Walking into the Void: A Historical Sociology and Political Anthropology of Walking*, London: Routledge.

Latour, Bruno and Vincent A. Lépinay (2009) *The Science of Passionate Interests: An Introduction to Gabriel Tarde's Economic Anthropology*, Chicago: Chicago University Press.

Lawson, Andrew J. (2012) *Painted Caves: Palaeolithic Rock Art in Western Europe*, Oxford: Oxford University Press.

Lorblanchet, Michel (2010) *Art pariétal: grottes ornées du Quercy*, Paris: Rouergue.

Kaplan, Robert (2000) *The Nothing That Is: A Natural History of Zero*, Oxford: Oxford University Press.

Leibniz, Gottfried W. (2014) *Monadology*, Edinburgh: Edinburgh University Press.

Mannheim, Karl (1940) *Man and Society in an Age of Reconstruction*, London: Routledge.

Meinecke, Friedrich (1972) *Historism: The Rise of a New Historical Outlook*, London: Routledge.

Montelle, Yann-Pierre (2009) *Paleoperformance: The Emergence of Theatricality as Social Practice*, London: Seagull.

Montesquieu, Charles de (1999) *Considerations on the Causes of the Greatness of the Romans and their Decline*, Cambridge: Hackett.

Mumford, Lewis (1973) *The City in History*, Harmondsworth: Penguin.

Nering, Evar D. (1970) *Linear Algebra and Matrix Theory*, New York: Wiley.

Nietzsche, Friedrich (1967) *On the Genealogy of Morals*, New York: Vintage.

Plato (1961) *Lysis/Symposium/Gorgias*, London: Heinemann.

Plato (1966) *Cratylus/Parmenides*, London: Heinemann.

Plato (1996) *Theaetetus/Sophist*, London: Heinemann.

Scheler, Max (2010) *On the Eternal in Man*, New Brunswick, NJ: Transaction Publishers.

Schmidt, Klaus (2010) 'Göbekli Tepe – the Stone Age Sanctuaries', *Documenta Praehistorica* 37, 239–56.

Sharpe, Kevin and Leslie van Gelder (2006) 'The Study of Finger Fluting', *Cambridge Archaeological Journal* 16, 3: 281–95.

Seife, Charles (2000) *Zero: The Biography of a Dangerous Idea*, London: Souvenir Press.

Szabo, Arpad (1978) *The Beginnings of Greek Mathematics*, Boston: Reidel.

Szakolczai, Arpad (2017) *Permanent Liminality and Modernity: Analysing the Sacrificial Carnival through Novels*, London: Routledge.

2 The meaning and meaninglessness of building walls

Arpad Szakolczai

Why do we build walls? Nothing seems more natural, if we look at it from the perspective of the present; and yet, nothing is more absurd, from a proper perspective. Building walls seems to be the most obvious of things, as houses have walls, even fundamentally consist of walls, and we live in houses, where we feel at home – in fact, the words for 'house' and 'home' are all but identical in most European cultures. But we also build walls to separate houses, evidently so that we would feel even more at home, in our own house; but also to surround entire villages, cities and states with them; civilisation, it seems, is founded on the building of walls. Yet, from a proper, genealogical perspective, not projecting our own taken-for-granted views backwards as 'rational' and 'natural', but rather looking at human life from its earliest times and thus moving forward, or from the perspective of *walking*, a wall is very troublesome.

Walling is a deeply unnatural and irrational construction, as it blocks the progress of walkers. Walkers anyway face many obstacles in their road: they must negotiate mountains and rivers, they need to climb up and down, they cross all but impenetrable forests and wide open plains under the sun, thus face enough challenges; why multiply these with walls? Not surprisingly walking cultures, or civilisations, in the Maussian and not etymological sense of the word this time (see Wengrow 2010), did not build walls.

The origins of walling: lessons from linguistics

As often, etymologies offer a helpful starting point. However, given the great antiquity of wall-building as a practice, one must be extra careful. In fact, the situation is even more complicated, as this practice, after all, is not *that* old. Walling only makes sense since settlement, and in fact there is no evidence of walls being built in the Palaeolithic. Thus, in tracing such etymologies one not only must avoid 'backward inference' (Nietzsche 1974, No. 370), as always, but also hope to find indications of a source beyond the horizon of settlement and the Neolithic (or the Epipalaeolithic).

At a first and most obvious level words denoting walls reflect military purposes of defence and possession, the purported most evident 'reason' why walls were made, and are connected to words denoting strength. Thus, *okhuroma*, one of the ancient Greek words for 'wall' also means 'fortress' and 'prison', to be traced to *okhuros* 'firm, lasting', connected to a verb meaning 'fortify' (Beekes 2010). The term is traced to PIE **seg* 'hold, have', an etymology similar to Sanskrit *sahati* 'conquers, is powerful' and *sahu* 'strong' (Turner 1966: 768). At a second level removed, terms for 'wall' derive from the material of which solid walls were made. Examples include Russian 'stjena', to be traced to PIE **stai*, just as English 'stone' or German 'stein', meaning a 'real', stone wall, in contrast to a mere wooden fence (Wade 1996: 209). However, one of the Latin words for 'wall', *vallum*, originally meant a 'palisade', or a circle of wooden stakes (de Vaan 2008); while *sien* or *siena*, denoting 'wall' in several Baltic languages, allude to the way such fences were actually woven together. This is quite similar to the second ancient Greek word for 'wall', *teikhos*, also meaning 'fortification, castle, fortified wall', and traced to PIE **deig* 'knead, form, fashion', having again a close relative in Sanskrit *dehi* 'mound, bank, surrounding wall' (see again Turner 1966: 374), but also Latin *fingo*, similarly meaning 'spread out, knead, build', but also 'alter the truth to deceive, feign, pretend'.

Here, however, we are already close to the third layer of meaning, connected not to the purpose of a wall, or the material of which it is made, but the very act of *making* it – thus, closer to our central interest concerning the reasons why such a stunning practice, the purposeful making of an obstacle, ever emerged in the history of humankind. The second Latin word for 'wall', *murus* 'defensive stone wall', and source of the similar Italian and French words, just as German *Mauer*, present in English in 'mural', is traced to PIE **moi-ro* 'to build', thus coming together with Greek *teikhos*, even though the root is quite different.

Teikhos is rooted in PIE **deig* 'form, fashion', thus similar to 'build', and also offering an intriguing – though etymologically not recognised – connection with *techné* 'craftsmanship, artifice, trick', rooted in IE **tek* 'produce', and/or **te-tk* 'build, timber'. Here 'building' is related to wood and not stone, and the term has some evident, and acknowledged, link to *tekton* 'carpenter', but one must wonder whether there was not some internal connection between these terms at a certain stage in the development of language, all the more so as the close semantic connection between Latin *fingo* and Greek *techné* evokes the kind of 'cunning intelligence' discussed in the classic work by Détienne and Vernant (1978).

This conjecture is all the more likely as at a fourth level etymologies for 'wall' are traced to a trick, but of a very particular kind. This applies for Hungarian *fal*, an ancient Finn-Ugric term traced to a tool for catching fish with some kind of 'dam' or 'weir'; while 'weir' is also an English term for 'dam, fence, enclosure', especially for catching fish, and also present in this sense in Old Norse, Old Frisian and Gothic languages. This is an extremely important finding, as the catching of fish is an activity predating settlement and agriculture and is closely connected to the figure of the trickster; in fact, apart from the invention of fire, widely assigned to trickster figures, the trickster is mostly credited, over the range of cultures, with the invention of traps for catching fish.[1] Such a connection with trickster figures is reinforced by the Old Norse term *veggr* 'wall', a word also denoting a dwarf in Norse mythology, dwarfs frequently being trickster figures.

This also suggests that, originally, the aim of building walls was perhaps not so much to defend from the outside, but to entrap inside.

As, for the moment, we do not have tools to connect these linguistic events to chronological history,[2] we need to turn to archaeological evidence.

The origins of walling: lessons from archaeology

There are three major, primordial wall constructions in distant history. Two of them, the walls of Jericho and Babylon, are extremely famous and since a long time, play a prominent role in the Old Testament. The third, in the megalithic sanctuary of Göbekli Tepe, was only discovered in 1994. Yet, arguably, it holds the key to the other two, and to some extent to the entire phenomenon of walling. The three also constitute a tight series: Göbekli Tepe is the first case of circular stone walls being made, and these surrounded sanctuaries; Jericho was the first case of a wall being built around a human settlement, which was a village; while the walls in Babylon and other Mesopotamian sites are connected with the emergence of the city.

Göbekli Tepe

Göbekli Tepe is in Southern Turkey, close to Syria, just south of the Taurus Mountains, thus at a highly liminal place then as now. Furthermore, it is about 15 kilometres north-east from Sanliurfa, historically called Urfa and also Edessa (with that name having some significance for the rise of Christianity). It is also close to Aleppo and Harran, and only about 120 kilometres away from Malatya (ancient Meliddu), with the important archaeological site of Arslantepe, central for the transition to the Bronze Age. Even further, it is just about a day's walk (20 miles) towards the east from the hilly flanks of Karacadağ Mountain, where the domestication of emmer and einkorn wheat took place.

The sanctuary was built just at the end of the Ice Age, around 9600 BC, by hunter-gatherers, and was intentionally and quickly buried around 8000 BC (Schmidt 2000, 2011). It was never inhabited according to its excavator, and even 'the use of fire at the site has not been noted' (Schmidt 2010: 241–2).

Göbekli Tepe is best known for its numerous and enormous megalithic pillars. Some of them are 5.5 metres high, weighing up to 50 tons, and there are possibly hundreds of them, as still only a small part of the site is excavated. However, for this book the central point is that these pillars, often with engravings and reliefs, were organised into a series of enclosures, surrounded by very substantial, circular-oval or square, stone-built walls. While the general function of these enclosures is still mysterious, as no traces were found yet either of burial practices or of rituals of sacrifice, they were probably some kind of sanctuaries. Some of these pillars were erected on pedestals cut out of natural bedrock, and they evidently represented powerful beings, with several showing anthropomorphic features. This led Schmidt to conjecture that, 'If gods existed in the minds of Early Neolithic people, there is an over-whelming probability that the T-shape is the first known monumental depiction of gods' (253).

If this were the case, it is all the more intriguing why these sanctuaries were surrounded by thick walls.[3] The enclosure-sanctuaries seem piled upon each other, with access to and between them being quite difficult.

A possible clue towards the answer is provided by the character of the representations. The images are in radical contrast to those painted on the walls of Palaeolithic caves – walls that were natural, not constructed, and internal, under the ground. While Palaeolithic cave imagery exudes unspeakable beauty and harmony, the Göbekli Tepe images are rather threatening and fearful. In the words of the excavator, in beholding them one feels 'danger, menace, fright, dread' (Schmidt 2011: 245); their presence exudes a 'supernatural and crashing force' (260). This is further supported by the character of the animals represented on the megalithic pillars. Most frequently depicted are the serpent (28.4 per cent), the fox (14.8 per cent) and the wild boar (8.7 per cent) (see Peters and Schmidt 2004: 185), and also insects, in particular spiders and scorpions.[4] The list contains some of the most widely identified trickster animals, the serpent being the prominent trickster of the Old Testament, the fox in the Middle Ages (Varty 1967), but also among the Dogon (Dieterlen 1989) and various other cultures, similarly to the spider (Horvath 2008), which was also rediscovered by the great novelists of the nineteenth century, Dickens and Dostoevsky, as representation of 'absolute evil' (Citati 2000; see Szakolczai 2016a). Thus, the great Neolithic sanctuary of Göbekli Tepe is nothing else but a trickster bestiary.

If this is so, then it offers us a cue about the strange innovation of stone walling. The sanctuaries possibly were not erected to venerate gods; rather the enclosures, with their walls, were used to capture, entrap and imprison harmful, demonic beings. This could have corresponded to the uncertain, threatening conditions experienced at the and of the Ice Age, with the enormous rise in the sea levels that occasionally produced calamities of apocalyptic dimension, and the first encounters with the dilemmas of settled existence in nearby Natufian Palestine.

The features of Göbekli are quite distinct from those of the Natufian. Natufian is the first settled culture, with signs about the storing of food but not of agriculture. There are also traces of sacrificial rituals, part of a cult of the dead, even of death, with no interest in the artistic representation of animals, while the area around Göbekli is the place where the first experiments with plant and animal domestication took place, with nearby Nevali Çori, which also had megaliths, playing a central role.

Jericho

Just when the Göbekli sanctuary was destroyed, around 8000 BC, a series of major stone buildings were erected in Jericho, at the heart of the Natufian. Studies of Jericho, literally up to our days, ignore Göbekli Tepe and the other southern Turkish discoveries of the past decades, even though Jericho can only be understood properly, genealogically, through Göbekli Tepe, as 'it had been at Göbekli and not Jericho that the history of the world had turned' (Mithen 2003: 67). Still, recent studies of Jericho offer a series of fresh insights concerning the two most famous attractions of the Neolithic part of the site, the Wall and the Tower.

While Kathleen Kenyon, excavator of the site in the 1950s, considered it as a defensive rampart, in the absence of any potential attackers or similar constructions the idea has been abandoned (Barkai and Liran 2008: 275; Bar-Yosef 1986; Naveh 2003: 86–7). The alternative suggestion of Bar-Yosef, that it was a flood defence system, against both water and mud, however, is similarly unsatisfactory, as there was simply not enough water in the area presenting a threat to justify such a construction. This explanation also failed to account for the particularly thick walls towards the West (Barkai and Liran 2008: 276). These two approaches are connected by their 'Cartesian point of view', limiting the building to a 'technological measure', imposing a 'physical modification of the material reality' (Naveh 2003: 87). New explanations favour a symbolic reason. However, one needs to find a very convincing argument why such a massive work was undertaken, as the wall has a width of about two meters, a height of 3.5 to 5 metres, is surrounded with a ditch cut into solid bedrock that is 8 metres wide and 2.7 metres deep, and has a circumference of about 600 metres. A recent approach suggests that this had to do with a particular geographical-astronomical constellation: there is a geographical alignment between the mountain, the tower, and the stairs inside the tower that gives access to its top (Barkai and Liran 2008: 278–9). Furthermore, the authors argue that it can be shown through computer simulation that at the time of building the Quruntul peak of the Judean Mountains, just west of the site, a major source of fresh water, cast a shadow in alignment with the Tower over the settlement during sunset at the Summer Solstice (Liran and Barkai 2011).

According to the researchers even a computer simulation of the events offers a 'powerful experience', which must have been even more 'dramatic' and 'awe-inspiring' in actual reality and ten thousand years ago. While their earlier article only focused on the perceived connection between the cosmos and the actual habitat, rendering evident that the alignment in the building was a conscious, planned, concentrated action (Barkai and Liran 2008: 281–2), the more recent article goes beyond such a cautious conjecture and voices the possibility of a purposeful and evidently quite sinister manipulation: the construction might be a sign that by them 'some individuals [. . .] took the opportunity to take control over the population. Jericho's Neolithic tower may very well be the first concrete evidence of organised civic manipulation, and of the use of architecture as a means of calculated human control' (Liran and Barkai 2011).

Still, questions remain concerning the reasons for such an undertaking. There are three main problems with the explanations offered by Liran and Barkai (2008, 2011), and also Naveh (2003). They assume some kind of 'metaphysical fear' as the primary human condition, an idea refuted by the cave art culture represented by Chauvet, Lascaux and Altamira; they consider the building as connected to the origins of settlement, which however go back almost five millennia earlier; and, most crucially, they ignore the nearby Göbekli sanctuary. Focusing on this latter, and with the help of Alfred Gell's theory concerning the tight connections between technology, magic and enchantment,[5] for the particular purposes of this essay the following suggestion is offered.

The builders of Jericho certainly knew about the Göbekli complex, as the distance of about 400 miles was by no means unbridgeable in a basically still walking culture. From the perspective of that sanctuary, the Jericho building are not so unusual and unique as it is repeatedly claimed; though the purpose has no doubt been modified. If the builders of Jericho indeed took Göbekli as a model, then two features of the complex had a particular effect on them. First, the sanctuary, especially through the huge pillar stones was indeed awesome, producing not simply fascination, but also 'captivation' and 'abduction', two words central for Gell (1998: 12–14, 68–72), originally both meaning to take hold of somebody as a prisoner. Second, the walls were evidently indeed built in order to 'entrap' or 'capture' (trickster) demons or 'evil spirits'. The pillars and the wall are the two most important features of the Göbekli complex, and they are one by one reflected or even 'mimicked' by Jericho, though applied to the concrete setting. Thus, instead of a number of pillars, requiring considerable artisanship as well as artistic skill to decorate them with animals, skills notoriously absent from the Natufian area, rather one huge tower was built, which also mimicked the nearby mountain, thus – using the celestial alignment – offering, with the sunset, an even more concentrated and dramatic effect; and furthermore, the walls were not built around an uninhabited sanctuary, rather the inhabited settlement. In other words, the wall was used to entrap not gods but humans, thus combining a kind of technological-astronomical magic produced by enchantment-abduction, with actual, physical enclosing. If one requires a close contemporary equivalent, this can be found in the Soviet Union, with its space programme on the one hand, which goes back to the 1930s, or the direst Stalinist times in Russia, and the tight sealing off of its borders, with nobody being allowed out of the country, passports being required even for leaving the big cities in order to visit the countryside.

The building of walls, as a practice, initially was a sacred activity, as originally almost anything was, eventually transferred to human settlements, first in Jericho. Jericho, however, was still only a village surrounded by walls,[6] while for us, based on a very long history, walls are identified with cities or towns, and with mostly defensive fortifications. The walls of Babylon are the most emblematic, though not the oldest examples for this practice, which goes back to the origins of cities, to be traced to the Mesopotamian area. The recent, magisterial work of Jean-Claude Margueron (2013), outcome of a life-work, offers here a precious guide, complementing the biblical storyline discussed in this volume by Marius Ion Benţa.

City foundations and foundational walls

Margueron's approach is particularly interesting, especially from the perspective of the etymological considerations sketched above, as he reproaches archaeologists (excepting a pioneering work by Henri Frankfort; see Margueron 2013: 11) for not paying enough attention to the architectural aspects of city-building. According to him, the building of a city was a radical novelty, to be traced not to Jericho, as often done, rather to Mesopotamia.[7] Even further, the novelty was indeed something like an actual and genuine *tabula rasa*, in the sense that the first cities were literally built on a flat and cleared surface, on which then an enormous, 1–1.5 m high stone foundation was built (8–10). The reason for this was climactic: given the specific characteristics of weather in Mesopotamia, any other kind of building structure would have been destroyed by the elements within decades (26–7).

However, such foundations also implied the fixing of limits to an area to be surrounded by walls. Such walls were fixed for over ten centuries, underlining the divine character of urban territories (595). It therefore implied the literal creation of an empty space, or a void, into which then, following a plan, buildings were placed. Before such building work, however, first the infrastructure of the new city, above all the streets, were set in place, often following canals (553–5, 580, 605, 611). This way of proceeding was radically different from the way villages developed, started by concrete houses, where streets simply did not exist. In fact, according to Margueron, streets, often also delineated by inner walls, are the most distinct features of cities. In order to implement such a design, however, at first a central tower had to be built from which construction works could be supervised. Thus, after all, there are close connections to Jericho, including the links between tower and walls as a central feature, except that with the building of cities these were not imposed on a pre-existing settlement, but rather were starting points for the creation of a brand new one.

In laying down such foundations, including the walls, there was a confluence of the symbolic, even sacred, and the material. Walls and stone foundations were very real, using enormous blocks of rock, and for a very 'material' reason, the destructive forces of water and winds; but their construction at the same time implied a sacred, religious activity. The technique used remained unwritten, due to the close connection between urbanistic and religious thinking; a well-guarded secret of a religious/ritual elite (611).

The origins of this idea are almost most interesting and relevant. The first 'global city', Uruk, centre of the Uruk culture expansion, was not originally built in this way, and in fact can be rather considered as a 'global village'. However, experiments with *tabula rasa* city building were attempted at the sites of Habuba Kabira and Tepe el-Gawra during the Uruk period (446, 557–67), and their effect can be shown even in the site of Arslantepe, a first centre of metallurgy. However, the first city fully built by the new method was Mari (26), another major metallurgical centre at the liminal borderline between Syria and Iraq near the Euphrates, where the river takes a turn and also the current borderline crosses the river, thus showing the tight connection between metallurgy and the new idea of *tabula rasa* settlement-construction.

The link to metallurgy not only raises the possibility of a connection between smiths and masons, both joint experts in transformative technology and rituals, but also suggests a source about a key ritual associated with city foundation, human sacrifice. Traces of both animal and human sacrifice were already found in the Natufian and on a much larger scale in Cayönü, a site connecting southern Turkish sanctuaries and post-Natufian Palestine, but the institutionalisation of the practice arguably only happened with the foundation of cities.[8] The tight connection between *tabula rasa* city building and human sacrifice can be understood through the void: as the foundation of a city was not based on something concrete and pre-existing, but the creation of an empty space, a void, it needed particularly strong means to ensure social cohesion – which in a concrete setting was pre-existing, thus could be taken for granted. This is a main reason why Durkheim's preoccupation with social coherence as a *general* problem is fundamentally misplaced. It also signalled, right at the beginning, the potential end of any newly founded city: once the violent mechanisms keeping together the city lost their force, the growing inner void could only be maintained by conquest. The case of Assyria offers a textbook example of empire building driven by the inner void,[9] as the greater and more powerful the Empire became, the more its inner substance was emptied out, so that already by Antiquity Assyrians simple no longer existed as an 'ethnic' group.

The connection between city building and rituals, even rituals of human sacri-fice, took up a central place in the classic work of Rykwert (1988), focusing on Rome and its Etruscan origins.[10] However, a crucial and still little-known discussion of foundational sacrifices can also be found in a work by Mircea Eliade (1990), classical figure of the history of religions.[11]

Foundational sacrifices

For Eliade, rituals, in particular rituals of sacrifice, only repeat a foundational act. In Antiquity the Phoenician cities were particularly renowned for such rituals (Eliade 1990: 33), but the idea, with analogies to the alchemic-transformative thinking characteristic of metallurgy (40–2), can be traced to Mesopotamia and India (80), present in particular in a 'geometric and cosmological system' (33–4), just the kind recently identified with Jericho. Such sacred cosmology played a central role at the confluence of city foundations and violent sacrificial rituals, as both were defined as being analogous to world creation, a repetition of the initial divine act of creating order out of chaos (8–12, 90). Here the actual struggle with nature was generalised and extended out of all proportion, creating a nature-hostile vision of the world, identifying some natural processes with a reversal into chaos, and *thus* positing the new, masonic-metallurgical elite as possessing the know-ledge for such world creation, even offering an ideological justification of violent death (91–3). Eliade argues that such knowledge was transmitted by secret societies organised by the holders of such professional knowledge, or the 'masters', connect-ing masons, smiths, architects and miners (99–101), evoking the connections in Greek mythology between demons and smiths, discussed in an important recent work by Sandra Blakely (2006), which also incorporated African ethnographic studies, focusing on the womb-like characteristic of the furnace, thus helping to connect, in the terminology of Horvath in this volume, the city-matrix with the furnace matrix, revealing the close affinity between human sacrifice and artificial matrixing and assigning – *pace* Durkheim – rituals of sacrifice not to the origins of culture and society, but rather to its perversion. The hubris implied in such acts was furthermore supported, and at the same time covered, by the highly taxing initiation rites that members of these secret societies were supposed to undergo (Eliade 1990: 101), or ascetic practices that Eliade traces to the origins of settlement (66), but that in fact can be traced back to the Palaeolithic.[12] Such acts of endurance increased the 'aura' of ascetic mason-smith-priests and, together with the – false – claims about 'world creation' helped to trick people into accepting the necessity of violent sacrifices, even convincing mothers to give up their children for such acts (40–4). The practice of sacred prostitution can also be connected to this ideology, as children born due to such activity could even more easily be used for sacrificial purposes (44–5).

Myths, or recollections of such rituals, were until recently still prominent in certain parts of Europe, and the motive is shown with particular, archetypal clarity in the Romanian myth of Master Manole (27–8).[13] This story not only captures the motive of a wife of the masons as sacrificial offering, but adds the theme of self-sacrifice as well.

Perhaps even more important for the history of walling is another point mentioned by Eliade, the quite different practice among the Greeks, where the foundation of the cities is to be traced to tombs erected for heroes, and related relics (87). The focus here is thus a *concrete* and not ritual death, and a *concrete* place visited, giving rise first to a sanctuary, and then eventually to a city (see also Polignac 1995). It can also be traced to the practices of burials, in the Palaeolithic, already recognised by Mumford as distant origins of the city, together with caves (Mumford 1961: 14–15). In this context it is relevant that it has been argued that there is no clear evidence that human sacrifices were ever practised by the Greeks (Hughes 1991); while the location of cities around the tombs of heroes can be extended even to pre-Roman Italy; especially to places associated with the Pelasgians (Briquel 1984), who were according to Herodotus (I.56-8; II.50-2) the inhabitants of Greece before the Greeks.

While the existence of Pelasgians is a quite contested theme, in particular through the unfortunate 'Pelasgian theory' in linguistics, which however has no bearing on this issue, it is necessary to extend the investigation to them, all the more so as it centrally touches upon the question of walling.

Pelasgians and their walls

One of the similarities between ancient Greece and Italy, well before classical Antiquity, concerns the presence of impressive, enormous wall constructions, called polygonal, Cyclopean or Pelasgian walls. In Greece, these are associated with Mycenaean culture and can be seen among others in Tiryns and Mycenae, but also in Athens. In Italy the most famous such cities, like Palestrina, Sora, Anagni, Alatri, Veroli or Ferentino, cluster just south of Rome, around the river Liri. The area also played an important, in a certain sense even foundational, role in medieval Christianity, containing the monastery at Monte Cassino (also site for polygonal walls), founded by St Benedict and centre for the Benedictine order in the medieval period; Casamari Abbey, a key Benedictine and later Cistercian monastery; the Church of Santa Salome in Veroli, containing the relics of St Salome, mother of the apostles John (the evangelist) and James (patron saint of pilgrims); while St Thomas Aquinas was born in Aquino. Pelasgian walls, however, also are present in Umbria (in Amelia) or Tuscany (in Orbetello), and for long were considered as built later than Rome. While such an idea was always highly puzzling, as the Mycenaean cities in Greece were clearly much older than Rome, it is increasingly questioned. But traces of the Pelasgians can also be found further south, especially in south-east Italy, for example in Otranto. Pelasgians and Etruscans were always connected, in ancient Italy as in Greece, and Dominique Briquel (1984) demonstrated that the classical accounts according to which the Pelasgians were the ancestors of the historical Etruscans should be given credit. Furthermore, recent archaeological evidence demonstrated that the first Neolithic communities in Greece were in the fertile Larissa basin in Thessaly (van Andel and Runnels 1995), an area classically called Pelasgiotis, just as the cities with Pelasgian walls south of Rome were in the fertile floodplains around the river Liri in Lazio. The Neolithic settlers of Thessaly came from Anatolia but – in contrast to previous belief – did not pass through the Balkans, rather by 'hopping' through the Islands (Perlès 2001). Thus, going back to very distant history, there were definite differences between the Graeco-Italic and Balkan cultures.

All this gains further importance through the striking character of these 'Pelasgian' walls. Though these walls are also enormous, they are still quite evidently different from Mesopotamian constructions. While the walls of Babylon or Niniveh attempt to overpower and crash those beholding them, the similar walls of Athens or Amelia are rather fascinating by their strange, enchanting beauty. Such impressions are due as much to the evident skills demonstrated in building them as their sheer visual impact. They cannot help recalling the maxim of Vitrivius, according to which architecture as an art implies the realisation of the unity of '*venustas, utilitas, firmitas*', or beauty, utility and skill. The building of a Pelasgian wall certainly required great skill, but even more communal efforts in fitting the carefully prepared bricks in place, quite different from the monotonous work and sheer physical force necessary for placing enormous square blocks upon each other. Thus, just as in their impression, also in their execution there is a wide gap between Near Eastern city walls, aiming at squashing those coming near to them, and employing sheer force and sacrificial rituals for their construction, which implied the mere execution of a preconceived master plan; and the Pelasgian walls, which rather astonish through their striking beauty, and whose building required a combination of artisanal – as opposed to geometrical-cosmological – skill and communal effort. These walls also closely recall the pattern of human skin.[14] Thus, it's as if they embody the difference between two visions of the city: the original, Mesopotamian *tabula rasa* construction on the one hand, and their pacification into the Pelasgian-Etruscan version on the other, which eventually gave rise to the Greek and Roman city states, flowering in a particular manner in Athens, and captured in the classic works of Plato and Aristotle.

The specific character of Graeco-Italian cities was also a subject of the classic work of Fustel de Coulanges on the ancient city. According to him, the central aspect of this city type was the connection with the cult of the dead, ancestors and heroes, and the sacred fireplace or the hearth (Fustel de Coulanges 1984: 7–31). Cities thus grew out of an alliance between closely knit ethnic groups, stability being maintained through property rights and the sacred character of city limits (62–72; see also Polignac (1995) and Finley (1977), who emphasises in particular the importance of autarchy for the ancient city). The European city owes its striking resilience over time to such origins in concrete communities and reliance on a degree of municipal autonomy, and not to purposeful state or city building (Clark 2009: 1, 7, 13). Even according to Paolo Portoghesi (2005: 44–5), an architect and historian of architecture, the greatest illusion of our days is the pretence to 'restart creation', resulting in cities that are impossible to live in. The desert metropolises are built for nomads who were nowhere at home, with the contemporary gurus of architecture propagating this same desert vision (22–5).

But how did all this eventually result in the contemporary, modern practice of walling? In order to offer a view on this, it is first necessary to give a short overview of the long-term historical process of which here only a few key elements were presented; then resume the main characteristics of the medieval city, according to the classic work of Lewis Mumford, all the more fundamental as Mumford was also a classic figure in the history of technology; and on this basis attempting to capture the main features of the related modern developments.

Overview, stocktaking

During most of their history, humans did not lead a settled existence, but walked.[15] This did not mean aimless and homeless wondering, but walking in a quite coherent manner, following the rhythm of seasons, in a wide area that for them was at the same time *the* world and their *home*. In this a crucial reference point was offered, eventually, but at least about half a million years ago, by the place where ancestors died and were buried, leading to a cult of the dead. Such a cult is widely considered as the origin of human culture, while according to Mumford (1961: 14) the permanent settlement of the dead, or necropolis, preceded human settlement. The reasons for the emergence of the first settlements around the end of the Ice Age still elude us, but at any rate these settlements were not surrounded by walls. The first walled spaces were the sanctuaries in Göbekli Tepe.

Settlement, and especially settlements surrounded by walls, represented a radical change in human history. This change, even etymologically, is generally associated with the rise of civilisation. However, it is rather doubtful that settlement can in any way be considered an 'advance' in terms of human values and 'quality of life'. What is certain, however, is that each step in the successive progress of settlement can be associated with a magnitude increase in violence, both with respect to the 'inside' and the 'outside'. Concerning the 'inside', this was first, in Natufian culture, due to the conflation of the space of the living and of the dead, strictly separated in the Palaeolithic, but also resulted in the emergence of sacrifices, as the artificial closing of humans into a limited space rendered inner coherence problematic, thus leading to the emergence of rituals of sacrifice, as analysed by Durkheim and Girard – except that this was *not* the origin of human culture, rather a consequence of settlement. Concerning the 'outside', such group identities also developed against those of similar neighbouring groups, resulting in the emergence and escalation of warfare. While we can only have conjectures about the distant origins of warfare, the manner in which the rise of Mesopotamian cities was accompanied by inter-city warfare, eventually empire building, and then the wars between empires, can be followed even in written evidence, as it increasingly dominated human history, up to the rise of the Persian Empire, the first 'ecumenic empire' (Voegelin 1974). In spite of a marked difference in their character, this was also the eventual fate of the Graeco-Italic cities, a line of development that first resulted, after the Persian Wars, in the Peloponnesian War (much under the 'guiding' influence of the Sophists, as the Sophists of all ages are great ideologues of global empire-building), then the rise of the Macedonian and Roman Empires, and eventually their collapse.

Here we arrive at the threshold of the modern world – but before entering there, let's turn to Mumford's work on medieval cities.

Lewis Mumford on the medieval city

Central for the medieval city, just as for any pre-modern city, was the relationship between the city and its walls. This relationship, Mumford (1961: 46) is well aware, was always and everywhere ambivalent: the walls separated as much as they protected, and even protective walls could turn into prisons. However, far from being static, medieval cities rather realised a quite harmonious balance between protection and growth (312–14), recalling classical Antiquity.

The medieval network of towns developed after the collapse of the Western Roman Empire, offering protection in particularly chaotic times. The towns, led by bishops, together with the emerging monasteries, served as 'islands of order'. Central to this development was a shift of focus from the Mediterranean and its ports to the inside of the continent. While this was much dictated by the Islamic conquest of Northern Africa, thus the break-up of the unity of the Mediterranean, the shift of focus towards the inside helped a return to the Palaeolithic culture of walking, away from the focus on sailing, central for metallurgy. The new balance was an organic, symbiotic and not forced or parasitic unity between towns and countryside, where for example the 'villages and towns of France could be plotted with amazing regularity, forming the pattern of a day's walk from the most distant point to and from the market', implying a significant return to walking culture, as in this new world order again 'the pedestrian's needs dominated' (314), which was also helped by the medieval focus on pilgrimage as a religious practice. Towns were surrounded by walls, which – apart from offering protection against raids and incursions – also set limits to growth, though such limits were not absolute as walls could be extended in case of reasonable needs. Mumford (312) among others uses the example of Florence, where city walls were widened several times from the eleventh to the thirteenth centuries. In fact, as a perfect illustration for the tight connection between the planning of walls and major municipal building works, at the end of the thirteenth century the walls were extended in Florence by Arnolfo di Cambio, who also built the Duomo, Palazzo Vecchio and the Franciscan Santa Croce Church, thus single-handedly forming Florence into the shape that is still seen with amazement by everyone.[16] In fact, the city walls he planned surrounded such a large area that it was only filled in by the eighteenth century, and the walls were only taken down in the late nineteenth century, in order to make way for the wide avenues now surrounding the city centre. According to Mumford (255–8), it was such a protection that secured the conditions under which capitalism, this 'cuckoo' inside the medieval order, could function, far from trade being the central driving force of medieval city development. The walls also rendered genuine self-government possible. For Mumford, the modern state, with entrusting such protection to the police, far from having increased individual and communal 'autonomy', rather 'both weakened responsibility and had done away with effective means of civic education' by a shift of emphasis 'from self-help to alms-giving and foundational philanthropy' (273–5), and increasingly state aid.

The unity of this urban network was maintained by the Church, for long preventing the escalation of inter-town conflicts into wars and rituals of sacrifice. Not surprisingly, the collapse of this network, and the entire medieval order, was part of the schismogenic developments ensuing the collapse of Church unity with the Reformation, a follow-up to the collapse of Byzantium.

The modern world order and its walls

Central to the new order was the idea of representation, both in political and intellectual life; another medieval idea, but given a new meaning. In politics, the medieval idea of representation as bringing the absent into presence in council meetings (Koselleck 1988; Gadamer 1989; Pizzorno 1994), was transformed into increasingly decontextualised and theatricalised governments guiding increasingly depersonalised and bureaucratised national states, with representation gaining an even more abstract and technical meaning. In thinking, the idea of representing became connected to the collection of knowledge (Foucault 1966), eventually culminating in the 'disciplinary society', in the manifold sense of the turn, in particular combining punitive and education governmental institutions. Central to this effort was the idea of arranging all knowledge into a singular, overriding scheme or table, with every single entity unambiguously given a name and assigned to classificatory group, separated by strict, universal barriers. Concerning politics, this was the core of the Westphalian framework, defining the relations between states after 1648; concerning knowledge, it culminated in the Enlightenment idea of an encyclopaedia. Joining the two, thus representing something like the paradoxical but effective archetype of contemporary modernity, is the coexistence of Prussian bureaucracy and neo-Kantian philosophy, based on the Newtonian-scientific vision of the world that does not start with whatever concretely exists, but with the void, and the subsequent identification of 'universal' laws that supposedly govern *the* world; a central aspect of the inversion of sacred order, in liminal times, to external boundaries and limits, discussed by Benţa in Chapter 3, and culminating in Kant's philosophy, ideal model of the thinking behind the European Union. It is a paradoxical ideal-type, as we prefer to connect modernity to the French Enlightenment and Revolution, and not to Prussia, which is rather considered as source of world wars and predecessor to Nazi fascism. Yet, it was indeed the effective source of our world, as the Prussian state defeated France in the Franco-Prussian War of 1870–1, becoming subsequently the model both for state-building, focusing on the military–business–technology–knowledge complex, and for academic life, as indicated by the way the main American scientific associations were founded by individuals educated in Prussian universities in the decades before the First World War; and as can be experienced by anyone currently working in academia, through the difference between the current managerial-administrative practice and the classical ideal of education, still present in American or English academic life half a century or so ago, now being expelled even from Oxbridge.

A crucial aspect of this world vision concerns the attitudes with respect to limits, boundaries and walls. Its specific character can be recognised through its difference from Neolithic and subsequent walling. There, the wall was first of all something very concrete and material; a construction effectively separating whatever lay on its two sides, gaining a powerful symbolic value through its concreteness. Here and now, with modernity, the situation is the exact opposite: the boundary, whether between states, human beings, or conceptual entities, is first of all an abstract idea, a mere line drawn in the mind, and subsequently made into reality through its enforcing by various, designated or delegated agents. Mesopotamian cities, with their *tabula rasa* foundations and planning design, probably offer a close precedent – certainly much closer than the towns of Graeco-Italic antiquity, or the medieval city.

In this way, we arrived at the present. Modern walling is fundamentally a mentality, a mind-set, a vision of the world, central part of the modern 'episteme' (Foucault 1966), based on the conviction that everything that exists can be unambiguously arranged into groups to be separated from each other by clear lines. It does not start from whatever concretely exists, as concrete beings always have manifold connections that can never be organised into completely separate and divisible sub-spaces. Yet, such artificial separating lines do touch upon the lives of all those who fall into an inside and an outside by them; are therefore disturbed, harmed, even feel oppressed by them, calling for their elimination and lifting. However, once put into place, thus becoming a reality, these artificial boundaries and borderlines also generate their own effects, literally entrapping people into these constructs, just as the walls of cities protected those behind them as much as they imprisoned them. Given the abstract and supposedly universal character of these boundary lines, the agencies entrusted to 'police' them became more and more powerful and, as Mumford already observed, the power and capacity of human beings to protect themselves therefore smaller and smaller, rendering them at the mercy of universalistic policing authorities, acting purportedly in their interest, but in the process at once infantilising and senilising them (for these pair of concepts, see Horvath and Szakolczai 2018), rendering them sleepwalkers. The result is the by now familiar, permanent oscillation between demands for more and more freedom for everybody, followed by similarly loud popular demands for more and more protection and defence for 'us' against 'them'; part of the 'linear transformation', in the terminology of Horvath in Chapter 1, that takes us further and further away from meaningful order and life, closing each and all into the 'iron cage' of a private fantasy world.

Can this self-sustaining and seemingly irresistible process ever be reversed? It certainly can, but only outside the horizons of modernity; a process that arguably started with the setting up of a first, universalising and absolutising boundary wall. Limits and borderlines of course always existed; no concrete being can exist without its own boundaries, which for a human being is best given by the skin – rendering them particularly vulnerable due to the absence of a fur, just as their balance is more difficult to maintain, moving on two legs and without a tail. Even animals have their own territoriality, which is scrupulously observed, but which must be *recognised* instead of being materially there. In fact, the growing up of a child is primarily not a cognitive process but a learning to *recognise* such boundaries: who is a family member and who is not; how far one can venture out and where does danger start; who can be trusted and who is not; and so on. But such a game of recognition is radically different from identification: recognition is about negotiation, dialogue, active learning, starting from existence as a *given*; while identification means to memorise, at a pure cognitive level, the strict separating lines that were artificially, though with a reason – but everything always has a reason! – placed there. The first is comparable to an adventure game where the only strict limits concern the rules within which the game must be played; while the second is equal to the memorisation of traffic rules or the penal code, where *everything* must follow the course of action set down previously. The first is burgeoning with the joy of living, while the second is deadly serious and also deadly boring. All this is necessary, it is said; and, to be sure, it is necessary once one accepted, or rather was lured into accepting, the world vision based on the presumed necessity and inevitability of the game of setting up 'universal boundaries' as a precondition for infinite 'progress' inside them.

The modern world, with its obsessive game of universal freedom combined with the setting up of artificial separating lines declared as having universal validity is on its way to destroy nature as it was given to us, human communities as they emerged over hundreds of millennia of history, and human personality, even threatening to destroy the planet on which we are living. This world order has no future, but it threatens the future of all of us. This threat can only be avoided if we strike at its core the very idea of a universalising knowledge, and especially its combination with universalistic rules and classificatory schemes, a project to which science no longer even adheres. After all, we live in this planet, having a quite specific nature and history. The universalistic knowledge offered by science can be a fascinating undertaking for some, but only if it is kept distant from our lives, which – apart from a very limited number of concerns – it does not help, but rather contributes to destroying.

We were led to believe, through centuries of education, that we should search for universal knowledge; and therefore, if we discover something truly universal, this should be followed and put into practice. But what if this very ideal were wrong? And what if exactly a truly universal knowledge were the greatest of dangers? Even here the history of wall-building offers a precious hint, as it was originally a kind of trickster knowledge – and, in fact, universalistic rationality, with its 'homeless mind', with its exterior perspective to everything, is indeed a kind of trickster knowledge, confirmed by the trickster character of the technology–magic–enchantment complex, analysed by Gell. Scientists are proud that their theories, if really true, would be as valid for any other planet as the Earth. But we live on Earth; this is our fate; and those who ignore this can and should be considered in a very serious sense as fools – much more so than those unfortunate ones who populate the mental asylums. Thus, if somebody tells us that the 'knowledge' he or she gained is valid for any planet that ever existed in the universe, we can be sure that it represents a mortal threat to *our* lives in *this* planet, as that knowledge is bound to erase the difference between our planet and those others – ending our existence not simply as humans, but as inhabitants of Earth.

These questions seem to be very distant from walling, but actually walling as a concrete practice was arguably at the origin of the kind of universalising knowledge which replaced acquaintance and familiarity based on walking culture, and that slowly but steadily turned the concrete order of the planet out of its corners. The first walls, in Göbekli Tepe and Jericho, were built in the context of a religious-cosmological world vision, setting up for a first time an 'absolute' limit between the inside and the outside. From this perspective, it is particularly intriguing that their destruction seems to carry a special meaning: the destruction of the Walls of Jericho in the Old Testament is identified, metaphorically, with the ending of an abusive civilisational order, while the people in charge of the Göbekli Tepe sanctuary eventually had the presence of mind to destroy their entire complex.

Perhaps the fate of Göbekli Tepe teaches us to possess the force of abandoning a misconceived enterprise – even though the same efforts were repeated, in a modified manner, in Jericho, and from there the spirit was as if liberated from its bottle. So we not only need to gather the force, but act better.

Notes

1 Concerning the trickster and fire, see Bright (1993: 24–9), Dumézil (1986: 128, 230–2), Hyde (1999: 15); concerning the invention of fishing nets or hooks, see Détienne and Vernant (1978: 27–47); Dumézil (1986: 217–18); Hyde (1999: 18–19).
2 For extremely interesting suggestions in this regard, see Alinei (2009).
3 For a particularly good image, see Dietrich et al. (2016: 54).
4 About them for technical reasons no percentages were offered.
5 For the use of Gell's idea in a similar archaeological setting, see Hodder (2006).
6 Note that 'village' in Hungarian is *falu*, which could grammatically be a derivative of *fal* 'wall', though the etymological dictionary denies such a connection. The validity of the standard Hungarian etymological dictionary, however, for reasons that go beyond the scope of this essay, cannot be accepted without reservation.
7 Even there, it was a novelty as compared to the earlier culture (see Szakolczai 2016b).
8 Concerning this, see the presence of a scapegoating myth among the tablets discovered in Ebla, at a site near Mari (Liverani 1998).
9 About this, see Szakolczai (2018).
10 For a detailed analysis, see O'Connor (2018).

11 For its English version, see M. Eliade, 'Master Manole and the Monastery of Arges', in *Zalmoxis: The Vanishing God*, Chicago: Chicago University Press, 1972.
12 See the 'room of monsters' in Pergouset cave, and the 'Shaft' in Lascaux cave (for details, see Horvath and Szakolczai 2018).
13 The Hungarian version of the myth about Clement the mason (*Kőműves Kelemen*), connected to the Transylvanian citadel of Déva, also mentioned by Eliade, has a particular interest in that St Clement, one of the first popes, is patron saint of smiths.
14 I owe this point to Agnes Horvath.
15 See again Horvath and Szakolczai (2018).
16 For details, see Szakolczai (2007: 83–5).

Bibliography

Alinei, Mario (2009) *L'origine delle parole*, Rome: Aracne.
Barkai, Ran and Roy Liran (2008) 'Midsummer Sunset at Neolithic Jericho', *Time and Mind: The Journal of Archaeology, Consciousness and Culture* 1, 3: 273–84.
Bar-Yosef, Ofer (1986) 'The Walls of Jericho: An Alternative Interpretation', *Current Anthropology* 27, 2: 157–62.
Beekes, Robert (2010) *Etymological Dictionary of Greek*, Leiden: Brill.
Blakely, Sandra (2006) *Myth, Ritual, and Metallurgy in Ancient Greece and Recent Africa*, Cambridge: Cambridge University Press.
Bright, William (1993) *A Coyote Reader*, Berkeley: University of California Press.
Briquel, Dominique (1984) *Les Pélasges en Italie*, Rome: École Française de Rome.
Citati, Pietro (2000) *Il male assoluto*, Milan: Mondadori.
Clark, Peter (2009) *European Cities and Towns, 400–2000*, Oxford: Oxford University Press.
de Vaan, Michiel (2008) *Etymological Dictionary of Latin and the Other Italic Languages*, Leiden: Brill.
Détienne, Marcel and Jean-Pierre Vernant (1978) *Cunning Intelligence in Greek Culture and Society*, Brighton: The Harvester Press.
Dieterlen, Germaine (1989) 'Masks and Mythology among the Dogon', *African Arts* 22, 3: 34–43, 87–8.
Dietrich, Oliver et al. (2016) 'Göbekli Tepe, Anlage H.: Ein Vorbericht beim Ausgrabungsstand von 2014', in Ünsal Yalçın (ed.) *Anatolia and Neighbours 10.000 Years Ago*, Bochum: Deutschen Bergbau-Museum, available at www.academia.edu, downloaded on 19 December 2016.
Dumézil, Georges (1986) *Loki*, Paris: Flammarion.
Eliade, Mircea (1990) 'Commenti alla leggenda di Mastro Manole', in *I riti del costruire*, Milan: Jaca Book.
Finley Moses I. (1977) *The Ancient City: From Fustel de Coulanges to Max Weber and Beyond*, Cambridge: Cambridge University Press.
Foucault, Michel (1966) *Les mots et les choses*, Paris: Gallimard.
Fustel de Coulanges, Numa D. (1984), *La cité antique*, Paris: Flammarion.
Gadamer, Hans-Georg (1989) *Truth and Method*, London: Sheed & Ward.
Gell, Alfred (1998) *Art and Agency: An Anthropological Theory*, Oxford: Clarendon Press.
Hodder, Ian (2006) *Çatalhöyük: The Leopard's Tale*, London: Thames & Hudson.
Horvath, Agnes (2008) 'Mythology and the Trickster: Interpreting Communism', in A. Wöll and H. Wydra (eds) *Democracy and Myth in Russia and Eastern Europe*. London: Routledge.

Horvath, Agnes and Arpad Szakolczai (2018) *Walking into the Void: A Historical Sociology and Political Anthropology of Walking*, London: Routledge.

Hughes, Dennis D. (1991) *Human Sacrifice in Ancient Greece*, London: Routledge.

Hyde, Lewis (1999) *Trickster Makes this World*, New York: North Point.

Koselleck, Reinhart (1988) *Critique and Crisis*, Oxford: Berg.

Liran, Roy and Ran Barkai (2011) 'Casting a Shadow on Neolithic Jericho', *Antiquity* 85, No. 327, see www.antiquity.ac.uk/projgall/barkai327/, downloaded 7/12/2017.

Liverani, Mario (1998) *Uruk: la prima città*, Bari: Laterza.

Margueron, Jean-Claude (2013) *Cités invisibles: la naissance de l'urbanisme au Proche-Orient ancient*, Paris: Geuthner.

Mithen, Steven (2003) *After the Ice: A Global Human History, 20,000–5000 BC*, London: Weidenfeld & Nicolson.

Mumford, Lewis (1961) *The City in History*, New York: Harcourt.

Naveh, Danny (2003) 'PPNA Jericho: a Socio-political Perspective', *Cambridge Archaeological Journal* 13, 1: 83–96.

Nietzsche, Friedrich (1974) *The Gay Science*, New York: Vintage.

O'Connor, Paul (2018) *Home: The Foundations of Belonging*, London: Routledge.

Perlès, Catherine (2001) *The Early Neolithic in Greece*, Cambridge: Cambridge University Press.

Peters, Joris and Klaus Schmidt (2004) 'Animals in the Symbolic World of Pre-Pottery Neolithic Göbekli Tepe, South-Eastern Turkey: A Preliminary Assessment', *Anthropozoologica* 39, 1: 179–218.

Pizzorno, Alessandro (1994) *Le radici della politica assoluta e altri saggi*, Milan: Feltrinelli.

Polignac, François de (1995) *Cult, Territory, and the Origins of the Greek City-State*, Chicago: University of Chicago Press.

Portoghesi, Paolo (2005) *Geoarchitettura: Verso un'architettura della responsabilità*, Milan: Skira.

Radin, Paul (1972) *The Trickster: A Study in American Indian Mythology*, with a commentary by Karl Kerényi and Carl G. Jung, New York: Schocken.

Rykwert, Joseph (1988) *The Idea of a Town: The Anthropology of Urban Form in Rome, Italy and the Ancient World*, Cambridge, MA: MIT Press.

Schmidt, Klaus (2000) '"Zuerst kam der Tempel, dann die Stadt": Vorläufiger Bericht zu den Grabungen am Göbekli Tepe und am Gürcütepe 1995–1999', *Istanbuler Mitteilungen* 50, 5–41.

Schmidt, Klaus (2010) 'Göbekli Tepe – the Stone Age Sanctuaries', *Documenta Praehistorica* 37, 239–56.

Schmidt, Klaus (2011) *Costruirono i primi templi 7000 anni prima delle piramidi: la scoperta archeologica di Göbekli Tepe*, Sestri Levante: Oltre.

Szakolczai, Arpad (2007) *Sociology, Religion and Grace: A Quest for the Renaissance*, London: Routledge.

Szakolczai, Arpad (2016a) *Novels and the Sociology of the Contemporary*, London: Routledge.

Szakolczai, Arpad (2016b) 'Processes of Social Flourishing and Their Liminal Collapse: Elements to a Genealogy of Globalisation', *British Journal of Sociology* 67, 3: 435–55.

Szakolczai, Arpad (2018) 'Empires: Rise, Decline and Fall', in B.S. Turner (ed.) *The Encyclopaedia of Social Theory*, Oxford: Wiley-Blackwell.

Turner, Ralph L. (1966) *A Comparative Dictionary of the Indo-Aryan Languages*, London: Oxford University Press.

van Andel, Tjeerd H. and Curtis N. Runnels (1995) 'The Earliest Farmers in Europe', *Antiquity* 69, 481–500.

Varty, Kenneth (1967) *Reynard the Fox: A Study of the Fox in Medieval English Art*, Leicester: Leicester University Press.

Voegelin, Eric (1974) *The Ecumenic Age*, vol. 4 of *Order and History*, Baton Rouge: Louisiana State University Press.

Wade, Terence (1996) *Russian Etymological Dictionary*, London: Bristol Classical Press.

Wengrow, David (2010) *What Makes Civilization: The Ancient Near East and the Future of the West*, Oxford: Oxford University Press.

3 Oppressive walling

Babel and the inverted order of the world

Marius Ion Benţa

Introduction

To understand from the perspective of political anthropology the meanings and the consequences of the proliferation of walls in the contemporary Western world, one needs to assume the risky enterprise of approaching fundamental problems, such as the philosophy of wall-building, the genealogy of walling across very distant historical periods, or the experiential substratum of walling provided by the mythical heritage of the Judeo-Christian tradition. In this chapter, I intend to embark upon such an enterprise with a main concern for the third task. I will try to clarify the novelty that the experience of building walls and tall structures brought to humanity and the way that element is still here with us in modernity.

Although they appear as two completely different, distant and unrelated spheres of culture and life, the modern world and the mythical heritage of the ancient Israelites share a genealogical connection. According to Eric Voegelin, the essential features of modernity can be traced back to the gnostic project (1999), which itself emanated as a response to – if not as an heir of – Christianity and Judaism. We consider that it is important, for a proper diagnosis of the problem of the inherent violence of walling in the Western world, to seek its mythical roots in what some scholars call 'the primeval history' (Gertz 2012: 108) of humankind. For this reason, I am going to analyse one of the ancient myths of this tradition, which accounts for the passage from nomadism to settledness and from tribal, village-based communities to more complex forms of social and political organisation.

The archetypal character of mythical narratives translates into the idea that they arguably account for a crucial and fundamental experience in the history of human societies, and for this reason are still here with us in some way or another. The explanatory power of a myth cannot lie in its historical factuality or in the wealth of its information, but in revealing with genealogical relevance certain fundamental experiences of humankind, which now constitute anthropological universals. I will analyse the story as both a mythical narrative and a theological history while drawing a parallel with the anthropological perspective on the experience of the passage to the city as a new form of social and political organization.

The myth

Mythical stories that refer to the construction of the first fortifications and monumental structures with ancient peoples can be encountered in various cultural areas, from Central America (the myth of Xelhua) to northern India, Africa and Australia, as scholars have noted (Kernbach 1989: 66); a version close to the biblical story is found in the Book of Jubilees (see VanderKam 1989). This chapter will be limited to examining the biblical version found in Chapter 11 of the Book of Genesis (see, for example, Berlin et al. 2004: 29), which is 'primeval in character', as it refers 'to humanity as a whole' (Gertz 2012: 109).

The Book of Genesis is the first book of the Pentateuch – or the five books of Moses – and the first book of the Hebrew Bible and the Christian canon. The critical reading of Genesis, which started in the Renaissance, questioned the conception of the Judaic tradition that the books of the Pentateuch were written by Moses (Ska 2012: 13). Many scholars today consider the Book of Genesis a collection of legends or 'popular tales' that give the book a composite character relying on multiple sources, as its various stories can be very different in the language used, in literary style, or in the political attitude towards other tribes, while the historical context of the events narrated in it remain a highly contested topic (Hendel 2012: 51). Some scholars believe that Pentateuch stories, such as the Babel narrative, had circulated orally for a long time (Barton 2000a: 2) before they were written by several redactors; analysing the way they were woven together makes the object of redaction criticism, which is prevalent in the German- and English-speaking academia (3). The actual writing of the texts may have been the work of several generations of writers (Barton, 2000b: 8), and took place roughly in the tenth century BC in the time of Solomon's monarchy or later, in the sixth century BC in the period of the Babylonian exile (Davies 2000). Concerning the Babel narrative, critical analysis has argued that this story, together with the story of Noah and his sons, does not belong to the initial versions of the book but was included later as a bridge between the account of the flood and the story of Abraham (Gertz 2012: 112). In its present form, the Book of Genesis has existed most probably by the fourth century BC (Barton, 2000b: 8).

Babel's story is a compact, short and self-contained narrative (Whybray, 2000: 66). It tells of a group of people (in fact, the entire humankind) who planned to build a tower so tall that it would touch Heaven. The project displeased God, who decided to hinder their plans by mingling their tongues, hence the inherent diversity of languages that humanity displays even to this day.

The Book of Genesis doesn't offer chronological details related to the event, but offers a genealogy in the lineage of the patriarchs along with their ages when their first child was born, which makes it possible to compute the chronology of the events, while the Book of Jubilees uses its own system of absolute chronology (Ruiten 2000: 310–11). In the lineage of the Patriarchs, the Babel event was located in the time of Peleg, a descendant of Noah, according to the Book of Jubilees (10: 18):

> During the thirty-third Jubilee, in the first year in this second week, Peleg married a woman whose name was Lomna, the daughter of Sinaor. She gave

birth to a son for him in the fourth year of this week, and he named him Ragew,[1] for he said: 'Mankind has now become evil through the perverse plan to build themselves a city and tower in the land of Shinar.'

(p. 344)

In terms of theological history, Ragew was born in 2903 *anno mundi* according to the computation based on the Septuagint version of the Genesis and in 1579 *anno mundi* according to the computation based on the Book of Jubilees (p. 311). Of course, the relevance of the Babel story cannot lie in its factual historicity, but in its mythical interpretive resources. In the anthropological framework of Malinowski, the Babel story may be located somewhere between a *myth*, in the sense that, 'as a statement of primeval reality which still lives in present-day life and as a justification by precedent, supplies a retrospective pattern of moral values, sociological order, and magical belief' (Malinowski 1948: 122), and a mere *legend*, in the sense that it lacks a clear connection with a living ritual in the ancient Israelite tradition.

In spite of its brevity, the story reveals a set of details that we will discuss here, as they may be particularly rich in meanings and relevant to the problem posed at the beginning of this chapter.

The culture associated with this myth tends to focus on the tower as a symbol of human arrogance and to overlook the fact that Babel was a complex project, a dual architectural structure with a symbolic overlay: *a city, a tower* and *a name* (Genesis 11:4). In historical terms, the complex structure must refer to the walls of a city built around a sanctuary in the shape of a tower, a ziggurat (Mumford 1961: 67, 74), or an *omphalos* (Szakolczai 2016: 442, following Eliade), which marked the experience of epiphany associated with the *name* of that collective identity.

This story's account of the birth of the city is paradoxical when confronted with the anthropological perspective. According to Lewis Mumford, the first cities must have taken shape in the cradles of ancient civilisations, such as Egypt and Mesopotamia (Mumford 1961: 55–93), following a constant trade-off between movement and security. In the tradition of Judaism, it is assumed that the event took place in the proximity of the rivers Euphrates and Tigris and that Babel was actually the ancient name of the city of Babylon (Berlin et al. 2004: 27). Mumford considers (1961: 43) that the structure of the city in general has deeply inscribed a germ of violence in it and even the institution of war. However, the biblical story, which exists in written form in the Book of Genesis only from the tenth century BC or even later (Davies, 2000), mentions that Babel people decided to build their fortress not out of fear of violence or as a result of some external threat, but as a result of a particular *anxiety*: the fear of being 'scattered all over the world' (Genesis 11:4), which was perhaps the fear of being separated from one another by large distances. The solution appears paradoxical given that the first thing a wall does is precisely to separate. The protagonists didn't experience this anxiety in the mountains, but while moving across a plain – the plain of Shinar, which was presumably the swampy Babylonian plain that was to become the incredibly fertile land of future civilisations – where they were surrounded by a constant and too distant line of the horizon.[2] This is probably the fear that one may not be able to meet another group once one moves away from their site in a space devoid of effective reference points. The story says they were moving from the east and settled in the plain, which can be understood simply as migration followed by a settlement. A physical map of Mesopotamia shows that the plain is walled in the east by the Zagros Mountains in today's Iran.[3] Their anxiety seems to have been the anxiety of a community that used to travel and live in the mountains perhaps for generations then tried to adapt to the completely different conditions of a settled, agricultural society in a low, flat territory.

Being devoid of landscape diversity, the geography of a plain is characterised by high simplicity and uniformity, which, in mathematical terms, translates into high entropy. This may appear counterintuitive, but it is true that a space of endless uniformity is closer to disorder rather than order, and it is known that all societies have a fear of disorder (Balandier 1972: 101–10). In the absence of mountains and hills to use as reference points, as backdrops and as objects to measure themselves against, humans may have experienced that particular anxiety. A wide landscape that lacks fixed marks is a space where people can easily get lost and risk not finding each other again *in the future*. The experience of an empty landscape, which may be related to what psychologists call fear of open spaces, somehow resembles the experience of the labyrinth: the problem with labyrinths is that they are difficult to chart in the memory of the experiencer, hence one may pass twice through the same place without *recognising* it as the same spot. When one is able to make use of landmarks, one is able to recognise places, and one can make projections (e.g. 'let's meet here again next month'). To organise space is, thus, an important condition for the organisation of a community's temporality, too. The desire to build the primordial city must have appeared with the realisation of the indefiniteness of the world in space and time: that the world may be larger than humans could chart in their memory and that the world may go farther in time (into the past and into the future) than humans could remember if they relied solely on their memory. To manage such an indefinitely extended world, they needed to organise it by creating *places* and by relying on the memory of stones and bricks.

Walking across the plain of Shinar, the Babel people must have had the nostalgia of their lost experiences of the mountain, the temporary shelter and the cave. The mountain offers an experience that is unimaginable if one never leaves the flat landscape. First, a cave in the mountains can be an excellent refuge in times of danger; like the womb of the mountain, the cave must have offered the first experience of the secrecy and security of a walled enclosure (Mumford 1961: 9). Second, when one lives in the mountain, one is constantly surrounded by these natural walls, and one perceives the horizon much closer than in a plain, which offers a completely different sense of ontological security. Third, from a height one can see much more of the world below where everything appears smaller. From a mountain one can observe and supervise others and one can have the experience of the immensity of the world and the smallness of the human condition. Moreover, one can have a completely new type of perspective: one can see things that other people cannot. It is not surprising that in many traditional cultures, the dwelling place of the gods was located in a mountain, which was believed to be the actual intersection spot with *Axis Mundi*.

As prehistoric tribes walked across the endless surface of the plains, they may have experienced a need for organising their world by raising tall and fixed structures to be used as reference points. However, their motivation should have been more complex than that. Drawing on archaeological findings and interpretive approaches, such as Mircea Eliade's view on the *omphalos* (see Eliade, 1958: 367–9), Arpad Szakolczai (2016) showed that such artefacts are indeed a mark of civilisation, yet they must be seen as manifestations of the sacred in the primitive societies, as places of worship and pilgrimage and as a source of subsequent flourishing in the communities that built them. Mumford noted that isolated sanctuaries and pillars are associated with the Palaeolithic age, which was dominated by weapons and tools associated with hunter societies. Such elongated structures can include the menhirs of Brittany (Tilley and Bennett 2004: 33–86), *omphaloi* or other megaliths. On the other hand, the construction of enclosures and villages is specific to the neolithic age, according to Mumford, as the experience of settlement emphasizes the aspects of containers,[4] specific to agricultural societies. Babel's protocity must have been an enclosure designed for both dwelling and worship, given that it contained the idea of an inhabited city built around a sanctuary. The novel architectural form incorporated dwelling and worship in complete union in the complexity of the city, which 'was the chief fruit of the union between neolithic and a more archaic paleolithic culture' (Mumford 1961: 27).

By building a city and a tower, the Babel people may have sought to re-create artificially their experience of the sacred mountain; it should be no coincidence that ziggurats and pyramids have the appearance of mountains. To organize a flat space means, first, to mimic natural verticality: one plants a pole into the ground – a physical re-presentation of arithmetic *one* – marks it as an immovable centre, and determines every object and human being's position and stature by the referentiality of that origin-spot. Collective identity becomes this way linked to a territory and it is no longer errant but anchored (Balandier 1972: 26) and, as Tilley and Bennett put it, 'these stones were the first culturally fixed and enduring points in the landscape and are closely associated with its post-Mesolithic transformation' (Tilley and Bennett 2004).

With the second step – walling – the limits of the inhabited territory were drawn around the centre and the opposition between homeland and alien land was defined. The central omphalos thus became the heartland, while the encircling wall drew the borderland.

The frontier and the capital are the two given principles of any collective identity at all the levels of human aggregation, from household and village to city and country. Even at the global level, modern geopolitics is based upon the notions of *heartland* and *rimland*, which were considered by Spykman and Mackinder as integral to any understanding of the world (see Gerace 1991). In the same way the membrane defines the physical area of a cell and the nucleus its essence, the border defines a community's geographical extension and the heartland defines its core. Any living cell has a membrane that delimits its entity and a nucleus that carries the essential information related to its identity. Any complex living being has a skin, which separates its body from its environment and a heart, which is the crucial organ for maintaining life and, for this reason, the most vulnerable one for the whole organism. Such notions as skin, heart, membrane and nucleus need to be understood as conceptual metaphors in the sense developed by Victor Turner (1975) in anthropology and Lakoff and Johnson (1980) in cognitive linguistics; they are but analytical tools available to both social scientists and people in every-day life in explaining social reality or conceptualising abstract experiences. Under such a perspective, the organisation of space via concepts of position, orientation and relationship provide the basic metaphors for social and political structures, such as centre is important, tall is powerful and peripheral is unimportant. In terms of symbolic or sacred geography, the central spot of a dwelling area is generally associated with purity, the sacred and political power, whereas the border areas are associated with the impure, danger and the outcast (Eliade 1958: 367–87; Balandier 1972: 108). Both areas are, in a way, liminal, in the sense that both the sacred and the impure are untouchable, uninhabitable and subjected to rituals of distinction and separation to the ordinary members of the community, as Mircea Eliade or Mary Douglas have noted (see Douglas 1984: 8–10). While it is improper to maintain that the centre has a liminal character, it is clear that there is a certain ambivalence of the sacred and the impure, which makes them actually replaceable elements under particular liminal conditions, such as periods of interregnum, ritualised rebellion or other types of controlled disorder when the laws of ordinary life are suspended and *inversions* in the social and political order can occur until order is gradually restored (see Balandier 1972: 101–16). The very possibility of such inversions during liminal times is remarkable, because it suggests that one should expect to identify similar inversions in societies that live in permanent liminality, too, as is the case of the contemporary Western world. It is important to note that, even if such liminal periods are said to be characterised by 'disorder' and 'entropy', the suspension of order is not always pure randomness or chaos, but often the precise inversion of opposite political terms, such as the king and the 'court captives' (116). I will come back to this point later when I will reflect on the connection between walling and violence, and argue that a similarly precise reversal of order characterises modernity's hubris, which followed the Babel hubris and led to permanent liminality, where wall and omphalos have switched their places.

The meanings associated with heartland/borderland, city centre/city wall, and so on, vary from culture to culture and depend on the complexity of that commu-nity's political organization. Generally, they are the sensitive areas of a community that need particular protection and are subject to particular taboos. Tilley and Bennett noted that such distinctions operate only in the case of settled (centred) populations and are absent in the case of non-settled (decentred) populations: 'all hunter-gatherers tend to view the land from a decentred perspective in which many places within it are of equal relevance, while farmers have a more centred or concentric frame of reference, focused on the village looking out' (Tilley and Bennett 2004: 36–7). The experience of settlement and the emergence of protourban architecture imply an increase in the complexity of political structures as well as more contrasting distinctions among the qualities of the sacred geography and sacred temporality, and the Babel myth arguably captures a set of mutations of this kind.

The third step, as the Babel story tells it, was to give the place and its inhabitants a *name*. Giving names is another way of transforming and organising space, time and beings, because it is a method that ensures remembering and recognition, and this is what the Babel society wanted: to build a name for themselves. Building a tall construction and a name are a way of fighting against decay and oblivion. Our identity is preserved through our remembering of our own yesterday and of our generational past. A city wall, a tower and a name are elements that are supposed to reinforce memory and to stand against forgetfulness. The Babel story has a particular significance related to the problem of language, and this fact is not accidental. Just like language and writing, the omphalos and the city were meant to provide people with ontological security, to help them remember and certify their past, and to legitimise their future. One can say that a wall, an omphalos and a name are the elements needed to organise knowledge into a cosmic geography and a cosmic history in which the city is seen as the centre of the world, the *hic et nunc* zero-point and the place of intersection of the surface of the earth with the *Axis Mundi* – that is the place of junction between the world and Heaven.[5]

This fact makes the Babel project not only an enterprise in organising space and the world, but in organising the community into a political structure connected to the divine power.

The hubris

In traditional societies from Mesopotamia to China or India, the world is organised when life follows the *rational* principles that seek the harmonious integration of the world into the order of being or the cosmos (Eliade 1958; Voegelin 1999; Yao 2000; Horvath 2013). This means that the act of building a tall structure, such as a wall or a tower, even though it is a disturbance or a distortion of the world, is not necessarily a hubris, as it can stem out of a positive mind-set. The action of building a structure, of creating material verticality on the earth, can have the character of either grace[6] or hubris: grace if it is a building of the gods or an act that derives its measure from the order of the world and a hubris if it is an act that is 'measured against Heaven'.

In the Hebrew text of the story (Genesis 11:4), the verb 'to build' is *banah*. The word appears 375 times in the Bible (Vine et al. 1985) in such contexts as Noah's building of the Ark, Enoch's building of a city, God's making of Eve and also in metaphorical senses, such as 'founding a dynasty' or Abraham's building of his house (literally, 'begetting children'). Its Greek counterpart used in the Septuagint is *oikodoméō*, which also means to build, to form, to restore, but also to conduct or to administer (Lust et al. 2003).[7] *Oikodoméō* was widely used in the Christian tradition with positive connotations to denote those experiences or teachings that bring spiritual growth and strength, edify and fortify one's soul, 'build someone up' and help them to stand and withstand trials and difficult times. For instance, St Paul uses this word in 1 Corinthians 10:23, when he says, 'All things are lawful for me, but all things edify not', while Matthew (21:33) uses it in the parable that tells of a man who built a fence and a tower to protect his vineyard, which is a metaphor for the community of faith. We may not be mistaken if we believe that this positive connotation of *oikodoméō* run on the same orbit as the 'care of the self', which was so important in Greek philosophy (see, for example, Szakolczai 1994).

The act of building is not necessarily a symptom of corruption as long as it reflects and enhances the virtue of *verticality*, which Béla Hamvas considers the essential virtue of the one who holds the political power, as it stands for lucidity, order, wisdom and force (2001: 217–30). As solid, sturdy, time-lasting and tall objects, walls may have reminded primitive people of the immovability and immutability of rocks and mountains and the verticality of secular trees, stirring up associations with such qualities as strength, oneness, righteousness, incorruptibility and resistance when confronted with strong wind and adversities. These kinds of objects have provided people in various cultures and traditional societies with powerful metaphors for the understanding of spiritual qualities and virtues. Verticality is a condition of *parousia*, the monarch's *presence* that imposes itself with majesty of the *one*.

Before the city, humans could have that feeling only in front of a mountain, a majestic tree or God. In most cultures, verticality is arguably associated with strength, vigour and domination as opposed to falling, lying down dead, being weak, sick, crooked, asleep or prostrated, which are all inactive, pathologic or vulnerable states. Verticality it is also associated with virtue and righteousness, and with the transcendental propension. The *omphalos* is not only a landmark for the organization of the inhabitable space, but also a device that accompanies the gaze and directs it upwards inspiring a movement of *ascension*, which imitates the escalation of a mountain.

Mumford, too, notes that a city is a tool for displaying political power through the image of strength, magnificence, firmness and monumentality (Mumford 1961: 65–8). A tall structure can be seen from afar and is meant to instil a feeling of inferiority into the viewer. On the negative side, tall and sturdy structures can project such meanings as arrogance, dominance, inflexibility and vanity, and the Babel enterprise turned into a failed project because of that. Theologians generally see the event as part of a wider series of events that constitute the eruption and proliferation of sin, as the situation of postdiluvian humanity is characterised as eminently violent and transgressive of right (Von Rad 1963: 141). It was 'an act Promethean hubris on the part of a humankind still unwilling to accept subordination to their Creator' (Berlin et al. 2004: 29), 'the ambition to rise above the human condition' (Whybray 2000: 66) and the arrogance of trying to give meaning to their relationship with the universe on their own terms. It was the first project of the collective human ego, which remained at the stage of a permanently unfinished project, a deconstruction project, as Derrida called it (1985). The Babel builders were punished for trying 'to make a name for themselves, to give themselves the name, to construct for and by themselves their own name, to gather themselves there' and for trying 'to assure themselves, by themselves, a unique and universal genealogy' (Derrida 1985: 169).

For those located inside, the city centre works somehow like an ancient theatre and has a magnifying power on the stature of people and the voice of the speaker (Mumford 1961: 115). The effect was the birth of 'personality itself', the 'self-directed, self-governing, self-centered, claiming for the single magnified "I" as divine representative of the larger collectivity' (Mumford 1961: 69). In other words, the building of the Babel compound was an account of the emergence of a complex political institution. Of course, it is debatable whether one can speak of political structures in the case of primitive communities before the appearance of the city, but the debate actually depends on the way one choses to define the political (Balandier 1972). If one reduces the political to the presence of power relations, then political structures are inherent in any type of society, including egalitarian communities. If, however, one assumes that the political implies apart from power a theatrical component in the sense of Szakolczai (2013), then one can consider the Babel story an account of the emergence of the political experience in the modern world, which institutionalises *political acting* and *spectatorship* as specific forms of social experience. In this line, Babel's hubris caused by people's decision to substitute the sacred with political power as an object of awe and glorification is still here with us in the form of the modern 'political stage' and the Habermasian 'public sphere'.

I noted that the initial anxiety that triggered the desire to accomplish the construction project was related to the experience of an unbounded, apparently endless environment and that the raising of a wall is ontologically paradoxical as it is responsible for creating both division and order in the world. The feminine aspects of walling noted by Mumford, which refer to such human drives as containing, storing, embracing, accumulating or protecting, must be responsible for the emergence of another form of human experience: that of measure. Storing various types of food in containers requires and implies the measuring of it in order to be distributed among the members of the community and to be offered to the gods. Consequently, the Babel construction is paradoxical in another sense in which it constitutes a hubris in its desire for limitless verticality and unstoppabble development (Szakolczai 2016) coupled with a desire to trace limits across the horizontal space and to solve the 'problem' posed by the endlessness of the plain. The '*apeiron* problem' of the Babel Tower can only be seen as a hubris – as Yahweh did, according to the story – if humans had a pre-existing sense of measure. Thus, the Babel story must account for that primeval experience of *measure* and *meaning*, when humans became aware of, and started reflecting upon, the fact that they could create and reshape the order of the world by the use of numbers and speech, that is, through their arithmetic and discursive abilities.

The work of laying down one brick after another is a perfect analogy and an invitation to meditate upon both the act of *counting* and the act of uttering words and meaning units in a sequential manner. The construction of such a structure required concerted action, synergy and efficient communication. Thus, in its positive manifestation, the protocity was the architectural expression of the various experiences of communitas, of being together: speaking and singing in harmony, dancing together in the same rhythm, assembling together for decision making or storytelling, working together in corroborated tasks, suffering together and worshipping together.

Building artificial structures mimic speech utterances. It is an act that mimics creation. It starts from bricks, constitutive elements that lack a meaning and place, but can be assigned one and can become a larger structure through inter-connectedness. Strangely, humans lost their ability of syntony and synergy once they became aware that their speech had an inner structure and that they were able to do engineering work and reshape the world using words the same way they used bricks.

If, in the visual register, the city provided new forms of social interaction and being together through the 'magnifying lens' configuration, in the register of sound and speech communication the city had a similar effect, which one could call 'resonator box'. Mumford spoke of the importance of vocal communication for summoning people, assembly calling, and so on: 'Early cities did not grow beyond walking distance or hearing distance' and 'Plato limited the size of his ideal city to the number of citizens who might be addressed by a single voice' (1961: 63). In a walled enclosure, polyphony is difficult if not impossible, which inevitably leads to a limitation of the number of voices who can express themselves at a time and a certain pauperisation of the discourse.

At Babel, they were not able to recognise each other and to recognise each other's God, to worship together, have rituals together and pray together. Babel did not disappear, but multiplied to this day: a multiplicity of communities and nations that refuse to recognise each other simply because they worship their own identities.

The name of the place – 'confusion', from the Hebrew verb *balal*, 'to confound' (Zschokke 1910: 50) – highlights the fact that collective identity to this day has in it something inherently confusing, which may be the paradox of modern ethnicity and nationhood, namely the idea that everywhere national structures appear to have emerged out of the same constructionist recipe. The world – traditional and modern – comprises a multiplicity of nations and collective entities that are con-structed in quite the same way. Each is unique, each has its sacred geography, each claims to be essential and each sees the other as foreign. The world exhibits indeed not only a multiplicity of languages and a diversity of cultures, but a multiplicity of 'cellular' collective identities, each with its own wall-membrane and omphalos-nucleus, driven by conflict and competition and, at the same time, by continuous mirroring, imitation and reflection. This diversity is somehow an illusion created by humans' loss of a basic faculty, as the biblical history depicts the pre-Babel humanity bearing a clear unity in the sphere of creation (Von Rad 1963: 144), which appears coherent with a unity of worship. Confusion of tongues certainly means the loss of harmony and the loss of a faculty of living in harmony with each other and the universe. It was a human faculty that was, as the story tells it, not lost but taken away.

Another reason for Babel being a hubris is that it was a failed project of self-assigned exceptionalism, of being a self-chosen people (who chose their area, their centre and their name) and a failed attempt at making *divine majesty* present. A tall, vertical construction that appears as majestic, lofty and monumental is an imitation of the monumentality of the mountain and is meant to raise a feeling of inferiority, fear and awe in the viewer. The outcome of the hubris was not disappearance of the omphalos-city-name structure but, on the contrary, its proliferation; as Eliade and others have noted it, *every* city is in the centre of the world and *every* capital city is located in the *ombilicus mundi*. This proliferation is related to violence: Mumford noted that the city has an inherent source of violence and is a 'container of disruptive internal forces, directed toward ceaseless destruction and extermination' (Mumford 1961: 53). After the Babel moment, humans may have received from God a tendency that was not here always, a tendency that ran against the positive forces of cooperation and synergy, which gave the city both a powerful proliferating force and an intrinsic propensity to war.

In the theological history of the Old Testament, the Babel story marks a major turning point. The story is mentioned in the Book of Genesis right after the story of the flood and right before the calling of Abraham, that is between two important biblical events that are associated with *covenants*: the covenant with Noah (which is a covenant with the entire humankind and indeed with all the living creatures of the Earth) and the covenant with Abraham (which is the first covenant with the Chosen People). The Babel story marks the passage from one type of biblical temporality to another: the biblical account of the origins, which is mythical, 'out of this time' and rather difficult to trace in terms of generations, and the time of the patriarchs, which is a worldly time, generational and historical. It stands between the primeval, ahistorical time (the mythical *illo tempore*) and the ancestral, historical time of *this world*. It ends the account of the origins, suggesting that the plurality of the nations was the goal of Creation, yet it leaves the reader with a large question mark: an unsolved problem between God and the nations (Von Rad 1963: 146). It explicitly makes this way the need for salvation, the need for transcending the *metaxy* gap and for the human need of reaching Heaven, and constitutes the framework in which the salvation plan begins with the calling of Abraham (Von Rad 1963: 141, 147) and, in the Christian tradition, culminates with another apparent 'confusion of tongues', the Pentecost's *glossolalia*, a symptom of the gift of the Holy Spirit offered to the nations, which supersedes Babel's linguistic complex and constitutes the exact opposite of a confusion of tongues, as noted by St Augustine, Thomas Aquinas and other theologians (see Zschokke 1910: 50).

The Babel story follows a covenant of universal character (with Noah) and anticipates the covenant of particular and exceptional character (with Abraham), which was to lie at the foundation of the Jewish collective identity. In the theological history of Israel, the Babel complex anticipates the true *Berith* – Moses's encounter and covenant with God – and the construction, following God's precise instructions, of the Tabernacle, which preserved some of the properties of the Babel complex, namely of serving as both a place of worship and dwelling and organising space into a sacred geography.

The Abrahamic project of the Chosen People showed quite a similar structure: it had a sacred spot, a well-defined area for the identity and a name (Israel), and was meant to be an encounter between the human being and the Divine along the vertical axis of the *metaxy*. The difference lay in the agent who performed the choice: not the humans, but God. The Tent of the encounter (then, later, the Temple) was a continuation of the Berith. To put it shortly, one can say that the Babel people tried to force God into a *Berith*, and God's answer was that this was not how the encounter and the covenant should take place: the proper metaxy experience was to take place on the Sinai mountain under harsh asceticism by a chosen man out of the chosen people and to take place by grace, not as a result of human effort. Babel tells the story of a hubris and a failed encounter with God, yet it acknowledges the human desire to transcend the *metaxy* gap and to experience ascension, a desire that is fulfilled later in the theological history when Moses meets God.

In his analysis of the relationship between the political power and the sacred, Balandier explains (1972: 99–122) that the political sphere is generally organised like a religion and that political structure and political domination are essential for maintaining the order of the world and for maintaining the social world in harmony with the universe. The Babel hubris may have been that of having disconnected the political religion from transcendence and having attempted to realise ascension by human means and human strength. This attempt is congruent with such conceptions of modernity as a gnostic project (Voegelin 1999: 243–311) or project of autonomy (Castoriadis 1991). The Babel story shows that there is a transcending movement inherent in human civilisation, which proves itself to be transgressive in its faulty actualisation. The Babel story is still running, the Babel complex is still here with us, as its 'deconstruction' did not bring its destruction, but its proliferation as an incomplete construction.

The Babel Tower, too, was generally seen by Bible experts as a symbol of the *lack of measure* (Powell 1998: 125). In an article on globalisation (2016), Szakolczai suggests that, at a certain point, the flourishing of social and cultural life in the ancient city suffered a certain *inversion*. Modernity generally considers flourishing and abundance as signs of progress, yet it is striking and even nonsensical that this very progress – such as *limitless expansion*, as noted by Szakolczai – exhibits negative effects and obvious signs of pathology. Voegelin remarked that it is difficult to explain how is it possible that a society could exhibit a tendency of progress and decay at the same time, as is the case of modernity, where technological and industrial progress can go uninhibitedly along with spiritual and moral regress.

I will turn now towards the importance of this story for the problem of walling in modernity and for understanding the ways in which the tendency of modernity to 'unreality' – mentioned in the Introduction of this book – is subversive for existing communities using a mechanism that reverses the proper life of collective identities.

Walling and violence

The first hubris, which led to the proliferation of the wall-*omphalos* urban complex as a specific type of political life while preserving the traditional societies' drive to staying connected with the transcendent order of the world was followed by a second hubris (or, one may say, 'a second confusion' or 'a second Babel') whose mechanism can be found in a different 'inversion', namely the kind of inversion specific to liminal times that I mentioned earlier following Balandier. What this inversion does in particular is to reverse the place of the *omphalos* and the wall in the life of the community by assigning the wall a central importance and sacred value and by imposing, this way, a distorted and corrupt geography with very damaging consequences for society. In traditional societies, the physical order of the world parallels the axiological and political order of the world in the sense that the important element is literally placed in the spatial centre of a collective assembly or in a ritual, while the impure, the liminal and the outcast are literally peripheral or outsider in geographical terms. In societies affected by the 'second hubris', walls are being metaphorically consecrated and turned into 'sacred shrines'.

The particular type of violence and painful experience that walls can induce stays in their power to press, to compress and to generate affliction and distress and is best described by the Greek verb *thlibō* and the corresponding noun *thlipsis* (*tribulatio* or *pressura* in Latin), which are used both in the Septuagint and in Christian texts, such as the Book of Revelation. *Thlibō* means to compress, to oppress, to afflict or to press upon, while *thlipsis* means oppression, affliction, anguish or distress (Lust et al. 2003), including the distress suffered by a woman who gives birth.[8] It is obvious that the form of violence specific to walling is quite different from that of arrows, swords or piercing weapons in general. Walling has the ability to create liminal spaces in the shape of narrow gates, straits or gorges, which can generate *tribulation* by pressing and compressing people and by forcing them into uncomfortable situations.

The main question related to the problem of the violence of walling in modernity is how this peripheral pressure comes to have a *central* position.

Sociologists have noted that the contemporary Western world is characterized by an expansion of the liminal areas and frontier lands motivated by the increasing fear of terrorism and illegal migration: border control is no longer limited to actual border crossing, but is increasingly expanded to other spheres of life and everyday life (Rumford 2006). Any type of transit areas, such as bus or rail stations, entry points to museums, large concert venues or holy sites, turn into institutionalised forms of liminality where security is commodified as scarce and expensive. The experience of airports – true *heterotopias* in the sense of Foucault (1984) – which is supposed to be transitory and marginal, seems to multiply itself and conquer more and more spaces where crowds are linearied and sorted through narrow gates and identity is reduced to the uniformity of the standard passenger.

New frameworks proposed for theorising the new modernity have shifted the focus from places, communities or nation-states to such ideas as cosmopolitanism, erosion of borders, proliferation of borders, relational space, network society, mobility and communication (see, for example, Beck 2000; Amin et al. 2003; Hannam et al. 2006; Castells 2010). All such notions are just expressions of the liminal experience and in-betweenness; the fact that sociologists place them in the spotlight in order to explain the complexities of contemporary society is the living proof of a *generalised inversion* that aims for hegemonic status in a 'globalising' world.

When walls and walling practices are being assigned a central position, the world acquires more and more the features of a permanently liminal setting, which can be described using various metaphors, such as a global monastery (Szakolczai 1998), a global confessional (Bauman 2000) or simply a 'global airport terminal'. This is the type of society where walling loses its power to contain and control violence and, instead, becomes the magical device of limitless and unrestrained worship of violence. It is certainly not a coincidence that European communism, which was a form of political governance eminently immersed in permanent liminality (Horváth and Szakolczai 1992; Wydra 2000), exhibited a particular fascination for metro stations and bus stops, whose elaborate architecture and artistic style paralleled the grandiosity and magnificence of religious sanctuaries, as it was artistically portrayed by the photographer Christopher Herwig (2017). Not surprisingly, a tradition has been established in Romania, a country that escaped the permanent liminality of communism and joined the European Union – a political structure equally immersed in a specific form of permanent liminality – to celebrate EU Day each year on 9 May in the capital city's underground metro stations. On that occasion, stations are decorated and filled with EU symbols while passengers can enjoy music, dance, circus, juggling shows and visual art exhibitions (see, for example, Petre 2016).

The migrating conception of citizenship (Somers 2008) is now reducible to the right of movement. Identity and citizenship are no longer legitimised via family genealogy, adherence to a set of values or loyalty to one's community, but via the possession of a document called a 'passport', which literally gives one the *right to pass through a narrow gate*; this document has entered the same logic of the market: it can be won or bought for a price, it can be of high quality or low quality (e.g. a US or EU passport is 'stronger' and more desirable than, say, a Mexican or a Syrian passport) and it can frame such notions as scarcity and poverty.[9] The passport is not only an identity document that ensures one's ordinary existence in the world, but also a potential liminality in the sense that the right to pass is a projection of one's future travels. The passport (or the ID) is an entry ticket into a different realm: owning a passport does not (only) give one the right to travel across the border, but to enter and exit safely the ever-growing number of liminal spaces that have inundated everyday life, and this right turns increasingly into a basic condition of human life.

Who governs airports and similar liminal spaces? Certainly, ordinary laws and principles of everyday life interaction are suspended in such spaces, which are true *heterotopias* in a militarised state of exception legitimated by an invisible yet omnipresent menace. Like in a monastery or a confessional, identity and behaviour are carefully monitorised and scrutinised in these wall-centred spaces, which give the individual an experience similar to passing through a strait or a gorge. People are lined up for individual checking while intimacy is being violated in many ways (Horvath 2013: 147); walling no longer protects or hides, but rather is praised as a device of theophany of the only security-provider entity, which is neither a particular state nor a nation, institution or person, just an evanescent, impersonal 'panopticon machine' that dominates the constantly expanding interstitial territory of the *passage*.

Such liminal spaces are sanctuaries of negative sacrality where the order of the world has been inverted in a way that walling has been raised to a status that demands 'robotic obedience' (Horvath 2013: 9), worship, fear and gratefulness. The constant expansion of these wall-centred *heterotopias* shows that ordinary life tends to become peripheral and squeezed into narrow spaces, while socially relevant places and events are being conquered by the liminal empire.

Conclusion

We have seen that the Babel story is an account of the human need for organising their world and for constructing and reinforcing their collective identity. The significance of the wall and the tower lies in their power to create or alter a sacred geography, which is essential for the emergence of any complex political structure. Following the first hubris, complex political structures have proliferated in the form of urban settlements, which could still be called traditional societies. Specific to modernity is what we called 'the second hubris', namely an inversion of the places that the practices of walling and the practices of the sacred have in society.

Modern society doesn't need more separation, as it sometimes claims, but just a wider network of border areas. The walls that seem to proliferate in the contemporary world are neither meant to protect nor to separate; they are meant to be looked at with awe and fear and to be recognised as generators of more liminal realms. As such, they are symptoms of corruption in the profound sense of the word, because life in a society that constantly contemplates its walls is an unnatural state that paralyses the natural forms of liminality and subverts both the balance of that community and the spiritual evolution of people.

A 'carceral society' is not necessarily a city surrounded by walls, but a world where the sacred of a community has been replaced by marginality, where the wall was placed in the centre; that is where the practices of walling and survival have replaced the practices of the sacred and cohesion.

Contrasting Shakespeare's *Measure for Measure* and *A Midsummer Night's Dream*, Martin Lings depicted in a condensed manner this state of corruption that menaces to conquer the world at the same speed of what sociologists call globalisation: 'What indeed could be more remote from an enchanted wood and an enchanted island than a corrupt city centred round its prison?' (Lings 1966: 49).

This was the drive of communist and fascist regimes and is indeed the drive of modernity, too: to turn the world into a global, corrupt city centred around its walling-machine where surveillance is universal and denouncing one's neighbour is a virtue. Such a world, which could not be more remote from grace, is a negation of the fundamental bounds of society; it is no longer a *one*, but a *zero*.

Notes

1 The name Ragew in Hebrew means 'bad', 'evil' (Ruiten 2000: 344).
2 For an extensive discussion of the experience of the flat land as *tabula rasa*, see Chapter 2 (Arpad Szakolczai) in this book.
3 In the Book of Jubilees (18:2), the builders reached Shinar after travelling eastwards from the land of Ararat.

4 'Containers' lead to the crucial problem of the nature of the 'substance contained' within them; for a thorough treatment of this problem, see Chapter 1 (Agnes Horvath), Chapter 2 (Arpad Szakolczai) and Chapter 4 (Glenn Bowman) in this book.
5 The Babylonian ziggurat that Herodotus visited in the fifth century BC, and which was seen by some as a possible source of inspiration of the Babel story, was called *E-temen-an-ki*, which means 'The Temple of the Heaven and Earth's Capstone' (Powell 1998: 127).
6 For the importance of 'grace' in the social sciences, see Szakolczai (2007).
7 The word *ziqqurat* is related to the verb *zaqaru*, 'to build high' (Powell 1998: 126).
8 For example in John (16:21).
9 See the problem of limbo identity and undocumentedness in Chapter 10 (Joan Davison) and Chapter 8 (Manussos Marangudakis) in the present book, as well as Chomsky (2014) or Gramer (2017).

Bibliography

Amin, A., Massey, D. and Thrift, N. (2003) *Decentering the National: A Radical Approach to Regional Inequality*. London: Catalyst.
Balandier, Georges (1972) *Political Anthropology*. Harmondsworth: Penguin Books.
Barton, John (2000a) 'General Introduction', in John Muddiman and John Barton (eds), *The Pentateuch* (1–6). Oxford: Oxford University Press.
Barton, John (2000b) 'Introduction to the Old Testament', in John Muddiman and John Barton (eds), *The Pentateuch* (7–16). Oxford: Oxford University Press.
Bauman, Zygmunt (2000) *Liquid Modernity*. Cambridge: Polity Press.
Beck, Ulrich (2000) *What Is Globalization?* Cambridge: Polity Press.
Berlin, Adele, Brettler, Marc Zvi and Fishbane, Michael (eds) (2004) *The Jewish Study Bible*. New York: Oxford University Press.
Castells, Manuel (2010) *The Rise of the Network Society*. Oxford: Wiley-Blackwell.
Castoriadis, Cornelius (1991) 'The Greek Polis and the Creation of Democracy', in D.A. Curtis (ed.), *Philosophy, Politics, Autonomy* (81–123). Oxford: Oxford University Press.
Chomsky, Aviva (2014) *Undocumented: How Immigration Became Illegal*. Boston, MA: Beacon Press.
Davies, Graham I. (2000) 'Introduction to the Pentateuch', in John Muddiman and John Barton (eds), *The Pentateuch* (16–53). Oxford: Oxford University Press.
Derrida, Jacques (1985) 'Des tours de Babel', in J.F. Graham (ed.), *Difference in Translation* (209–248). Ithaca, NY: Cornell University Press.
Douglas, Mary (1984) *Purity and Danger: An Analysis of Concepts of Pollution and Taboo*. London: Routledge.
Eliade, Mircea (1958) *Patterns in Comparative Religion*. New York: Sheed & Ward.
Foucault, Michel (1984) 'Des espaces autres', *Architecture/Mouvement/Continuité 5*: 46–9.
Gerace, Michael P. (1991) 'Between Mackinder and Spykman: Geopolitics, Containment, and After', *Comparative Strategy 10*, 4: 347–64.
Gertz, Jan Christian (2012) 'The Formation of the Primeval History', in Craig A. Evans, Joel N. Lohr and David L. Petersen (eds), *The Book of Genesis: Composition, Reception, and Interpretation* (107–16). Leiden: Brill.
Gramer, Robbie (2017) 'In Asylum Limbo, Europe's Forgotten Refugees Are Dying of Cold and Aid Groups Accuse EU of Inaction'. Retrieved 2 December 2017, from https://goo.gl/LKwDba
Hamvas, Béla (2001) *Scientia Sacra, Vol. 2*. Parma: Edizioni all'Insegna del Veltro.

Hannam, Kevin, Sheller, Mimi and Urry, John (2006) 'Editorial: Mobilities, Immobilities and Moorings', *Mobilities 1*, 1: 1–22.

Hendel, Ronald (2012) 'Historical Context', in Craig A. Evans, Joel N. Lohr and David L. Petersen (eds), *The Book of Genesis: Composition, Reception, and Interpretation* (51–82). Leiden: Brill.

Herwig, Christopher (2017) 'Soviet Bus Stops'. Retrieved 2 December 2017, from https://goo.gl/BtuSxH.

Horvath, Agnes (2013) *Modernism and Charisma*. Basingstoke: Palgrave Macmillan.

Horvath, Agnes and Szakolczai, Arpad (1992) *The Dissolution of Communist Power: The Case of Hungary*. London: Routledge.

Kernbach, Victor (1989) *Dicţionar de mitologie generală*. Bucharest: Editura Ştiinţifică şi Enciclopedică.

Lakoff, George and Johnson, Mark (1980) *Metaphors We Live By*. Chicago: The University of Chicago Press.

Lings, Martin (1966) *Shakespeare in the Light of Sacred Art*. London: George Allen & Unwin Ltd.

Lust, Johan, Eynikel, Erik and Hauspye, Katrin (2003) *Greek–English Lexicon of the Septuagint, Revised Edition*. Stuttgart: Deutsche Bibelgesellschaft.

Malinowski, Bronislaw (1948) 'Myth in Primitive Psychology', in R. Redfield (ed.), *Magic, Science and Religion and Other Essays* (72–124). Glencoe, IL: The Free Press.

Mumford, Lewis (1961) *The City in History: Its Origins, Its Transformations, and Its Prospects*. New York: Harcourt Brace Jovanovich.

Petre, Roxana (2016) 'Cum se sărbătoreşte Ziua Europei în Bucureşti'. Retrieved 21 December 2017, from https://goo.gl/17EuEj.

Powell, Marvin A. (1998) 'La tour de Babel: ici le ciel rencontre la terre', in A. Lemaire (ed.), *Le monde de la Bible* (125–7). Paris: Gallimard.

Ruiten, J.T.A.G.M. van (2000) *Primaeval History Interpreted: The Rewriting of Genesis 1–11 in the Book of Jubilees*, Leiden: Brill.

Rumford, Chris (2006) 'Theorizing Borders', *European Journal of Social Theory 9*, 2: 155–69.

Ska, Jean-Louis (2012) 'The Study of the Book of Genesis: The Beginning of Critical Reading', in Craig A. Evans, Joel N. Lohr and David L. Petersen (eds), *The Book of Genesis: Composition, Reception, and Interpretation* (3–26). Leiden: Brill.

Somers, Margaret R. (2008) *Genealogies of Citizenship: Markets, Statelessness, and the Right to Have Rights*. Cambridge: Cambridge University Press.

Szakolczai, Arpad (1994) 'Thinking Beyond the East–West Divide: Foucault, Patočka, and the Care of the Self', *Social Research 61*, 2: 297–323.

Szakolczai, Arpad (1998) 'The Global Monastery', *World Futures: The Journal of New Paradigm Research 53*, 1: 1–17.

Szakolczai, Arpad (2007) *Sociology, Religion, and Grace*, London: Routledge.

Szakolczai, Arpad (2013) *Comedy and the Public Sphere: The Rebirth of Theatre as Comedy and the Genealogy of the Modern Public Arena*, London: Routledge.

Szakolczai, Arpad (2016) 'Processes of Social Flourishing and Their Liminal Collapse: Elements to a Genealogy of Globalization', *The British Journal of Sociology 67*, 3: 435–55.

Tilley, Christopher and Bennett, Wayne (2004) *The Materiality of Stone: Explorations in Landscape Phenomenology: 1*. Oxford: Berg Publishers.

Turner, Victor (1975) *Dramas, Fields, and Metaphors: Symbolic Action in Human Society*, Ithaca, NY: Cornell University Press.

VanderKam, James C. (1989) *The Book of Jubilees: A Translation (Corpus Scriptorum Christianorum Orientalium 511; Scriptores Aethiopici 88)*, Louvain: Peeters.

Vine, William Edwy, Unger, Merrill F. and White, William Jr. (1985) *Vine's Complete Expository Dictionary of Old and New Testament Words*, Nashville, TN: Nelson.

Voegelin, Eric (1999) *Modernity Without Restraint: The Political Religions, The New Science of Politics, and Science, Politics, and Gnosticism*, Columbia, MO: University of Missouri Press.

Von Rad, Gerhard (1963) *Théologie de l'Ancien Testament*, Geneva: Labor et Fides.

Whybray, Roger Norman (2000) 'Genesis', in John Muddiman and John Barton (eds), *The Pentateuch* (53–92). Oxford/New York: Oxford University Press.

Wydra, Harald (2000) *Continuities in Poland's Permanent Transition*, Basingstoke: Macmillan.

Yao, Xinzhong (2000) *An Introduction to Confucianism Society* (Vol. 54). Cambridge: Cambridge University Press.

Zschokke, Hermannus (1910) *Historia Sacra Antiqui Testamenti*. Vindobonae et Lipsiae: Braumüller.

Part II

Contemporary examples for transformations through walling

4 Walling as encystation

A socio-historical inquiry

Glenn Bowman

Cyst: 1. *Biol.* a thin walled hollow organ or cavity in an animal body (or plant) . . .
2. *Path.* a closed cavity or sac of a morbid or abnormal character . . . 3. *Biol or*
Cryptogamic. A cell or cavity containing reproductive bodies, embryos . . .
(Oxford English Dictionary)

Although in reading of walling one tends to think of 'walling out' – the building of defensive walls against an outside seen as hostile or predatory – the practice of 'walling in' – enclosing a group or community behind walls that separate it from the encompassing society – is an important strategy engaged in by societies that contain minority groups seen to be temporarily or permanently unassimilable; we can think here of prisons, refugee camps, ghettoes and the like. Many of the same socio-psychological effects of walling discussed in this volume – paranoia, curtailment of communication, rage – are produced by walls in those 'walled in' as in those who 'wall out', and the same affects seen in societies that wall themselves off from an outside are mirrored in their inhabitants' attitudes towards 'walled in' populations.

In this chapter I will look at a particular instance of 'walling in' – which I term 'encystation' – in terms of its genealogy and its effects on both the wallers and those enclosed. I contend that the structure of this particular practice, while in some ways very much shaped by the specific historical, cultural and political setting of Israel/Palestine, can be seen in many other instances worldwide where, to borrow a term from Giorgio Agamben, societies produce 'states of exception' (1998 [1995]) and enclose their internal others within prisons, ghettoes, camps or analogous cells.

In January 2015 the Egyptian government under Abdel Fattah el-Sisi completed the extension of a free-fire buffer zone from 500 to 1000 metres at the Egyptian–Gazan border. This 'construction' (which involved the destruction of at least 1200 houses in Rafah) consolidates the process of closure of Gaza which the military regime inaugurated soon after coming to power, cancelling the policy of his predecessor's government of permanently opening the Rafah Crossing to movement in and out of Gaza. El-Sisi's buffer zone links up with the 'shell' Israel has – since its early efforts at walling Gaza in 1991 – built up around the whole of Gaza incorporating palisades, fences, three hundred metre buffer zones (these expropriating Gazan land unlike that of the Egyptians which is on Egyptian territory), naval blockades, air-space closure and sealed gates. Israel has, with the connivance of Egypt, literally closed the population of Gaza within a sac; this essay will examine the metaphorical implications of that 'encystation' – metaphorical implications with deep historical roots and very literal consequences.

Encystation as the process of enclosing within a cyst is more than a metaphor for the encirclement of Palestinian communities within the territories over which Israel claims sovereignty insofar as both are acts of quarantining 'matter' believed to put the surrounding social body at risk. Although Israel, as now Egypt, claims that walling is a matter of security (used, as the former claims, for the prevention of Palestinian attacks on Israeli civilians[1] and, as the latter claims, for the prevention of Salafist entries into Egyptian territory from Gaza), 'encystation' is – at least in the Israeli instance – a long-standing practice that works to very different ends on both the Palestinian and Israeli populations. In this chapter, I will stress that 'encystation' differs from the term 'encapsulation' as used by Frederick Boal (1994) and 'enclavement' by Mary Douglas (2001) in that it emphasises a bodily metaphorics of disease and generation that resonates with a biopolitics deeply embedded in Israeli conceptions of nation and statehood.

The question of borders

The use of the metaphor 'encystation' to describe Israeli practices draws on the idea that the 'shell' surrounding encysted materials is analogous to the walls[2] Israel erects to divide Israeli and Palestinian populations. 'Walling' is an act of asserting and enforcing borders, and, as such, an examination of the concept of border in Israeli discourse enables us to assess differences in the practices of 'walling' as they are applied to and in Gaza, the West Bank and Israel.[3]

The concept of 'border' has been both central to, and multivalent in, Israeli practice and discourse since the early days of the state, as Adriana Kemp has shown in her study of the role of the border and of military border violations in the shaping of Israeli identity. Kemp contends that

> the territorialist idiom of settlement, which presented the boundary as the ultimate symbol of state sovereignty, did not take root in the Israeli mind. The army gradually initiated practices which transferred activity to the other side of the border . . . [so that] the breaching of the border became a symbolic practice, a genuine territorial ritual, which had the effect of both trivialising the border and instilling a sense of lordship over the territories across the lines.
> (Kemp 1998: 89–90, 92)

Kemp details cross-border violations in the period when the West Bank was in Jordanian hands (although a favourite Israeli destination for the incursions of that period was Petra, well to the east of the Jordan River). In the period she discusses (1949–1957), border crossings by the Israeli military were designed to punish

Palestinian communities for allowing attempts to access Israel by refugees (who, for the most part, were attempting to return to houses and properties from which they had been forced in the course of the 1948 war and subsequent 'mopping up' operations):

> crossing of the lines by the Palestinians was portrayed as a 'gross violation of the armistice agreements' and was called 'infiltration'. However, when border-crossing became a habit of the Israeli army, even if unacknowledged, it was known as 'routine security measures' and depicted as part of the attempt to achieve 'border discipline'.
>
> (Kemp, 1998: 87)

Michel Warschawski, in *On the Border*, writes that

> in May 1966, while out hiking with some friends, I wound up in Jordan without knowing it, and it was an Israeli patrol that brought us back to the railway zone, an extraterritorial zone, and made us get on the next train. None of us even questioned then what an Israeli patrol was doing inside Jordanian territory.
>
> (Warschawski 2006 [2002]: 12)

The 'frontierist' conception of borders Kemp claims then characterised Israeli attitudes towards state and sovereignty is still in play in Israeli state policies not only towards Lebanon and Syria but also with regard to the illegally occupied territories of the West Bank, the Golan Heights and (until recently) the Gaza Strip where the state establishes settlements, builds roadways and other infrastructural 'facts on the ground', and maintains the citizenship of 'extraterritorial' settlers. Settlements are simultaneously 'walled in' to protect them from surrounding Palestinian communities, and connected – by Jewish-only bypass roads – to Israeli territory so as to in effect superimpose a contiguous Israel over West Bank Palestine (Rotbard 2003: 52 and *passim*).

At the same time Palestinians are always susceptible to being 'walled off' from their surroundings. This is strikingly manifest in the operations of the Border Police, a 'police' unit under the command of the Israeli military which is supposed to patrol borders as well as ports and airports. In practice, the Border Police go into operation wherever Palestinians confront Israelis in what the authorities perceive as a political manner.

When Ariel Sharon's 28 September 2000 'visit' to the Haram ash-Sharif (which provoked the Second Intifada) sparked demonstrations in Arab towns and cities within Israel's 1949 borders, it was the Border Police that was sent into Galilee to suppress these, at the cost of 13 'Israeli Arabs' shot dead. Borders, whether those drawn by the Wall or those of 'Closed Military Areas' which any officer can declare at whim, pertain to Palestinians and are erected wherever and whenever a Palestinian is seen to impinge upon or question Israeli sovereignty over 'the land'. A similar logic allows Israeli incursions into Gaza and the West Bank to assassinate activists or arrest government ministers, invasions of Lebanon, and the 18 January 2015 air strike on the Syrian Golan Heights; 'Arabs' must remain passive and in place while the Israeli military can go anywhere to ensure that quiescent immobility.

If borders for Israelis exist in large part for what Kemp calls the 'symbolic practice' of breaching them, how does one discern the limits of 'the land of Israel'? This question concerns not only the legal rights of settlers to benefits accruing from Israeli citizenship, which are refused their 'Arab neighbours' in the Occupied Territories, but also has 'extraterritorial' applications. Israel's 'Law of Return 5710-1950' promises that 'every Jew has the right to come to this country as an *oleh* [an immigrant]'[4] which in practice has come to mean that any person claiming to be a Jew, either by descent or recognised conversion, is granted automatic citizenship as well as guaranteed housing, full tuition for language and university education, and significant discounts on cars, appliances and other aids to settlement.[5] Beyond, however, easing *aliyah* [immigration], the Law of Return implies that, by virtue of being Jewish, Jews outside of Israel are in effect always already Israeli citizens (a parallel instance from Former Yugoslavia is analysed in Dimitrijevic 1993: 50–56).

In line with the effective extension of Israeli state sovereignty this guarantee of automatic citizenship entails, Israel has, in the past few years, intervened in cases in which Jews were on trial for crimes committed outside of Israel, as though these were cases in which its own citizens were being tried by a foreign state. It has also organised massive 'rescue missions' in Iraq, Iran and Ethiopia to take Jewish citizens of other countries out of these countries and 'resettle' them in Israel. If Israeli sovereignty is extensible to anywhere Jews exist, then there are in effect no borders constraining its population.

Gaza and the West Bank are clearly delineated by borders, marked by the aforementioned eight-metre tall walls and buffered and ditched fences (effectively sealing the territories to Palestinians but leaving them permeable to military assault from Israel and, in the case of the West Bank, the free movement of settlers). The logics of encystation operate differently in the two cases however, and I will investigate the operative and conceptual differences between the two applications through examining the relevance of Agamben's concept of the 'sovereign exception' to both Gaza and the West Bank.

Sovereign exception

Agamben, in *Homo Sacer: Sovereign Power and Bare Life* (1998 [1995]), speculates on the 'extra-territoriality' of persons excluded from the conceptual and legal domain of the nation state within which they nonetheless live. Unlike the diasporic extra-territoriality of persons or communities belonging to a national collectivity but located outside national territory (such as Israeli settlers or Jews outside of Israel), the 'outside inside' that Agamben examines is exemplified by the situation of detainees in Guantanamo Bay: 'the detainees of Guantanamo do not have the status of Prisoners of War, they have absolutely no legal status. They are subject now only to raw power; they have no legal existence' (Raulff 2004: 610). These detainees, who Agamben explictly compares with Jews in the Nazi camps (ibid.), are held within the embrace of the state but without the protection that state affords its citizens:

> Here what is outside is included not simply by means of an interdiction or an internment, but rather by means of the suspension of the juridical order's validity – by letting the juridical order, that is, withdraw from the exception and abandon it. The exception does not subtract itself from the rule; rather, the rule, suspending itself, gives rise to the exception and, maintaining itself in relation to the exception, first constitutes itself as a rule.
>
> (1998 [1995]: 18)

As was the case for those imprisoned in the concentration camps at the core of Agamben's argument, the withdrawal of the juridical order from the Palestinians 'behind the wall' is not a matter of disregard but one of dehumanisation (the production of what Agamben terms 'bare life' which can be defined as 'life exposed to death' (Agamben 1998: 88) at the hands of sovereign violence). The 'enclosed' populations are carefully regarded – profiled, branded with identity cards, confined to specified areas, tracked – while simultaneously being denied the rights or legal status accruing to citizens of the incorporating state. The encysted are brought far more under the control of the state than its citizens but, rather than enjoying protection by the state correlative to that control, stand in constant risk of extermination by it.

For Agamben this construction of an 'inside' (the sovereign juridical order of the state) by the inclusion of an excluded population (the threatening 'other') is a central rhetorical (and practical) move by modern sovereign powers. This interiorisation of a national exteriority not only provides its citizenry with evidence of the protective power of the state but simultaneously grounds – on the threat the incorporated other presents – that state's demands to increase its power over, and reduce the rights of, that citizenry (see Agamben [2003] 2005; King-Irani 2006).

Yehouda Shenhav and Yael Berda commend the analytic grip of the concept of sovereign exception, but query its apparent lack of a genealogy (its a-historicism) and, in rectifying that, show not only how it evolved in British colonial practice under Lord Evelyn Cromer in Egypt and Lord George Curzon in India but as well how its application by the British and later the Israelis changed from the Mandate Period until the wake of the Second Intifada. Constant to the sovereign exception's colonial application is the assumption of the potentially violent irrationality of the colonial subject and the consequent necessity of revealing colonial sovereignty to that subject as 'a phantom organ that manufactures miraculous decisions, but that conceals the locus of the decision making process, the inner working of its machinery, and its criteria of judgment' (Shenhav and Berda 2009: 342). That sovereignty, in other words, manifests itself as a simultaneously illegible and irresistible power which, in its unpredictability and brutality towards the Palestinian population, shares much in common with the power of the trickster figure (see Radin 1956 and Chapter 1 by Horvath in this volume). In the contemporary Israeli instance, racialised profiling of 'the Palestinian' is 'based on an all-powerful instant *classification as security threat* . . . rel[ying] on the belief that inside every Palestinian – regardless of age, residence or profession – hides the ghost or demon of a Palestinian terrorist' (Shenhav and Berda 2009: 355). Earlier profilings acknowledged inherent violent irrationality, but were accompanied by different strategies for bringing control.

Historically, the face that the sovereign exception shows to the subject population will very much depend on that population's perceived 'use value'. As Neve Gordon shows, Israeli policy between the 1967 occupation and the First Intifada was that of employing 'numerous forms of control to craft an economically useful Palestinian society while reducing the inhabitants' political aptitude' (Gordon 2008: 206, see also Bornstein 2002).[6] With the First Intifada Israel radically curtailed its dependence on Palestinian labour and simultaneously withdrew from managing Palestinian civil life, shifting 'the governing paradigm . . . to control of the Palestinian population seen from the single vantage point of 'Israel's security'' (Shenhav and Berda 2009: 338).[7] Although orders were given to the military to avoid killing civilians, Israel emphasised its sovereignty over the Palestinians through 'the implementation of the entry-permit regime and the pervasive practice of incarceration, torture and beatings in order to repress the population's political aspirations' (Gordon 2008: 206, and see Kimmerling 2003). However with the Second Intifada

> Israel adopted a new approach toward the Palestinians which rendered them, in many respects, expendable . . . In place of the politics of life that had characterised the OT until the second intifada, a politics of death slowly emerged. The paradigmatic practice of this new politics is the extrajudicial execution which in contrast to incarcerations or even torture does not intend to shape or alter Palestinian behavior, but to do away with 'recalcitrant' individuals.
> (Gordon 2008: 206–7)

Gordon notes the escalation of killings of Palestinians after September 2000 (the number of Palestinian fatalities during each year of the Second, or al-Aqsa, Intifada was more than all of those killed during the first 20 years of the occupation), an escalation highlighted by its savage attacks on Gaza in 2008–9, 2012 and 2014. Concurrent with the institutionalisation of assassinations and other forms of extermination of Palestinian militants was that of a policy of weakening the general population so as to sap its will to resistance. Dov Weissglass, in 2006, announced a policy, grounded on research by the defence ministry into minimal daily caloric needs, of taking the Gazan population to the edge of, but not into, starvation: 'the idea is to put the Palestinians on a diet, but not to make them die of hunger' (quoted in Rabbani 2013: 8).

The path mapped here between valuing a subject population as a labour pool and judging it expendable and collateral to the extermination of resistance activities traces the development of Israeli policy towards Gazans from surveilled incorporation to the isolated 'bare life' of the camp.

A Matter of Degree

I initially assumed (see Bowman 2007) that there was a qualitative difference between the walling of Gaza and that of the West Bank insofar as the encystation of Gaza seemed much more brutal and all-encompassing than that of the West Bank. Gaza's wall tightly encysts a population which is exclusively Palestinian and the area is, aside from military incursions, closed to Israelis. Israeli policies, not to mention invasions and bombardments, have effectively destroyed the economy, radically restricting the provision of water, electricity and, as mentioned above, food. The 'expendability' of the Gazan population was made very clear in Operations Cast Lead, Pillar of Defense and Protective Edge through Israeli willingness to destroy occupied apartment blocks in putative pursuit of Hamas or Islamic Jihad militants as well as, on 1 August 2014, to raze an entire neighbourhood, killing its inhabitants, so as to prevent the incarceration of a single Israeli soldier. The West Bank wall appears to operate according to a different logic in drawing a border between Israel and the West Bank (a border which massively violates the 1949 armistice line but only so as to expropriate Palestinian territory) and allowing, within that border, a significant degree of mobility as well as supply of goods and services to West Bank Palestinians. What Gordon refers to as the 'politics of death' is not there endemic; although assassinations and targeted killings – both at the hands of the IDF (the sole military wing of the Israeli security forces) and militant settlers – are far from infrequent, collateral damage is nowhere near as extensive as it is in Gaza. However, further investigation of the implications of post-Oslo developments has shown that Israeli policies are fundamentally the same for both areas but that Gaza is further along the road to encystation and bare life than the West Bank. The difference is temporal rather than qualitative.

Oslo II (1995) divided the West Bank (excluding East Jerusalem) into three administrative divisions: Areas A, B and C. Area A was designated as being under full civil and security control by the Palestinian National Authority (PNA) and closed to Israelis other than Israeli security forces on raids against militants. Joint Israeli and Palestinian policing would take care of security concerns in Area B, although all civil issues (water, electricity, sewage, health provision, education, etc.) pertaining to Palestinians living in Area B would be the exclusive concern of the PNA. Area C was placed under full Israeli security and civil control. The 'Interim Agreement', signed by Yitzhak Rabin and Yasser Arafat under the aegis of US President Clinton, stated that areas B and C would, aside for concessions to be negotiated, be handed to full Palestinian control in the wake of the permanent status agreements. In the subsequent two decades no moves towards any agreement over permanent status have been reached[8] and, insofar as it is evident that Israeli state policy is to ensure that no such moves can occur, it is important to investigate the status quo established by areas A, B, and C.

Area A, that under full civil and security control of the PNA, makes up no more than 3 per cent of the West Bank,[9] and is effectively the territories occupied by the major cities: Bethlehem, Jericho, Ramallah, Qalqilya, Tulkarem, Jenin, Nablus and 80 per cent of Hebron (the remainder of which is designated as settler property).

East Jerusalem, annexed by the Israelis in 1980, is not included. Although the agreement referred to the cities and their 'surrounding areas', the latter are continually being encroached on and expropriated by settlement expansion, road building and the declaration of closed military zones. In the Bethlehem District, the wall has voraciously bitten off olive groves and agricultural lands right up to the edges of the inhabited areas. The aquifers underlying the region have been tapped by the Israelis for supplying water to Jerusalem and the surrounding settlements, and Palestinians are not allowed to draw from them. Although Israeli civilians are legally forbidden from entering Area A (which impedes not only contacts between Israeli peace activists and Palestinians but also economic interaction – supply and services – between the two populations), settlers and soldiers make frequent incursions into the regions.

Area B makes up 24 per cent of the West Bank and contains some 450 Palestinian villages and their surrounding lands. In this region civil affairs are purely the concern of the PNA while 'security' is the 'joint concern' of the Palestinian Authority and the Israeli military. The protocols, however, point out that 'the [Palestinian] Council will assure responsibility for public order for the Palestinians. Israel shall have the overriding responsibility for security for the purpose of protecting Israelis and confronting the threat of terrorism.'[10]

The PNA, in other words, polices the Palestinian population but is required to step aside to make way for IDF intervention when Palestinian activities are seen to threaten Israelis or Israel's security concerns; such activities include responses by Palestinians to attacks by settlers on individuals or communities, and civilian resistance to settlement expansion onto Palestinian lands. Settlements, nominally restricted to Area C, frequently expand into Area B expropriating private lands for building or cultivation and sparking local resistance which is then suppressed by the Israeli military (see Eldar 2012).

Area C is by far the largest portion of the West Bank, making up approximately 73 per cent of the whole. Of this, 68 per cent is allotted to settlements and their lands, 21 per cent is designated as closed military zones and 8 per cent is made up of 'nature reserves'. The entire region is under Israeli civil and security control, but the civil administration concerns itself only with the resident 341,000 settlers leaving a substantial majority of 300,000 Palestinians who live there without connection to the water network, blocked from building by restrictions on Palestinian construction, and deprived of basic amenities such as schooling and medical facilities.[11] Palestinian movement through Area C is fiercely monitored and restricted by a permit system, permanent and 'flying' checkpoints, roadblocks and settler-only roads.

In effect, despite the impression that the West Bank is 'encysted' as a unit within the 'Wall' or 'Separation Barrier' as it was called by journalists, the facts on the ground reveal that the region is itself shattered into a multitude of discontinuous Palestinian 'cysts' encompassed by Israeli territory under the sovereignty of a combination of Israeli state military and armed settlers. As the UN Office for the Coordination of Humanitarian Affairs argued strongly in May 2006, it is difficult to any longer speak of the West Bank as an entity:

a combination of checkpoints, physical obstacles and a permit system has effectively cut the West Bank into three distinct areas . . . Within these areas further enclaves have been created – also bordered by checkpoints and road-blocks – that has led to one Palestinian community being isolated from its neighbour.

(UNOCHA 2006)

Here the vast majority of the 2,362,043 resident Palestinians live amidst 385,900 settlers (*CIA World Factbook*, July 2017) on 27 per cent of the land with only 3 per cent of that territory under 'full' civil and security governance by the PNA. The speed and efficiency with which Israeli troops are able to impose full closure on the cities and towns of the West Bank was first demonstrated during the 'reconquest' of the West Bank during the Al-Aqsa Intifada of 2000, while the militarisation of Areas B and C by a combination of the IDF and settlers renders the villages in those regions highly susceptible to expulsions in the event of Israeli percep-tions of their, or Palestinians in general, posing heightened 'security threats'. The current state of affairs, in which right-wing nationalist provocations by Israel threaten to spark a third intifada, could well bring about such actions at any time, especially in the light of Israeli sabre rattling towards Iran and the general tumult of the Middle East. Were that to happen the situation of Gaza could easily be reproduced in the urban areas of the West Bank with open warfare on an encysted population swollen by refugees flooding into the cities from the villages of Areas B and C.

What I have sketched above might be seen as an apocalyptic scenario, and there are forces at play – even though they appear to be fairly muted in the current Israeli climate – which are working against its possibility. It is important, however, to stress that the groundwork is very much in place to allow its enactment when Israeli politicians judge that the time is right. Gaza, like the Gazan population, has been judged expendable by Israel; its groundwater is salinated and heavy with pollutants and it does not have the biblical aura that makes 'Judea' so desirable to religious ethno-nationalists. It would be difficult – politically, practically and ideologically – to do with the people of the West Bank what has been done with those of Gaza (so many of whom are themselves refugees, or descendants of refugees, from the ethnic cleansing of the territory that became 1949 Israel) but this may simply be a matter of waiting for the opportune moment. At present escalating emigration, particularly of those with the potential to build a viable Palestinian entity to counter Israel's project (see Kårtveit 2014), is quietly carrying out the labour of politicide while encirclement and etiolation of those that remain works to fragment the sense of national community and substitute a simple will to survive for aspirations for self-determination and national sovereignty. The question of whether and when Israel will opt for surgical intervention depends on many factors, but the equipment for reducing and in time removing the cyst is already at hand.

Imperial sovereignty

I return, in closing, to the concept of 'encystation'. Like the term 'border' in Israeli discourse and that of 'extra-territorial' in this essay, 'cyst' has a double meaning; it is both a closed sac in which morbid matter is quarantined so as to protect the surrounding body and a cell 'containing reproductive bodies, embryos etc.' which provides a defensive membrane within which a foetal entity can develop until it has grown sufficiently strong to emerge into the world outside. It is in the latter sense that Israel, as a homeland for the Jewish people, was conceptualised by Herzl and the late nineteenth-century Zionist pioneers who saw the land as a place distant from Europe and its anti-Semitism where Jews, weakened by centuries of discrimination, could shelter while developing into what Herzl termed 'real men' (*Complete Diaries* I, 19 cited in Kornberg 1993: 166; see also Bowman 2002: 456–63 and Bowman 2010). This programme of leaving Europe, with its discriminatory laws against Jewish participation in civil society, in order to establish a state where full civil rights would enable Jews to develop into the social and political maturity Europe denied them, was key to Herzl's project.[12] It is also intriguingly analogous to the liminal passage charted in Victor Turner's *The Forest of Symbols* (Turner 1967: 93–111) insofar as it proposes separation and encystation as a means of reaching a civil and political maturity legitimating its participants' claims to participate in their 'home' society.[13]

As a protected space within which a people could shelter and grow strong without encountering debilitating competition and challenges, Israel's founders envisaged not only the need for strong defences against an 'outside' but also means for ensuring that any internal challenge to the development of sovereignty would be contained, expelled or destroyed.[14]

It is tragic but unsurprising that the solution to Jewish exclusion and ghettoisation involves the exclusion and ghettoisation of a population native to the liminal zone in which Herzl imagined the Jewish people maturing into 'real men'. Nonetheless, in addition to the 'problem' of territory (solved in large part by expulsion and then settler colonial expropriation of land), a very real internal challenge to the existence of Israel as a Jewish state was and is the radical diversity of both the cultural backgrounds (Ashkenazi, Sephardic, Mizrahim, African, Asian, etc.) and the socio-economic conditions of the diasporic Jewish populations that immigrated into Israel. One can argue, counter-intuitively, that current Israeli practices of surveillance, control and walling are not primarily meant to protect the Jewish civilians and state institutions from attack by a hostile non-Jewish population, but more vitally to protect Jewish identity, and the state that has founded itself on it, from dissolution from within by producing a scapegoat population whose exclusion strengthens the solidarity of the community out of which it is driven. By 'encysting' Palestinians Israel stages for its own population a continuous performance of threat on their own doorsteps, impelling that population to huddle defensively together despite its radical heterogeneity and simultaneously guaranteeing that the contained and curtailed Palestinians (and their supporters) produce dramatic yet relatively impotent gestures of resistance. Any questioning of state policies, and of the politics of fear, from within the Jewish community is deemed treasonous because suicidal, and can only be the result of Jewish self-hatred; criticising Israel from 'outside' is viewed as simply and purely anti-Semitic and proof of the necessity of a militarised defensive state. All of these attacks serve to fortify further the walls the Jewish state and its 'supporters' have thrown up around an essentialised, and constitutionally incohesive, Jewish community.

Israel is, of course, no longer the enclave state of a previously ghettoised people; with its massive army, its nuclear capabilities and its high-technology economy it has entered forcefully into the global community of mature states. Nonetheless, in still wanting to pose itself as a protective womb for a threatened people, it engages in policies both at home (refusing Palestinians even the semblance of self-determination (see Kimmerling 2003) and in the global setting (where it seeks to extend its protective wall outwards so as to encompass and protect all the members of a globally distributed ethno-religious population it sees as its 'concern') that increasingly make it appear as a pariah state whose values are incommensurate with international standards and whose claims to represent the Jewish people are facing challenges from an influential portion of that community. The processes of walling the Israeli state has set in play are proving counterproductive. As David Biale points out in *Power and Powerlessness in Jewish History*:

> Instead of sovereignty turning the Jews into a nation like all others, the Jewish state has become a new expression of the separation between the Jews and the rest of the world. Instead of sovereignty bestowing a sense of security, it has led to contradictory feelings of inflated power and exaggerated fear.
>
> (Biale 1986: 146)

Notes

1 The Israeli Ministry of Foreign Affairs asserts unequivocally that 'it cannot be clearly stated that the Palestinians' right to freedom of movement must take precedence over the right of Israelis to live' (http://securityfence.mfa.gov.il), accessed April 2011, since removed, but available at www.aboutisrael.co.il/eng/site.php?site_id=307&parent_id=296, accessed 17 September 2017.
2 Whether these be buffered bulldozed strips of between 20 and 40 metres in width containing two three-metre barbed wire topped fences, a ditch, another fence with electronic movement sensors, two raked sand 'trace strips', and a paved patrol road or eight-metre-high stretches of concrete wall crowned with smoked-glass windowed watchtowers protected by ditches, patrol roads and supplementary fences. Other 'walls' may be mobile such as the 'Closed Military Areas' declared by Israeli soldiers or 'Border Police' to seal off sites of real or potential confrontation between Israelis and Palestinians.
3 Ibrahim (2005) documents the growing popularity in Israel proper (behind the 'Green Line') of municipalities and developers constructing (without the consent of the Palestinian communities) four-metre-high concrete walls between Jewish and Arab communities. Case studies are presented from Qisariya, Lid and Ramle.
4 www.mfa.gov.il/mfa/mfa-archive/1950-1959/pages/law%20of%20return%205710-1950.aspx, accessed 17 September 2017.
5 www.jewishagency.org/aliyah, accessed 17 September 2017.

6 Gordon notes that during this period 'Israel invested considerable resources in closely monitoring the nutritional value of the Palestinian food basket in order to ensure that its policies were decreasing Palestinian susceptibility to disease and making inhabitants more useful in economic terms' (Gordon 2008: 207–8).

7 Israeli policies of curtailing its dependence on Palestinian labour and importing immigrant workers to replace it undermines parallels between Israel and South Africa. South Africa's apartheid regime, and the neo-liberal systems that have replaced it, reflect that country's dependence on black labour; Israel, in the wake of the First Intifada, no longer *needs* its Palestinian population, and this puts that population at greater risk than simple exploitation.

8 Only 2 per cent of promised interim withdrawals from 13 per cent of the West Bank were carried out after the Wye River Agreements, and these were reoccupied during Operation Defensive Shield.

9 Whereas the Oslo Accords of 1993 designated 316.9 square kilometres of the West Bank as Area A, the subsequent Oslo II Agreement (1999) reduced this to 96.3 square kilometres. www.arij.org/atlas40/media/18.jpg (Applied Research Institute Jerusalem) see also www.mafhoum.com/press/mapsbs.htm (Maps of Israeli Interests in Judea and Samaria: Determining the Extent of the Additional Withdrawals, Haim Gvirtzman, Hebrew University), both accessed 17 September 2017.

10 Israeli–Palestinian Interim Agreement on the West Bank and the Gaza Strip, Annex I: Protocol Concerning Redeployment and Security Arrangements, Article V.3 (Areas B and C); http://mfa.gov.il/MFA/ForeignPolicy/Peace/Guide/Pages/THE%20ISRAELI-PALESTINIAN%20INTERIM%20AGREEMENT%20-%20Annex%20I.aspx last accessed 17 September 2017.

11 www.ochaopt.org/content/area-c-west-bank-key-humanitarian-concerns-august-2014 last accessed 17 September 2017.

12 Herzl argued that as Jews were made 'Jewish' by exclusion and Europeans could only see Jewishness when it saw Jews (henceforth insisting on maintaining the exclusionary policies that made Jews 'Jewish'), Jews would have to leave Europe in order to stop being 'Jewish' and reveal themselves as European. The Zionist state, wherever it was to be established, would be a place where Jews could act just like – and thus become just like – other Europeans. In the wake of the 1895 Vienna city council elections in which the overtly anti-semitic Christian Socials won a majority Herzl wrote in his diary that 'in the election the majority of non-Jewish citizens – no, all of them – declare that they do not recognize us as Austro-Germans. All right, we shall move away; but over there too we shall only be Austrians' (Herzl in Patai 1960: I, 246–7).

13 Intriguingly although the full analogy with the rites of passage can be contested with regards to present-day Israel, for which emigration is anathema, in Herzl's envisaging of the process it was signally the image of the Jew that was to be transformed (through a partial emigration of Jews to the Jewish state), enabling the rest of the population – no longer recognisable as 'Jewish' – to reside in Europe. The hard labour of 'redeeming the land' (Sufian 2007) would, in the agenda set out in *Der Judenstaat*, be carried out by a 'Jewish proletariat' (Herzl 1993 [1895]: 18), for the most part the loathed *ostjude* [Eastern Jews of the ghettoes], that would itself be transformed by a regime of work and social engineering from 'good for nothing beggar[s] into . . . honest bread winner[s]' (Herzl 1993 (1895): 39). Subsequently, via 'an ascent of the classes' (Herzl 1993 [1895]: 20), the Jewish parvenu with their 'taint of commerce' (Kornberg 1993: 76) would in turn emigrate to the Jewish state, thus clearing Western Europe of the presence of the 'disquieting' presence of 'foreign' and 'faithful Jews' (Herzl 1993 [1895]: 18–19) who would now 'become stationary [in the Jewish state] . . . Jewish Frenchmen, no more than . . . the "assimilated" of other countries . . . would no longer be disturbed in their "chromatic function", as Darwin puts it, but would be able to assimilate in peace' (Herzl 1993 [1895]: 18 and Bowman 2010).

14 This position is elaborated by Ze'ev Jabotinsky, Zionist leader and founder of the clandestine anti-British militant organisation Irgun, in his 1923 manifesto for a Jewish state, *The Iron Wall (We and the Arabs)*; see Shlaim 2000: 11–16.

Bibliography

Agamben, Giorgio (1998) *Homo Sacer: Sovereign Power and Bare Life*, Stanford: Stanford University Press.

Agamben, Giorgio (2003) *State of Exception*, Chicago: University of Chicago Press.

Biale, David (1986) *Power and Powerlessness in Jewish History*, New York: Schocken Books.

Boal, Frederick (1994) 'Encapsulation: Urban Dimensions of Ethnic Conflict', in Seamus Dunn (ed.) *Managing Divided Cities*, Keele: Keele University Press, pp. 30–40.

Bornstein, Avram (2002) *Crossing the Green Line: Between the West Bank and Israel*, Philadelphia: University of Pennsylvania Press.

Bowman, Glenn (2002) '"Migrant Labour": Constructing Homeland in the Exilic Imagination', *Anthropological Theory* 2, 4: 447–68.

Bowman, Glenn (2007) 'Israel's Wall and the Logic of Encystation: Sovereign Exception or Wild Sovereignty?', *Focaal – European Journal of Anthropology* 50, 127–36.

Bowman, Glenn (2010) 'A Place for the Palestinians in the *Altneuland*: Herzl, Anti-Semitism, and the Jewish State', in Elia Zureik, David Lyon and Yasmeen Abu-Laban (eds) *Surveillance and Control in Israel/Palestine: Population, Territory and Power*, New York and London: Routledge, pp. 65–79.

Dimitrijevic, Vojin (1993) 'Ethnonationalism and the Constitutions: the Apotheosis of the Nation State', *Journal of Area Studies* 3: 50–6.

Douglas, Mary (2001) *In the Wilderness: The Doctrine of Defilement in the Book of Numbers*, Oxford: Oxford University Press.

Eldar, Akiva (2012) 'West Bank Outposts Spreading into Area B, in Violation of Oslo Accords. Ha'aretz'. 18 February 2012. www.haaretz.com/west-bank-outposts-spreading-into-area-b-in-violation-of-oslo-accords-1.413390. Accessed 17 September 2017.

Gordon, Neve (2008) *Israel's Occupation*, Berkeley: University of California Press.

Gordon, Neve (2009) 'From Colonization to Separation: Exploring the Structure of Israel's Occupation', in Adi Ophir, Michael Givoni and Sari Hanafi (eds) *The Power of Inclusive Exclusion: Anatomy of Israeli Rule in the Occupied Palestinian Territories*, New York: Zone Books, pp. 239–67.

Herzl, Theodor (1993) *The Jewish State: An Attempt at a Modern Solution of the Jewish Question* (trans. Sylvie D'Avigdor), London: Henry Pordes.

Ibrahim, Tarek (2005) *Behind the Walls: Separation Walls Between Arabs and Jews in Mixed Cities and Neighborhoods in Israel*, Nazareth: Arab Association for Human Rights.

Jabotinsky, Vladimir (1923) '*O Zhelznoi Stene* (The Iron Wall – We and the Arabs)', *Rassvyet* 4, www.marxists.de/middleast/ironwall/ironwall.htm. Accessed 17 September 2017.

Kårtveit, Bård Helge (2014) *Dilemmas of Attachment: Identity and Belonging among Palestinian Christians*, Leiden: Brill.

Kemp Adriana (1998) 'From Politics of Location to Politics of Signification: The Construction of Political Territory in Israel's Early Years', *Journal of Area Studies* 12: 74–101.

Kimmerling, Baruch (2003) *Politicide: Ariel Sharon's War Against the Palestinians*, London: Verso.

King-Irani, Laurie (2006) 'Exiled to a Liminal Zone: Are We All Palestinians Now?', *Third World Quarterly* 27, 5: 923–36.

Kornberg, Jacques (1993) *Theodor Herzl: From Assimilation to Zionism* (Jewish Literature and Culture), Bloomington: Indiana University Press.

Patai, Raphael (ed.) (1960) *The Complete Diaries of Theodor Herzl*, New York: Herzl Press and Thomas Yoseloff.

Rabbani, Mouin (2013) 'Israel Mows the Lawn', *London Review of Books* 36, 15: 8.

Radin, Paul (1956) *The Trickster: A Study in American Indian Mythology*, New York: Philosophical Library.

Raulff, Ulrich (2004) 'Interview with Giorgio Agamben', *German Law Journal* 5, 5: 609–14.

Rotbard, Sharon (2003) 'Wall and Tower (Homa Umigdal): The Mold of Israeli Architecture', in Rafi Segal and Eyal Weizman (eds) *A Civilian Occupation: the Politics of Israeli Architecture*, Tel Aviv/London: Babel/Verso, pp. 39–56.

Shenhav, Yehouda and Yael Berda (2009) 'The Colonial Foundations of the State of Exception: Juxtaposing the Israeli Occupation of the Palestinian Territories with Colonial Bureaucratic History', in Adi Ophir, Michael Givoni and Sari Hanafi (eds) *The Power of Inclusive Exclusion: Anatomy of Israeli Rule in the Occupied Palestinian Territories*, New York: Zone Books, pp. 337–74.

Shlaim, Avi (2000) *The Iron Wall: Israel and the Arab World*, London: Allen Lane.

Sufian, Sandy (2007) *Healing the Land and the Nation: Malaria and the Zionist Project in Palestine, 1920–1947*, Chicago: University of Chicago Press.

Turner, Victor (1967) 'Betwixt and Between: the Liminal Period in "rites de passage"', in *The Forest of Symbols: Aspects of Ndembu Ritual*, Ithaca: Cornell University Press, pp. 93–111.

UNOCHA (2006) 'Territorial Fragmentation of the West Bank', May 2006. www.ochaopt. org/content/territorial-fragmentation-west-bank-may-2006. Accessed 17 September 2017.

Warschawski, Michel (2006) *On the Border*, trans. Levi Laub, Cambridge, MA: South End Press.

5 Border-crossing and walling states in humanitarian work in Kolkata

Egor Novikov

Introduction

In the political clashes of today the notions of 'walls' and 'borders' at large serve as either negative metonymies for disjunction and isolation or positive ones for order and protection. Meanwhile, the public discourse leaves the transformative force of walling unattended: the complex mechanics of trespass lie in obscurity, beyond the spotlight of the ideological stand-off. This chapter, studying the enactment of this transformative force in the ecstatic experiential education at one of the oldest and most legendary charity institutions of Kolkata, is based on my own participant observation.

Saint Teresa of Calcutta, or Mother Teresa, established Kalighat Home (Nirmal Hriday) in 1952 in a former dharmashala[1] side by side with a major Hindu Kali temple. Here, an unlikely encounter takes place between the outcast inhabitants of Indian streets on the verge of death, the Western-educated and rather wealthy volunteers, and the international community of nuns living a life of prayer and service. In spite of the rather limited capacities of the shelters to accept people in comparison with the enormous destitute population of the metropolitan agglomeration, the order is a highly influential social institution associated with the charismatic figure of the canonised founder. Although the commonly reproduced mission of the shelter is providing a place for the poor 'to die in dignity', one of the sisters also called Kalighat a 'classroom' thereby offering me a clue to another vision of the institution. The references to the 'revelations of the hidden' and 'true experience', which I have encountered in various personal accounts of the nuns and the volunteers, also point out the specific educative function of the shelter. Although rarely explicitly pronounced, this transformative function arguably underlies the official humanitarian mission of Kalighat.

As a part of the urban landscape, the shelter forms a fertile *cyst* of structured liminality, which allows a union and an ideological fecundation amidst the emotionally aggressive otherness of Kolkata (see Chapter 4 on encystation by Glenn Bowman). Within this moulding place (see Chapter 1 by Agnes Horvath) dwells a polarised social structure, saturated with suffering, monstrosity, filth and proximity of death. This enclosed environment promotes a direct, immediate touch to death and sickness, employing it as an education/cultivation resource. Among other things, the subjects of this experiential education obtain a non-dual sense of the transcendental, which provides them with a peculiar ethical solution for the tensions and contradictions inherent to the humanitarian activity.

The trespass is the transformation

An understanding of the multi-layered entanglements of walling and transformation is necessary to palpate the undercurrents of the volunteers' experience at Nirmal Hriday. The theoretical optics capable of grasping this irregular experience necessitates a combination of a somewhat eclectic variety of concepts. For the starting point, I employ Turner's liminality, but also turn to the structures of dirt and purity, analysed by Mary Douglas (2003), the post-structuralist concept of transgression seen as a basic faculty of experience and Agambenian bare life as an originary sacred product of walling.

To begin from the structural point of view one can say that limits are established to be crossed: penetrability is a structural characteristic of a wall, just as trespass is a function of a border. Or, more precisely, borders and transgressions are mutually constituent: 'A limit could not exist if it were absolutely uncrossable and, reciprocally, transgression would be pointless if it merely crossed a limit composed of illusions and shadow' (Foucault 1977: 34). This means that the figure of trespasser is a generic feature of a border: a limit reveals itself as a reality through various effects that it summons on the trespasser – from a physical transformation (e.g. death or injury) to a symbolic one (e.g. change of social identity).

Originating from the Latin word for threshold, the term 'liminality' in its broad sense embraces the social aspect of the dialectic bind of limits and transformations. Departing from Arnold van Gennep's analysis of the rites of passage in small cyclical societies Victor Turner developed a broader theory of liminality as a border state of transition. Turner (1967) describes it as an interstructural inbetweenness where the former integrity of the subject can be dissolved and rearranged. Furthermore, he states that the liminal bind of localised destructurisation and confrontation with the limits of existence composes a universal facility of identity-formation: 'once previous certainties are removed and one enters a delicate, uncertain, malleable state'; as Arpad Szakolczai summarised Turner's idea, 'something might happen to one that alters the very core of one's being' (2009: 148).

Meanwhile, in the dialectics of liminality establishment and dissolution of borders always go hand in hand. For instance, a ritualised transformation of identity, such as rite of passage, is usually enabled by a separation of those undergoing it from the regular social structures behind a symbolic or a physical barrier (Turner 1967). At the same time, the transformation requires transgression of social as well as cognitive divisions within the liminal subject or community. Thereby, the wall, which isolates the liminal from the regular, is prerequisite to enable the dissolution of the borders within the encirclement. Meanwhile, a demolition of this outer border means re-incorporation of the previously fluid liminal group or individual in the outside social structures and reestablishment of regular solid divisions.

Often, the realisation of the outer border securing the liminal employs the mechanism of defilement by marking the liminal subjects as impure (Turner 1967). In her structural anthropological enquiry into the dirt/purity opposition Mary Douglas (2003) differentiated at least two functional realisations of social borders: the strict lines protected by physical sanctions, such as the outer boundaries of a territory, and the vaguer precarious borders protected by the mechanism of pollution – usually, the internal divisions structuring a social body. In spite of the uncertain nature of such internal borders, the sanctions of pollution can be severe and lasting, involving complex mechanisms of exclusion, contagion and purification: 'The polluter becomes a doubly wicked object of reprobation, first because he crossed the line and second because he endangered others' (Douglas 2003: 140).

According to Douglas the social danger of pollution is related to the cognitive nature of the dirty/pure dichotomy: 'Dirt then, is never a unique, isolated event. Where there is dirt there is system. Dirt is the by-product of a systematic ordering and classification of matter, in so far as ordering involves rejecting inappropriate elements' (2003: 36). Representing cognitive categories, the structures of purity/ dirt define one's perception of the reality. In the modern West as well as in traditional societies dirt is a relative attribute of an object hardly connected to bacteriology and other rationalistic categories. What one perceives as dirt is an ambiguous sensual image, which cannot be certainly categorised within her cognitive structures or occupy place, thus falling out from the subjectively meaningful image of reality (Douglas 2003).

Douglas's idea casts light on the profound role of dirt in Turner's theory of social transformation. The sense of purity crumbles in liminality, where the 'ideas, sentiments and facts, that have been hitherto for the neophytes bound up in configurations and accepted unthinkingly, are, as it were, resolved into their constituents' (Turner 1967: 105). Thereby, an identity transformation requires the borders of purity to be dissolved in the first place, before the cognitive structures of an individual can be reassembled into a new shape. Being an attribute of solid division, 'purity is the enemy of change, of ambiguity and compromise' (Douglas 2003: 163). That's one reason why the transformation rituals and rites of passage are strongly bound to pollution and purification dynamics, often marking the neophytes in a liminal period as impure or as sacred in the original ambivalent Latin sense – meaning not belonging to the world of humans but to that of the transcendental, thus dangerous and indefinite.

The ambivalent connection between sacredness and pollution is one of the starting points of Giorgio Agamben's investigation into the proto-ethical roots of the modern biopolitics (1998). It is well known that already in late Victorian anthropology the puzzling proximity and even coincidence of defilement and consecration had been a source of concern and inspiration: '*sacer* designates the person or the thing that one cannot touch without dirtying oneself or without dirtying; hence the double meaning of 'sacred' or 'accursed' (approximately)' (Ernout and Meillet, as quoted by Agamben in 1998: 79). Following Robertson Smith, James Frazer, for instance, treated this paradox as a generic feature of the 'primitive', means 'hazy state of religious thought in which the idea of sanctity and uncleanness are not yet sharply distinguished, both being blent in a sort of vaporous solution to which we give the name taboo' (as quoted by Douglas in 2003: 10).

For Agamben, this symbolic ambiguity is nothing of a meaningless cultural rudiment, but a surface trace of the originary political exclusion of classical Rome inherited by the structures of modern biopolitics. This exclusion is embodied by the Roman sacred man – homo sacer. The sacred man is one captured in the political vacuum between the political (*bios*) and the natural life (*zoē*). It is the life included in the order of the city only through exclusion from it – the bare life, which can be killed but cannot be sacrificed (Agamben 1998: 90). The moribund poorest of the poor at Nirmal Hriday represent this primary biopolitical antimatter: lost in the void between the city and the home they are not only nameless and forsaken – like the perfect outcasts of Rome they are given out to death but not dead.

Significantly, in ancient Rome one of the acts inflicting the fundamental exclusion of 'sacratio' was a negation of borders (Agamben 1998: 85). This brings us back to the myth of the foundation of Rome (see Introduction in this volume). The establishment of the border by Romulus and its instant negation by Remus are followed by the punitive exclusion of sacratio resulting in the fratricide, which manifests the border as a sacred 'pomerium'. Brought together in one instant the three events detonate in the originary big bang of the city. This eruption charged the encircled structure of the city with an amplified power of the divine, giving momentum to the historical spiral of the urban wallings and trespasses. Meanwhile, the bare life of the excluded is the negative sacred product of this originary bordering, multiplied in the countless reproductions of the city and the empire throughout Western history.

Coming back to the ambiguous connection between sanctity and impurity, Mary Douglas points at Christianity accomplishing a revolutionary subversion of its traditional forms. As Douglas notes, in traditional societies sacredness (whether in the sense of dirt or purity) is seen as a material attribute of a substance, while 'Christian rules of holiness, by contrast, disregard the material circumstances and judge according to the motives and disposition of the agent' (2003: 11). Thereby, in Christianity the transition of an object from dirty to pure and from profane to sacred (and vice versa) can be navigated by the attitudes and intentions of the subject. Caroline Walker Bynum (1991) provides some revealing examples of such transitions in her profound study of medieval mysticism. One of these is the case of St Catherine of Siena, who is believed to have deliberately eaten pus from an ill woman's breast and drunk a bowl of water mixed with pus and fetid blood:

> Filled with a holy anger against herself, she said, 'thou shalt swallow what inspires thee with such horror,' and immediately, collecting in a saucer the water in which she had washed what flowed from the wound, she went aside and drank the whole.
>
> (Raymond of Capua 1860: 93)

Significantly, the transgressive act arose from the disgust and nausea caused by the smell of the wound she was treating and was supported by a moral imperative:

the shame for lacking compassion towards the impure one means being possessed by the materialistic dualism expressed through the rejection of dirt. The immediate effect of the transgression was bliss: 'In my whole life, I never tasted anything so sweet and so agreeable' (Raymond of Capua 1860: 93). By her selfless trust into the non-dual all-embracing God, the saint has turned the dirtiest profane substance into sacred nectar. In the aftermath of this triumph over her subjectivity Catherine had a vision in which Christ fed her with the sacred blood from his wound as a reward for selflessly consuming the dirt in His name as she consumes his flesh in daily communion. This pattern of ecstatic transgression of the division between the dirty and the clean, while comforting and serving the excluded life comes up in biographies of various saint mystics including St Francis, Catherine of Siena and Angela of Foligno. St Teresa of Calcutta and her Missionaries of Charity in a broad sense continue the ancient mystic linage, like their medieval predecessors reaching to the transcendental through subversive descent into dirt and ecstatic touch to the excluded sacred life.

Bynum's insights demonstrate how the mystic self-cultivation employs transgression of the emphasised borderline between dirty and pure to overcome the preservative nature of the dualistic cognitive structures of the subject. The transformative force of transgression is deeply analysed in postmodern philosophy, where it is a key concept. Michel Foucault assumed that the experience of transgression one day would seem as obviously fundamental to our culture, 'as the experience of contradiction was at an earlier time for dialectical thought' (1977: 33). Foucault does not see transgression as a counterpart of limit, but rather as a dynamic dimension of it: the never ceasing breaks through the continuous borderlines highlight the actual divisions, constituting a dynamic spiral of limitations and trespasses. A transgression affirms the limit by breaking it into limitlessness, being a 'solar inversion of satanic denial', which 'opens the space where the divine functions' (1977: 37).

Pre-dating Foucault's insights, Georges Bataille also saw transgression and taboo as two sides of the same cultural mechanism. The two forces affirm the limit of the sacred, towards which 'men are swayed by two simultaneous emotions: they are driven away by terror and drawn by an awed fascination' (Bataille 1962: 68). By accomplishing the transgression an individual incorporates the limit relating it to the transcendental beyond. To invoke the feeling of the transcendental in the individuals through a personal experience, religions inspire limited transgressions beyond the regular structures of meaning in rites and celebrations, all kinds of carnivalesque disorder (Bataille 1962).

In the act of transgression emotional tension prevails over the cognitive structures. As the subject approaches to the usually forbidden limit, the pressure of fear increases reaching a top point just to suddenly evaporate in the act of trespass. In that moment, the immense ecstasy pours out as the subject touches the non-structured unconditional being, where the individual identity melts and transforms: 'ecstasy begins where horror is sloughed off. [. . .] More than any other state of mind consciousness of the void about us throws us into exaltation' (Bataille 1962: 69). The ecstasy of the transgression resonates and reigns freely in 'the empty place filled with emotions' (Chapter 1 by Horvath), in the transformative pre-dual womb beyond the structure where nothing can hold the exaltation back. The touch to the infinite, which neither can be grasped nor defined, effectively throws structures of perception into a transformative movement, releasing them from the binds of purity. Like the sun at noon, the pre-structured beyond does not allow a direct gaze, but with sharp dramatic light backlights the dissolution of the firm binary structures. It reveals itself in the horror and bliss of the unintelligible *sacred*, where there is no more meaningful distinction between dirt and cleanness, health and sickness, subject and object, or death and life.

The three halves

At each moment about a hundred people live in the sacred ambiguity of Kalighat Home for the Dying Destitutes, including a half-dozen nuns, a few residential workers, and up to 50 men and 46 women[2] suffering from severe health conditions. Predominantly, Kalighat functions as a transit institution from where most residents leave in the course of a month or two in one of three ways: they die, recover and return to the streets, or are transferred to another of the ten shelters in the city.

On the apparent, practical level, the volunteers are playing a secondary role in the shelter by helping the sisters do their job, which is the impression accepted and reproduced in private conversations by some nuns and volunteers themselves. The volunteers serve meals and do the laundry, clean wounds, pick up dying people from the streets, help those patients who cannot manage to move and maintain hygiene, and deliver dead bodies to cemeteries and crematoriums. Tasks requiring specific professional skills – the physiotherapist, the accountant, the therapist physician – are also usually performed on a voluntary basis.

Yet if one looks at the genealogy of the institution, the volunteers are embedded into the very structural core of the shelters playing the role of indispensable witnesses. As a matter of fact, a volunteer was accompanying Mother Teresa in the slums of Kolkata on the very first day, before the order of sisters existed to support her.[3] Witnessing is a key element of the Christian cultivation doctrines, primarily affirmed by the biblical apostles who were witnessing the way of Christ by their presence and later by mimetically reproducing it in their own martyrdoms and labours. The nature of the Christian apostolate is based on salvation of souls through spreading the teaching of Christ. Such educative activity requires a witness – the one to be impregnated by the word of truth through evidencing its enactment. The volunteers are the ones who witness the shelter's missionary service to the destitute, their apostolate.

Therefore, the three categories of actors – the nuns (the missioneers), the volunteers (the witnesses) and the suffering (the saved victims) – form the threefold structural core of the Kalighat shelter. In this triangle each segment is defined by its relation to the other two. All three groups are explicitly distinct in their functions and attributes. And all three engage in a ritualised interaction in structured liminality – a de-structured liminal zone within the stable social structure, which does not threaten the bigger whole but serves as a legitimate transition mechanism within it (Thomassen 2014).

All three types of actors are also essentially liminal in their peculiar ways. In their symbolic status of the bare life, the destitute residents of Kalighat Home exist in the liminal gap between the home and the city. In this limbo between life and death they are stripped of the last attributes of subjectivity having no possessions (everything is taken away, stored and returned if they leave), wearing uniforms, following the daily schedule of the shelter and being completely dependent on the other actors. Meanwhile, the sisters of the order live in institutionalised liminality (Turner 1967). While the volunteers and the residents can to an extent re-aggregate with the profane world outside the borders of Nirmal Hriday, the sisters bear their separation from the regular with them wherever they go. Their lives in this world are but a prelude to the encounter with the Lord and the eternal life after death. As one sister said to me: 'if you feel agreed and comfortable with this world, something is wrong'.

Liminality of the volunteers is multi-layered and can be analysed in various aspects of their experience, from passage through a delible re-identification period of life, to the daily rituals of separation and re-aggregation as they cross the borders of the shelter. The witnessing role of the volunteers is liminal in itself. Witnessing results in a transformative intimate experience, which affirms a truth – a universal foundation of a moral subject. Thereby, Nirmal Hriday combines all three liminal aspects as described by Bjorn Thomassen (2009): spatial liminality (a walled space amidst 'otherness'), temporal liminality (periods of social suspension for the volunteers and transition between life and death for the residents) and social liminality (the suspended social status of the nuns, the foreigners and the outcasts).

Walled and dissolved

On the macro level, most of the volunteers interviewed in the shelters were undergoing a liminal period of life. Many of them were in a 'travelling' state when they took a year off work, after graduation, or after a personal crisis looking for a transformative experience. 'I am like in between' is one typical expression from a Western volunteer, often accompanied with a feeling of necessity for a change and a search for self-identity. 'People come from very different backgrounds, but here they are like blank paper', as another volunteer noted, clearly revealing the liminal nature of the volunteering experience, characterised by 'creation of a tabula rasa, through the removal of previously taken-for-granted forms and limits' (Szakolczai 2009: 148).

On the micro scale of daily experiences, the separation and aggregation phases at Nirmal Hriday are enabled through the facility of walling. According to Van Gennep, the transformative rites of passage are accomplished in three steps: the phases of separation and aggregation part the subject from the social structures of everyday life, while the actual transition occurs in the liminal margin phase between the two (Van Gennep 1960). The disturbing street turmoil functions as a symbolic threshold of transition, in accordance with Van Gennep's idea of the spatial origin of rites of passage (1960: 22). When volunteers reach the doorway of the shelter, they enter a different world: the kaleidoscope of the overpopulated

Bengali capital gives way to the warm still frightening murmur of the liminal bubble where the laws of the intensive outside social world cease to function. The ancient doorkeeper in spectacles (a former moribund resident himself) finds the volunteer's name in a thick copybook and marks the date of visit with his crooked brown fingers, slightly waving towards the hall: 'Pass . . .'.

When seen in the context of experiential education, the setting of the shelters is anything but unimportant. The pattern of sharp contrasts between the outside and the inside is generic for the entire experience of volunteering. That's how Lucia describes the daily route from her hostel to one of the shelters where she was volunteering:

> The trip is neither easy nor pleasant. [. . .] Crows, cats and dogs trying to tear off parts of scattered animal corpses, blood-stained sidewalks, garbage covering every centimetre of every and each street, tram rails full of kids who put their arms forth begging for food but happy to get just a tickle, a smile, or a little sympathy. [. . .] Forty minutes of a permanent kaleidoscope of feelings ultimately ends up when we arrive to Prem Dan.[4]

Upon entering a building of the congregation, the volunteers are in an abrupt manner cut off from the disturbing urban turmoil as well as from their previous lives focused on material needs and individual successes. After a trip through the streets of Kolkata, the solemn morning Mass with over a hundred sisters and novices feels like an island of clearness and harmony. The serenity of the Mass permeates the flock with the liminal ambience of its own. The mimetic flow of the ritual saturated with Christian symbolism immerses the participants into the mysterious metamorphosis of sacrifice and resurrection. According to Thomas Aquinas (2013), in the mass's celebration of the act of the crucifixion of Christ, the symbolic roles of a priest (the subject of sacrifice) and a victim (the object of it) merge together. Thereby, the ultimate sacrifice of Christianity subverts the traditional binary mechanism of scapegoating through the unification of its oppositions in the universal transcendental subject. Furthermore, in this painful humiliating death of the universal subject 'human suffering itself has been redeemed' (Pope John Paul II 1984).

The figure of suffering Christ is the focal point of the liturgy – the ambiguous and paradoxical dominant symbol (Turner 1967), which unites and concentrates all the tensions and contradictions of meaning into a coherent symbolic structure producing a potential to transform cognitive structures of meaning and affirm collective truths. On the one hand, the re-enactment of the death and resurrection and the consumption of his flesh prepare the participants to interpret the sufferings of the residents of the shelter in the context of the transcendental, embracing them as meaningful experiences. On the other hand, the conflux of subject and object in the non-duality of God invoked in the liturgy prepares the participants to embody the concept of 'caritas', which plays a crucial role in the practice of volunteering. This idea of the transcending selfless love towards the neighbour is pivotal for the ethics of Catholicism. Conceptually, caritas is not a love that one individual feels towards another individual, but it is love of God's creature towards God Himself embodied in another creature of His. It is the ecstatic love, which overcomes any individual traits of subjectivity. Thereby, caritas plays a key role in the transgressive education of the volunteers: just as eroticism or cruelty for Bataille, it wells up as an emotional disposition, which resolves the transgression into a usually forbidden field of behaviour (1962: 80).

Coming back to the striking contrasts of the volunteer experience, the impact of the liturgy is interrupted and enhanced by the occasional intrusions of city life into its scripted flow. Occasionally a barbaric sound of drums or a deafening thunder of an old Kolkatan tram drowns the priest's sermon or the 'Halleluiah' hymn. A few seconds later, the noise passes, and the sounds of the ritual reclaim their dominance in the sanctuary of the chapel. In general, the firm religious core of the sisters provides a strong contrast with the sense of fluid insecurity, which soaks the volunteers' being. In the liminal state of uncertainty and lack of established structures of meaning, which would allow a rational choice, mimesis and imitation gain a central position among the modes of interaction (Turner 1967). Spending their days in an essentially uncertain being the volunteers start attributing much more value to the firm religious concepts embodied by the sisters.

Within the shelter the volunteers are secluded from the swarming myriad values and meanings that exist outside the walls. In this rarefied symbolic air the concrete is subordinated for the general through codification in rituals. The volunteering is a pilgrimage with an egalitarian ambience of 'communitas' typical for liminal communities (Turner 1967). At Nirmal Hriday communitas is maintained through the non-hierarchical organisation, prohibition of property and gifts and the general attitude of voluntary self-sacrifice for the neighbour. It is reflected in the ways of referring to one another: sister, brother, auntie, baba.[5] Nevertheless, the sense of communitas does not dissolve the underlying threefold structure: the three groups differ in attributes, roles and grades of political agency. Such rigid bordering is generic for the situations of sanctioned transgressions instigated by a religious authority: 'Transgression outside well defined limits is rare; within them taboos may well be violated in accordance with rules that ritual or at least custom dictate and organize' (Bataille 1962: 71). The carcass on which the ecstatic flesh of daily transgression dwells is composed of the basic rules securing the desexualisation and depersonalisation of social relations (mainly related to the religious restrictions of the monastic order), the cyclical daily schedule, repetition of rituals and the definite power divisions between the three categories of actors.

Societies, in the same way as physical bodies, tend to gradually slide towards chaos and disorder, 'dissolve into error, nonsense, ambiguity, vagueness, hypocrisy and meaninglessness unless continually clarified, corrected and re-established' (Rappaport 1999: 461). In the case of the liminal cyst of Kalighat Home, this centrifugal force is balanced by the ideological charisma of the convent, enforced by a high grade of ritualisation of everyday life. On the individual level, the voluntary subjection to the conventional rituals of the institution, mainly short prayers and daily liturgies, works as a certain practice of freedom aimed at a conscious transformation of the architecture of self (Mahmood 2001). The mode of action embodied through the rituals 'endows the self with various kinds of capabilities that form the background of moral and political judgment' (Mahmood 2001: 845). Thus, the abundant rituals not only balance the entropy of liminality by affirming the form and the rhythm of the service, but also sanction the transgressive service by introducing non-dualistic attitudes, which dissolve symbolic divisions. Thereby, the rituals bind together the limits, the sacred and the transgression in one ecstatic cultivating performance.

Additionally, the period of volunteering itself can be seen as a peculiar irregular ritual. Although built into the doctrinal context of the routinised charity, the cultivation strategy implemented at Kalighat Home works in imagistic mode, which 'relies mainly on unverbalized, emotionally arousing experiences and episodic memory of a spatiotemporally localized and autobiographical sort' (Atran 2004: 153). The transgressive experience of volunteering in Kalighat is an exemplary case of a sensorially invasive imagistic non-routine rite, which resists communication to others and remains mainly unspoken but creates a profound and lasting sense of community and cultural affiliation. For the religious volunteers this intimate imagistic installation into the doctrinal fabric opposes the 'tedium effect' of repetition (Atran 2004: 155) – a by-product of daily routine and restrictions resulting in decay and washout of rituals and norms. Such invasions of imagistic events into the regular life revive its insipid repetitious pattern with injections of ecstatic personal experience.

It is worth mentioning that the architectural shell that Nirmal Hriday now occupies originally belonged to the famous Kalighat temple complex devoted to Kali. Usually depicted with a sword in her hand and a necklace of freshly cut heads upon her breast, this goddess among her qualities embodies dissolution of limits and purifying destruction, change and renewal, and the death, which enables birth. She is a precise impersonation of liminality as a phase of existence. Significantly then, Mother Teresa entered inside the deserted walls of the dharmshala originally raised to shelter Kali worshiping pilgrims, and deployed her realm of the selfless transgression to care for moribund sacred life with her hands. Thereby, the building has been turned into a sacred wall, which separates the liminal foundry where identities are melted and forged from the Brownian motion of the city. Although its only keeper is the ancient 'Charon' at the main door, the cyst of Kalighat Home does not require a physical protection from potential invasions. The ambiguity of the liminal, where purity and dirt collapse and entangle in the prism of the sacred, protects itself naturally from intrusions falling into a hole on the map of the everyday structures of meaning. One popular anecdote tells that once an angry mob of the local Kali worshipers came to the building demanding that the Christians return it to their temple. Mother Teresa invited the people to come in and see. The story relates, the noise dissipated as soon as the protesters entered the shelter. They then left quietly and never raised the issue again.

Transgressed and fecundated

At the entrance to Nirmal Hriday there is a metal jar labelled 'gloves'. This jar was empty whenever I looked into it. Only once did the sisters suggest that I find and use gloves – to apply an ointment on the skin of residents infected with scabies, though the proposition did not make much practical sense, as those were the same patients we carried around and dressed every day without any protection. Very few people regularly protected their hands from contacting dirt with polyethylene gloves. One was Stefano, who worked on an ambulance in Italy, and maintained a medical approach in that his perception of the structural division of dirt and purity apparently was not as blunted as it was with the majority of the volunteers. Also, his persistence in avoidance of direct contact with dirt might correlate with the outside purpose he had: just as I was gathering material for my research (I also used gloves more often than others did) he was writing a magazine article. Though basic hygienic standards are followed, the sisters avoid medical formalisation. A Catholic female physician from the UK once tried to introduce hygienic require-ments for the volunteers (wearing masks and gloves, regularly washing hands, measuring time with the Hail Mary prayer, etc.) but her attempt failed, and for a reason: Kalighat Home is not a medical institution, but rather a spiritual and reli-gious space. The prevailing practice among volunteers, sisters and workers remains direct contact with bodies and their waste products. Day by day volunteers learn to touch dirt and sickness without hesitation. The introduction into the transforming service of the shelter occurs each morning when volunteers put on aprons and gather around stone basins to do the laundry under the silent gazes of freshly washed and dressed male residents. The first daily transgressive experience occurs when the volunteers dip their hands into soapy, antiseptic water, grab a dirty wet piece of cloth and start laundering it. Thereby, they celebrate immersion into the fluid ambience of liminality enriched with dirt, suffering of the bare life and the detergent of Christian love, which turns this filthy solution into a sacralised educative resource.

The physical space of the Kalighat Home is filled with human bodies: 100–120 workers, nuns, novices, volunteers and residents at each moment. The con-stant contacts between the intensely different bodies of residents and volunteers reveal a plethora of social tensions between dirt/purity, health/sickness, security/ vulnerability, West (North)/East (South) and domination/service. Meanwhile, the internal social structure of the shelter does not level these tensions through a symbolic unification, but rather amplifies them through the explicit distribution of roles and attributes. The increased tensions are resolved on the level of a personal psyche, which bring the opposites together through acts of sanctioned transgression. Particularly, the fluid ambience of liminality makes the borders – including those between the dirty and the pure – permeable while at the same time emphasising grotesque and monstrous features. The more explicit the border is, the stronger is the composition of the desire to transgress it and the fear of such trespass, and the stronger is the exaltation evoked by the accomplished transgression. Interviews with volunteers and observations of daily work in Kalighat Home demonstrate that people perceive such transgressions as simultaneously attractive and frightening. Contact with a sick body is challenging in many ways. First, there is the rationally justified fear of contagion. 'Risk of contagion is not big, it is often exaggerated. But it exists and taking it, being ready to suffer for another is a part of this [Christian] love', said one of the sisters. On the symbolic level, the touching of a sick body is a touch of impurity in two senses. Besides the obvious material impurity of sickness revealed through specific smells, fluids and deformations perceived as dirty, disease is also traditionally perceived as contagious social impurity, which gravely impacts the social status of the diseased with the attached underlying connotations of moral failure.

Being of cognitive origin, the fear of pollution is invoked by the necessity to build culturally sensible experiences: dirt and uncleanness are structural attributes of everything ambiguous, undefined and contradictory (Douglas 2003). The epistemological categories of dirt/purity are not given a priori but depend on cognitive structures of the subject and can be revised on an individual level. But such revision might need an essential outer justification from a cultural authority (40). Possessing the symbolic authority of Mother Teresa provides enough weight to sanction within the shelter's walls a transgression of the limits usually protected by the forces of fear and disgust. This description of a transgressive experience by a volunteer reveals the mechanism of the sanction through a reference to the non-duality of the transcendental presented in the framework of Catholic Christianity:

> When one of the sisters asked me to wash this woman I thought there is no way. I just couldn't. [. . .] So she said, 'Alright, come with me,' and she picked up this little bundle of bones, because that's what this lady was, and took her into the bathroom. Even now it makes me cry – there wasn't a lot of light in the room and I was still absolutely catatonic. Then all of a sudden the whole room just lit up! One minute I was saying 'I can't' and the next I realized, of course, I could. It suddenly struck me, seeing one of those religious pictures they have on the wall – it was the body of Christ – that anybody, whoever they are, can be Christ. It wasn't just that old little lady who was covered with scabies, it was the whole world that was the body of Christ.
>
> (Vardey 2011: 143)

As mentioned, Nirmal Hriday is commonly presented and perceived as a place where the poor can die in dignity – significantly bringing into one semantic construction dignity, poverty and death. But the dignity mentioned in the formula has little to do with the dignity of human rights or that of a free capable man of the Enlightenment. In her Noble Prize speech, Mother Teresa told a story about one of the first residents of Kalighat Home, who was dying there infested with maggots, when he said: 'I have lived like an animal in the street, but I am going to die like an angel, loved and cared for' (Mother Teresa 1979). This dignity of an angel has no personal identity – St Teresa does not speak about a transition from an objectified animal to a political subject, but rather from an individualistic animal to union with the divine. This Christian idea of dignity is based on the concept of 'Imago Dei' – the image of God embodied in every human being without exception. The love towards God in any human not only invokes Imago Dei in the victim, but simultaneously restores the Imago Dei of the loving subject through the re-enactment of

God's loving attitude towards his creature (Aquinas 2013). This love towards the image of God in every human being is the conceptual core of caritas. In Nirmal Hriday, the volunteers witness the force of caritas in practice, relying on it as they transgress the walls into the liminal area of the sacred beyond the structures of regular.

The touch is the point of trespass, the moment of truth on which many volunteers reflect in private conversations. Over the obvious fear and rejection of touching the body of the Other or waste products, volunteers express striving for a superior reality more real than their everyday life at home. That is how Romaine post factum reconstructs his original motivation to volunteer in Kolkata: 'I felt like my soul was dying while working in the office. I had to touch some real life, feel it, *touch it.*' The reality of poverty and suffering comes in the shape of monstrous bodies with missing or swollen limbs, rotting wounds, open fractures, skin and nervous disease, enormously attenuated or crooked. Through the direct contact with the Otherness the volunteers obtain the feeling of encounter with the inexpressible real, sparkling with the ecstasy of transgression.

The counterintuitive desire to touch anthropogenic dirt and dead bodies is a typical case of what Bataille describes as the paradox of forbidden fruit. As opposed to other social taboos such as incest or murder, the act of touching dirt naturally 'has no complementary desire running counter to the revulsion' (1962: 71). Developing on the Freudian reading of taboo as an auto-disciplining mechanism of the super-ego, Bataille concludes that the taboos restricting manipulations with human corpses (which might be reduced to the restriction of cannibalism as their core meaning) are an exemplary case of limitations constructed to instigate the wish to overcome them.

> the object is 'forbidden', sacred, and the very prohibition attached to it is what arouses the desire. Religious cannibalism is the elementary example of the taboo as creating desire: the taboo does not create the flavour and taste of the flesh but stands as the reason why the pious cannibal consumes it.
>
> (Ibid.: 72)

Similar to the desire of cannibalism, quenched in various transgressive rituals (including the Christian communion), the desire to touch and embrace dirty and diseased bodies is instigated by the very prohibition to do so.

According to Turner, death and growth yield together in the interstructural unity of the liminal (1967). The liminal status means a structural death of a social subject, which is a necessary step in the transformation process. The structural death is symbolically equalised to the physical death as liminal existence is approximated to the posthumous existence (Turner 1967). The proximity of this perfect symbolic border of existence backlights the entire volunteering experience of Kalighat. Regular deaths of the patients personally known by the volunteers often produce a strong psychological impact. The necessity to wash, dress, carry and deliver the dead bodies to crematoriums and cemeteries also forces the volunteers to establish a certain intimate relationship with this ultimate limit.

Encounters with monstrosity and death form an essential part of liminal trans-formation. Rearrangement of reality into monstrous patterns allows a symbolic deconstruction of the social structure (Turner 1967). At the same time, the monstrous deformations of bodies and minds encountered by the volunteers at Kalighat serve other didactic purposes. In a way, death and sufferings of Nirmal Hriday are a live enactment of *vanitas* – one of the popular genres in the fine arts since the Renaissance. These images create an impression of vulnerability and vanity of corporeal life in opposition to the spiritual life promoted by the sisters. Proximity of physical death enforces this impression of the elusiveness of the physical being, disturbing the most sensitive strings in the volunteers' psyches.

The Catholic mystics of the past are known to have increased the degrees of transcendence far beyond the obvious limits of fear and disgust in search of the union with God (Bynum 1991). Similarly, the intensification of the border experiences typifies the educative trajectory of the volunteers. They begin their transformation laundering dirty clothes, continue with rubbing scabies affected skin with a medical solution, wash the patients, and clean, dress and carry dead bodies. They can be assigned to a scout team, which performs the hardest job of picking up the future patients from the streets of Kolkata. Besides the massive responsibility of the decision-making, these volunteers handle people in terrible physical condition, sometimes stained with filth, invaded by maggots and other parasites, and suffering severe pains, fractures and flesh injuries.

Conclusion

Arguably, liminality is an essential characteristic of the whole project of modernity stuck in an impetuous leap into a continuum of transformations (Thomassen 2014; Horvath et al. 2015). Seen through the optics of political anthropology contemporary humanitarianism is the flesh and blood of modernity. Based on 'the diptych of life as highest good and suffering as redemptive ordeal' (Fassin 2012: 251), the human-itarian episteme operates in a continuous state of emergency, perceiving the reality as constantly sieged by calamities and social pathologies. Thereby, it propels a self-instigated armaments race of development – a constant reformation where the salvation is at stake. While being based on 'the inequality of lives, often invisible' (Fassin 2012: 242) between the politically potent providers of aid and the object-ified recipients, humanitarianism inevitably reproduces cultural and economic hierarchies of modernity, from the colonial ideological domination, to the toxic social effects of victimisation and non-reciprocal gift giving (Bornstein and Redfield 2011). Moreover, all the internal tensions and power misbalances inherent to the ethics of human rights and development are often amplified when intersecting with the complex social reality into which they bluntly are introduced.

According to various anthropologists (Bornstein and Redfield 2011; Fassin 2012; Muehlebach 2013), Christian discourse is profoundly interwoven into the contemporary humanitarian field, shaping and influencing its structure on many levels. From the explicit presence in local subsidiarity and international charity missions to the subtle religious moral imperatives and imagery of self-sacrifice, it impacts on all kinds of humanitarian activity. During the 'aggiornamiento' reforms in the middle of the twentieth century, the Catholic Church adopted the mainstream humanistic discourse of human rights and claimed the role of a major humanitarian authority worldwide (Casanova 2006). About that time Mother Teresa founded Kalighat shelter, and became an international media icon.

On a symbolic level the Christian embrace of humanitarianism has organically coalesced with the cult of suffering as a source of redemption. The acknowledgement of pain and misery as meaningful experiences constitutes one of the basic motives of Christianity deriving from the passions of Christ. In charity, the attribution of essential meaning to suffering allows one to process the experience of encounter with misery beyond the borders of a biopolitical norm, which considers suffering but a negative sign of pathology. Thus, the categorical condemnation of poverty and suffering on the side of mainstream biopolitics and rationalistic utilitarianism is opposed by the embracement of these conditions as merited or meaningful experiences in religious ethics.

Different from both the cold formalism and the humanistic pathos of secular humanitarianism, the non-secular charity invites one to immerse into the warm abyss of non-structured being – as terrifying as attractive in its incomprehensibility. The normalising secular approach tends to minimise the transgressive character of the service through the medical and bureaucratic formalisation of the interaction. In this segregating framework, the objectified recipients of aid are subtly branded with abnormality, pathology, poverty and underdevelopment. Thereby, the humanitarianism of development restricts its responsibility to the attempts of moral and physical administration of the object of aid on the background of recursive repetition of the humanistic ethical dogmas. Being epistemologically disconnected from the transcendental in the biopolitical framework of modernity, the secular humanitarianism proves to be unable to transcend the administrative grid and critically account on the subjective side of its own performance.

Representing a different episteme, the charity of Kalighat Home emphasises the direct touch, informal power relations and rejection of the medical technology. While reaching out to the excluded bare life of the forsaken street dwellers, the volunteers actually abandon the biopolitical episteme of modernity as they transgress its originary political division. Such a different approach to service enacts the symbolic potential of transgression, which 'does not seek to oppose one thing to another' but 'affirms the limitlessness into which it leaps as it opens this zone to existence for the first time' (Foucault 1977: 35). This is the moment of a highly emotional filling-up which re-builds the individual. The encircled bubble of the shelter becomes the ultimate external realm, defining the perspective of the subject in the moment of ecstatic reconstruction of her internal walls of individuality.

Beneath the official mission of charity Kalighat Home functions as a classroom, where the actors coming from completely different social realities engage in a transformative interaction. As a humanitarian institution, the shelter bears traits of modern political alchemy (Horvath et al. 2015: 89–90), being a transforming body where identities are melted in exaltation and cast into new forms under the artificially created and maintained structured liminality. Nevertheless, that is only the surface layer – Kalighat Home genealogically pertains to a pre-modern tradition of religious cultivation and missionary work. While formally embedded in the fixed liminality of modernity as a variety of a humanitarian non-governmental organisation saving sacred human lives in the continuous state of emergency, the shelter does not act within the dualistic episteme of modernity. Enacting the transformative powers of the sacred with its walling/transgression machinery, the home dwells in the religious liminality of the Christian mystic and monastic traditions, which predate and in a way presage modern morals of charity. As a charismatic leader, Mother Teresa stands in line with the icons of Catholic female mysticism of the High Middle Ages. Like Catherine of Siena or Angela of Foligno she cultivated an ecstatic union with God through the deliberate descent into the world of social exclusion and suffering. Following her path, the sisters employ the same ecstatic technique of cultivation in the liminal space behind the walls of Kalighat shelter.

As a key point of non-secular humanitarianism, the transformative cyst of Kalighat Home is effectively positioned amidst concentrated disturbing otherness of the Bengali capital. On the one hand, wanderlust brings individuals of the globalised age looking for essential, life-changing experiences to the exotic turmoil of Kolkata. On the other hand, being the major human dump of Asia, the city is a bottomless source of forsaken bare life to be subjected to charity. Between those hands at the heart of an alien religious life pulsates the hermetic, walled body of the shelter – a limbo between life and death. While dwelling in the firm frame of religious rituals, spatial divisions and distributions of social roles, the social fabric of the shelter is permeated with liminal fluidity and self-tuned under the moral imperative of caritas.

The walling facilities of Kalighat shelter enable the transformation of the volunteers' identities as they embody the sense of sacred. As Agnes Horvath notes in Chapter 1, an actuality of the existence can be only born from a union of finite and infinite. The case of Kalighat demonstrates how the idea of the unlimited transcendental fecundates the volunteers' identities in the course of the transgression, backlit by the ecstatic touch to the void. At first hand, the transgression of symbolic limits invokes the ecstasy of leaping out from one's own identity into the transcendental. The ideas of 'caritas' and dignity defined through a reference to the non-duality of the transcendental allow the subjects of aid to cross the limits of normality secured by disgust and fear.

While backed by the life-changing border experience, these ethical values are acknowledged by the volunteers as essential truths of life. As a result, in the mystic experience of service the volunteers obtain a dynamic view on the limits of existence, witnessing that: 1) the sacred reveals itself beyond the limits of the regular; 2) the limits are conditionally permeable; 3) caritas and oneness in God can serve as cognitive/emotional tools permitting the ecstatic transgression of the limits; and 4) the descent into the non-structured being can approve fundamental truths and be used for self-cultivation.

Acting in the fixed liminality of modernity, the charity service of Nirmal Hriday suggests an alternative approach to the continuous emergency of humanitarianism. Without neglecting the modern episteme, it adds a transcendental underlayer to it, which subverts the constant state of emergency, embracing it as a meaningful constant of the real. Through the reference to the transcendental, the non-secular mode of charity reaches beyond the modern semiotic ideology of 'distinction between object and subject, between substance and meaning, signifiers and signified, form and essence' (Mahmood 2009: 843), offering a non-dualistic solution for the basic tensions of objectification and inequality, which tear the humanitarian field apart from within.

Notes

1 A dharamshala (Hindi: *dharmaśālā*) is an Indian religious rest house (*The Imperial Gazetteer of India, v. 11*, p. 301).
2 According to an information board at the entrance.
3 According to the Sisters and the common legend of Mother Teresa; e.g. see Chawla, Navin. 1996. *Mother Teresa*. Rockport, MA: Element.
4 My translation from Spanish; the original version was retrieved 7/5/2016 with a generous permission of the author from the Facebook page of Lucia Valenzuela at www.facebook.com/luvabu/posts/10153622375692337?pnref=story
5 Baba – Bengali, Hindi and Marathi: father; grandfather; wise old man; sir – Platts, John T. 1884. *A Dictionary of Urdu, Classical Hindi, and English*. London: W. H. Allen & Co.

Bibliography

Agamben, Giorgio (1998) *Homo Sacer: Sovereign Power and Bare Life*, Stanford, CA: Stanford University Press.
Atran, Scott (2004) *In Gods We Trust: The Evolutionary Landscape of Religion*, Oxford: Oxford University Press.
Bataille, Georges (1962) *Erotism: Death & Sensuality*, New York: Walker.
Bornstein, Erica and Peter Redfield (2011) *Forces of Compassion: Humanitarianism Between Ethics and Politics*, Santa Fe: School for Advanced Research Press.
Bynum, Caroline Walker (1991) *Fragmentation and Redemption: Essays on Gender and the Human Body in Medieval Religion*, New York: Zone Books.
Casanova, José (2006) 'Secularization Revisited: A Reply to Talal Asad', in *Powers of the Secular Modern: Talal Asad and His Interlocutors*, Stanford: Stanford University Press, pp. 12–31.
Catherine of Siena, Saint (1994) *The Dialogue of the Seraphic Virgin*, London: Routledge.
Chawla, Navin (1996) *Mother Teresa*, Rockport, MA: Element.
Davis, Mike (2007) *Planet of Slums*, London: Verso.
Douglas, Mary (2003) *Purity and Danger: An Analysis of Concepts of Pollution and Taboo*, London: Psychology Press.
Fassin, Didier (2012) *Humanitarian Reason: A Moral History of the Present*, Berkeley: University of California Press.
Foucault, Michel (1977) 'A Preface to Transgression', in *Language, Counter-memory, Practice: Selected Essays and Interviews*, Ithaca: Cornell University Press, pp. 29–52.
Horvath, Agnes, Bjorn Thomassen and Harald Wydra (2015) *Breaking Boundaries: Varieties of Liminality*, Oxford: Berghahn Books.
John Paul II (1984) 'Salvifici Doloris', available at https://w2.vatican.va/content/john-paul-ii/en/apost_letters/1984/documents/hf_jp-ii_apl_11021984_salvifici-doloris.html (accessed on 14 August 2016).

Mahmood, Saba (2001) 'Rehearsed Spontaneity and the Conventionality of Ritual: Disciplines of "Ṣalāt"', *American Ethnologist* 28, 4: 827–53.

Mostafanezhad, Mary (2016) *Volunteer Tourism: Popular Humanitarianism in Neoliberal Times*, London: Routledge.

Mother Teresa (1979) 'Mother Teresa – Nobel Lecture', available at www.nobelprize.org/nobel_prizes/peace/laureates/1979/teresa-lecture.html. (accessed on 14 June 2016).

Mother Teresa and Brian Kolodiejchuk (2008) *Mother Teresa: Come Be My Light: The Private Writings of the 'Saint of Calcutta'*, Waterville: Wheeler.

Muehlebach, Andrea (2013) 'The Catholicization of Neoliberalism: On Love and Welfare in Lombardy, Italy', *American Anthropologist* 115, 3: 452–65.

Rappaport, Roy A. (1999) 'Enactments of Meaning', in Michael Lambek (ed.) *A Reader in the Anthropology of Religion*, New York: Wiley, pp. 446–68.

Raymond of Capua (1860) *Life of Saint Catharine of Sienna*, Philadelphia: P. F. Cunningham, Available at http://archive.org/details/lifeofsaintcatha01raym.

Szakolczai, Arpad (2009) 'Liminality and Experience: Structuring Transitory Situations and Transformative Events', *International Political Anthropology* 2, 1: 141–72.

Thomas Aquinas, Saint (2013) *Summa Theologica, Volume 1*, New York: Cosimo.

Thomassen, Bjørn (2009) 'Uses and Meanings of Liminality', *International Political Anthropology* 2, 1: 5–27.

Thomassen, Bjørn (2014) *Liminality and the Modern: Living Through the In-Between*, Farnham: Ashgate.

Turner, Victor Witter (1967) *The Forest of Symbols: Aspects of Ndembu Ritual*, Ithaca: Cornell University Press.

Vardey, Lucinda (2011) *Meditations for a Simple Path*, London: Ebury.

6   Liminality and belonging

The life and the afterlives of the Berlin Wall

Harald Wydra

The Berlin Wall was a constant presence as I was growing up in the Federal Republic of Germany (FRG) in the 1970s and 1980s. The nature of its significance is highlighted in that I would not actually see the wall until 1986 when I first visited the West and East parts of Berlin, but still its influence pervaded. Nevertheless, I was persuaded that most West Germans would consider the wall a monument of shame and repression. When Berliners literally overran the wall in the evening hours of 9 November 1989, a new era of freedom finally seemed to break. The collapse of the wall became an instantaneous worldwide event, gripping tens of millions of observers and turning it, in a way not dissimilar to the Parisian Bastille, from a symbol of oppression into the iconic symbol for the spring of peoples. From the vantage point of 1989, the story of a divided Germany would turn into a feast of unity in freedom. Now it was possible, following ex-Chancellor Willy Brandt's dictum 'to grow together what belongs together'.[1] This claim expressed the deep feelings of an overwhelming majority of East Germans and probably of many West Germans as well. Yet, it was clearly counterintuitive, if not even inappropriate. Over 40 years, the division of Germany had created two different societies, which had built divergent economic, social and political systems that would also deeply affect collective identities.

In this chapter I shall argue that Brandt's dictum – whilst spoken with genuine conviction and momentous hope – only makes sense if we accept that the division of Germany had transformed Germans in East and West. Whilst earlier generations of Germans might have taken for granted an undivided nation, that is one Germany, such a mentality had increasingly become alien to those Germans who had formed their lives in the face of the wall. The wall indisputably created two Germanys, whose elective affinities pushed each other apart, whilst always maintaining attraction, which pulled them together. In the following I would like to explore some of the 'creative' capacities of the Berlin Wall. By 'creative' I do not refer to the beginning of a new political and social order, which would sustain and complete the ideological programme of the Socialist Unity Party (SED). Rather, I would like to emphasise the role of the wall as an active carrier of images of belonging. The wall produced many fractures because its original aim was to close the watershed that allowed a mass exodus from the Soviet occupation zone towards West Germany. The political imagination of Germans on both sides was shaped precisely because the wall never could produce the limits that its builders had intended. It is true that the wall, like any border and territorial limit shaped identities and political existence. As social theorist Georg Simmel lucidly saw a long time ago, a society is characterised as internally belonging by the fact that its existential space (*Existenzraum*) is enclosed by sharply conscious borders (Simmel 1992: 694). What Simmel called 'sociological centripetality' referred to 'spiritual coherence of persons that grows into a sensuously felt picture of a tightly enclosing borderline' (Simmel 1992: 69).

My proposition, however, is to suggest that the Berlin Wall failed to create such an enclosing borderline. It failed to do so on two major accounts. First, as the German Democratic Republic (GDR) had rejected the heritage of the former German Reich and had invented itself as a socialist Germany it was plagued by a profound legitimacy deficit. Placing a taboo on the historical emergence of its statehood out of post-war destruction and by the grace of the Soviet Union it nevertheless had to legitimise itself by mythological references to the past and by utopian constructions of 'second realities'. In doing so, it fundamentally relied on mythological accounts of its anti-fascist credentials, which presented the GDR not as a successor state of Germany but universalised its experience as a frontrunner of a socialist modernity.

Second, in spite of closing off relations with West Germany, the wall became a site of negotiation regarding belonging and national consciousness of Germans on both sides. In the shadow of the wall two divided Germanys not only pursued different economic and socio-political models but also built collective identities. By becoming more 'Eastern', Germans in the GDR also become more originally German, something they had initially rejected. Conversely, whilst West Germans saw the wall as an object of shame and repression, which stood in the way of German unity, they grounded their identity of being German not in a particular pride about their Germanness but in international values such as freedom, democracy and the rule of law. When the wall finally collapsed, East Germans felt much more intensely and profoundly German, whereas many West Germans saw unification not as a goal of fulfilling a national duty but rather as the imposition of the West German political and economic model on the new territories in the East.

The fundamental reason for why in spite of its materiality as a *fait accompli* the wall could not produce longer lasting thriving social conditions and sociological centripetality lies in the fact that it was a deeply ambivalent 'solution' to different dimensions of social and political liminality, which had imposed on post-war Germany a sense of fluidity, uncertainty and, quite literally, in-betweenness. Within the fractures that the wall aimed to transcend, new fractures emerged. As the editors point out in the Introduction to this volume, walls create different dimensions of liminality.

First of all, they generate spatial liminality, which turns the area affected by the wall into an in-between space. Not accidentally, the width of up to 500 metres between the West and East wall became colloquially known as the death strip (*Todesstreifen*).

Second, walls also represent temporal liminality. The immediate reason for building the wall was the survival instinct of a regime that faced the prospect of a government without a population. Unlike the FRG, which considered itself as the legal and legitimate successor state to the German Reich, the Soviet occupation zone had a problem of legitimacy. The creation of the GDR on 7 October 1949 was not the original intention of Stalin, nor were the authorities of the SED regime always absolutely certain of the loyalty of the Soviet Union. In spite of its ideological claims to construct a forward-oriented socialist modernity, the GDR drew legitimacy nearly exclusively from the past. The closure produced by the wall had a paradoxical effect. Whilst it was aimed to end the in-betweenness of a divided nation, whose parts belonged to different ideological blocs, it actually established a new liminal space. As the exit option of regime critics and other citizens was now closed, the SED regime was harder pressed to provide the symbolic meaning to the existence of the wall. Whilst this closure might have signified a rupture with the past, in reality it forced the authorities to re-mythologise the past.

Third, walls require understanding the dimensions of social liminality. The wall reassured the political authorities of the GDR of relative stability in order to pursue their project of socialist modernity. This stability was relative in the sense that it would guarantee control of the population but it would also make the system more liable to internal dissidence and potential unrest in the case of economic crisis. In terms of the effects on the whole of Germany, it also served the purpose of a simplified identity binary, which reassured each side of its moral superiority. The 'other' side was portrayed as possessing all the evil attributes that would warrant the separation of two hermetically closed parts of Berlin. The wall was, so to speak, the GDR's last resort to guarantee the integrity of its territorial frame. This sense of assurance might have been a kind of protection, both in political and epistemological terms. Yet it also fired the imagination both as a symbol of the division of the world during the Cold War but also as an artefact around which two versions of German identity and German statehood evolved.

Towards closure

A first dimension of liminality concerned the political fluidity and the constitutional in-betweenness of Germany after total defeat in 1945. Total surrender in May 1945 would entail the end of German statehood as well as the loss of substantial territories east of the rivers Oder and Neisse. With the Potsdam agreement in early August 1945, Germany lost eastern territories and throughout the late 1940s would receive approximately 11 million refugees who mainly came to the occupation zones of the Western Allies. The later division of the former German Reich into four different occupation zones would make multiple liminalities a normality; the end of the German Reich, the end of patriotic feelings, the division of the nation. The result in 1949 would be the formation of two different political societies with opposed socio-economic and political models.

In May 1949 the FRG passed its provisional constitution (*Grundgesetz*). The nascent West German republic focused on the integration into Western political and economic structures. The fundamental political choices of domestic political and economic organisation as well as foreign policy options had been forged in the early 1950s. The constitution of a federal democratic government laid the basis for what would later become the economic miracle (*Wirtschaftswunder*) but also further integration into Western alliance structures – first the European Coal and Steel Community in 1951 and later membership of the North Atlantic Treaty Organization (NATO) in 1955. On the territory of the Soviet occupation zone, the socialist GDR was founded in October 1949. However, the Soviets did not fully commit to transforming East Germany into a socialist system. Until as late as March 1952 Stalin continued to lure West Germany's government with the proposition of national unification on the basis of neutrality.

One of the key problems of the 'German question' concerned the role of the former capital Berlin, which had become a liminal space of its own within the broader liminality of two provisional German states. This was due to a momentous decision at the end of the war. In May 1945 the Western Allies held more than a third of the territory of what later would become the Soviet occupation zone (SBZ) and, eventually, the GDR. Yet, they pushed for exchanging these territories for a substantial part (concretely 12 out of the 20 sections of Great Berlin) in order to ensure a presence in the former capital of Germany. In the following 16 years, this status of Berlin would become deeply contested.

The first major stand-off occurred in 1948. When the currency reform was introduced in the zones dominated by the Western Allies in June 1948, Stalin reacted with the blockade of all land communications between Western zones and the Western sectors of Berlin. The Western Allies responded with an unprecedented airlift, which lasted for nearly 12 months (June 1948 to May 1949). They supplied the population in the western part of the city with food, medication and other goods. The resilience and resistance of the West Berlin population also galvanised the West German population. Conversely, capitalist West Germany remained a magnetic attraction for East Germans. Between 1948 and August 1961 nearly three million people crossed from the Soviet sector in Berlin to the western sectors of the city, making up approximately 16 per cent of the GDR population. Whilst many of those who crossed the border were well educated, after the riots of 17 June 1953 workers and peasants increasingly left the Soviet occupation zone. When SED Chairman Walter Ulbricht declared in a press conference on 15 June 1961 that 'nobody has the intention to build a wall', there is little doubt that he was honest about it. And yet, the open nature of West Germany society and the difficult ideological and economic position of the GDR had indeed become an existential problem for the SED. The continuous bloodletting threatened the viability of the system with more than 30,000 people crossing from East to West in July 1961 alone. This 'voting by feet' threatened the spectre of a government without people.

When on 13 August 1961 units of the National peoples army (*Nationale Volksarmee*) blocked all passages from East to West Berlin, the population in West Berlin was under shock. Moreover, reactions from Western powers and from the West German government were hesitant or lacking. The heads of state or government of the United States, Britain and France were on summer holidays. Chancellor Konrad Adenauer did not come to visit the city until the 22 August, that is three days after US Vice President Lyndon B. Johnson. Whilst officially claiming he did not want to accelerate escalation, the real reason might have been that West Berlin Governing Mayor Willy Brandt was Adenauer's opponent in the forthcoming parliamentary elections scheduled for 17 September. In an extraordinary measure Brandt wrote a direct letter to President Kennedy, claiming that the Western Allies should insist on their right to be in control of the city.[2] Brandt suggested that failing a single solution from the Western Allies, perhaps they could at least send a clear signal to reassure the population in the western sectors. Most importantly, he argued that by accepting the construction of the wall, the Western powers had de facto acknowledged the existence of something that did not exist according to the official policies of the Western Allies: the GDR as a state. This acknowledgement is remarkable in the sense that the wall – which could only be built with the consent of the Soviet Union – was a political victory for the regime in the GDR. It allowed the minister of interior to issue orders to the Western Allied powers, which they grudgingly had to obey.

The wall also aimed to preserve and to protect. The authorities of the GDR used to refer to the wall as '*Anti-Faschistischer Schutzwall*', an anti-fascist wall of protection. At first sight, this was a propaganda trick. The complex defence mechanisms within the strip between the West and the East part of the wall aimed entirely at preventing East German citizens from *Republikflucht* (flight from the republic). And yet, this closure provided reassurance about each side's political and economic trajectory. It is quite uncontroversial that the building of the wall in August 1961 'solved' the permanently contested status of Berlin as an open city. Whilst it shocked the citizens of Berlin living in the western part of the city, the lukewarm protests by the Western Allies could not conceal the fact that the building of the wall not only formalised the stand-off between the occupation powers in Berlin but also became a crucial milestone in the acceptance of the second German state.

It would be presumptuous, however, to think that the wall did not have a protective 'function' for West Germany as well. Beyond the utter destruction of German cities and infrastructure across the Western occupation zones, West Germans had also been defeated morally. The 'we' identity can never be fully distinguished from the 'they' identity. They rely on each other and often have mimetic effects. Already before the construction of the wall in the summer 1961, the West German government under Konrad Adenauer had insisted on the alien nature of East Germany and its total dependence on Moscow. Adenauer rejected any offers regarding unification – such as Stalin's note of 10 March 1952 – as he saw them as strategic attempts by the Soviets aimed at weakening West Germany's efforts to further integration into democratic structures of Western Europe. In his 1957 campaign for federal parliamentary elections – which he won with an absolute majority of seats – Chancellor Adenauer had used the famous campaign motto 'No experiments', indicating his firm disposition to stick to West integration at any cost. The presence of Soviet communism in Eastern Europe and in the Soviet occupation zone in particular provided an image of the enemy and strengthened the will to freedom. After all, the existence of the wall (and the heavily guarded and nearly impenetrable inner-German border) was fundamental for the domestic perception of West Germany as being bordered and framed by sharply delineated limits.

Legitimising the wall

The second layer of liminality refers to the ways in which the Berlin Wall determined the self-understanding of the socialist regime in East Berlin as a socialist state and, later, as a socialist nation. The wall became a cornerstone of the project of a socialist modernity on the territory of the GDR, which was directed towards the future but, paradoxically, generated its legitimacy from the past. The SED in East Germany had a difficult stance in many respects. The Communist Party in the SBZ lacked international recognition. Against its ideological premise, it had not come to power by a workers' revolution but on the back of complete defeat of Nazi Germany. Under the pressure of the Soviet occupation authorities, the German Communist Party (KPD) and the Social Democratic Party (SPD) were united in April 1946 in order to form the SED. After 1949, the two new German republics had not only to build the material bases of new political and economic institutions but also to create political consciousness that would correspond to their new international orientations. In terms of state security, the wall cut apart and closed off. Although its construction has been considered as the second foundation of the GDR, the wall primarily caused alienation, greater estrangement, even hostility. Some 156 kilometres of wall surrounded West Berlin, nearly 44 kilometres of which divided the two parts. This separation tore apart many social ties and relations, cutting people's communications and leaving thousands of families and friends disheartened and abandoned. During the 28 years of its existence more than a hundred people were killed when trying to cross the wall, whilst several hundreds more died when attempting to cross the checkpoints.

In spite of this closure it would also remain a contact zone and site of cultural negotiation. Whilst the forced division of the city seemed nearly impenetrable, political imagination became increasingly driven by second realities. Eric Voegelin introduced the concept of second reality to explore how our selective consciousness can be attracted by imaginary worlds that become socially relevant. Eventually, they can even become constitutive of political hierarchies, legitimacy and truth claims (Voegelin 1999). Whilst the very centre of Berlin was literally turned into a no man's land, the wall assumed a life of its own, becoming a living organism in the minds of people, shaping consciousness and the mentalities of Germans on both sides. It therefore shaped underlying bonds that attracted both sides towards each other. The wall reassured the political authorities of the GDR of relative stability in order to pursue their project of modernisation. However, it also meant that potential regime critics had to be accommodated, as they could not exit the system. The wall structured specific life-worlds and the political will addressing such life worlds.

Second realities became authoritative frames of the symbolic order of political existence. As a prime example of a regime created by liminal outsiders, the establishment of communist regimes anywhere in Eastern Europe required – in accordance with ideological precursors both in Marxist-Leninist theory and in the practice of Soviet Russia – a break with the past and a projection in a brighter future. As I have shown elsewhere, communism, in its Soviet version, was a programme of utopia based on dream-like fantasies with a belief in complete harmony for the future by destroying the past (Wydra 2015). The gap between existing reality and desired future required legitimation strategies. *The Communist Manifesto*, not the most systematic but no doubt the most influential of Marx and Engels' writings, suggests that in the wake of the abolition of all class differences public force (understood as oppression of one class by the other) will lose its political character. The proletariat's fight against the bourgeoisie will unite them and produce the new ruling class by means of revolution. Crucially, as Marx and Engels put it, 'as a ruling class it will eliminate the old means of production (by violence), and then it will also abolish the conditions of existence of the class struggle, the classes altogether, also its own domination as a class' (Marx 1971: 548).

For Marx, the classless society could not arrive by means of technological progress. The state would not represent but rather alienate, pauperise and enslave the proletariat. Marx had the idea to turn the reality of degradation of manual labour through machinery and modern industry into a different type of reality. Here the workers would convert from the cogs in the wheel into the 'ruling class'. Marx remained quite abstract about the transitional phase. Lenin, however, linked the achievement of freedom to the massive and complete destruction of the remnants of the old order. Following closely Marx's idea – expressed in the 18th Brumaire of Louis Bonaparte – Lenin insisted on the absolute need to break (*zerbrechen*) and shatter (*zerschlagen*) the machinery of the old state.

Following similar lines, the GDR established the promise of a socialist modernity as a programme of truth. This 'truth' drew upon the fact that the creation of a socialist state on German soil had not followed the ideological blueprint of a workers' revolution. Quite the opposite, the 'beginning' was one of utter destruction and despair. The GDR's programme of truth was no intellectual fantasy but rather a discursively produced mythical narrative that aimed to transcend the utter destruction of the defeated and occupied Germany. The total destruction of German cities, for instance, left the population traumatised and disoriented. As Wolfgang Engler has shown, the devastation of Berlin after 1945 was deeply traumatic. In 1945, 80 per cent of the buildings of Berlin were destroyed and the immediate aftermath was utter desolation, fear and confusion. Many school essays written by youngsters in early 1946 report the *Ur-scene*: the first encounter with the victor who does not enter triumphantly but exhausted and grim. The defeated crouched in the basements of their houses and wait for the inevitable: the first Russians to arrive.

The authorities placed a taboo on these moments of destruction and despair. As Günter de Bruyn put it, if one mentioned events that occurred during the war or shortly after, everything that had been frightening had to become taboo. Soviet soldiers did not rape or loot, no German prisoners of war could have died in a concentration camp or in Siberia. The pervasive continuity of the consequences of the war kept the GDR in a double-bind between negating the concrete destruction and constantly referring to the past. As Lutz Niethammer has argued, the war for the East Germans remained much closer than for the West Germans; their destiny remained chained to the war, everywhere one could read its signs and its consequences reached deep into many families who had to carry the burden for the care for war victims, widows, and orphans.

(Quoted in Engler, 1999: 20)

The experience of time in East Germany would keep the war (and thus the immediate past) in communicative and social memory. The ideology of the SED, however, which required a reorientation of this memory, aimed to lay the ideological foundations of a new society. The denial of reality became the correct line by which the outcome of history, law, politics or economic development would be known in advance. The horizon of expectation was, so to speak, concentrated not as experience but against all experience. Hypermodernity in the Soviet Union was aimed at industrialisation, which would overhaul and reject the past. As Stalin put it in 1931: 'We are fifty or a hundred years behind the advanced countries. We must make good this distance in ten years. Either we do it, or we shall go under.'

The conditions of the GDR were different. Up to the very construction of the wall (which started in the late evening of 12 August 1961), Berliners could freely cross between the occupation zone of the three Western powers into the Soviet zone. Therefore, the primary necessity in establishing a convincing socialism was to prevent citizens of the GDR from exiting the territory to capitalist West Germany. Although the task of the SED regime might have seemed more down to earth and parochial than the aspirations of Marxist theory, their myths gained enormous power because they became a public force in a liminal situation. The authors of *The Communist Manifesto* claimed that in bourgeois society, the past rules over the present, whereas in communism, the present rules over the past (Marx 1971: 41). Marx and Engels here learnt their lesson from the French Revolution, after which 'History' was to become a function of political engineering. A revolutionary dictionary suggested writing no history until the constitution was completed. The past would become the creation of the political will.

Indeed, Soviet communism based its promise of a radiant, bright and harmonious future on victimhood, suffering and resentment. Memories of victimhood and suffering and their transformations into myths have existed in all phases of human history, especially in transition zones or times of great transformation. As structured narratives, myths are of an ahistorical nature thus giving them a natural or eternal justification. Yet, as social phenomena, myths have a concrete historical basis, where people need to make sense of extreme experiences. People believe myths not because the historical evidence is compelling but because they are attempts to make sense of uncertainty by 'structuring' events. Myths are not ontologically stable, they are interpretations that draw on perceptions about people's social experiences for the sake of setting out definitions of knowledge, loyalty and belonging for the political reality to come. In Victor Turner's terms, myth relates to how one state of affairs becomes another: how an unpeopled world becomes populated, how chaos became cosmos, how immortals became mortal, and so on.

Myths are liminal phenomena; they are frequently told at a time or in a site that is 'betwixt and between'.

The GDR had to legitimise its political order through a major exercise in myth-making. First, it justified the existence of its own state by its anti-fascist credentials. The GDR considered itself a state with revolutionary intentions but it paradoxically anchored its own self-understanding much more within German history. The GDR authorities were very much aware that there had been no revolution, as the Nazi regime was defeated in a war by foreign powers. Therefore, the official narrative spoke of upheaval (*Umwälzung*). The GDR regime desperately relied on this con-stitutive mythology in order to make up for the lack of legitimacy. There was a heroic component to this myth of anti-fascism that portrayed the communists as resistance fighters who were not victims of Nazi dictatorship but actively sacrificed themselves for the common cause. The sacralisation of anti-fascism happened by means of a series of publicly staged rituals and public holidays. The political authorities used the disciplining function of this anti-fascist myth in a very rigorous way. As Engler put, whilst West Germany converted destroyed buildings and deso-late spaces into new modernist architecture, in the East even decades later the original situation transpired. Roads and pavements were only gradually renovated, whilst the network of motorways essentially remained the ones constructed under the Nazis. The façades of the city centres would for a long time witness the damage of the fights of the last weeks of the war (Engler 1999).

Second, the claim to universalisation and the overcoming of German history plunged the GDR more than its counterpart in the West into the past. The wall was the peak of a response that silenced debate over historical events for the sake of an ideologically manipulated second reality. The three successor states to the German Reich, Austria, West Germany and East Germany, dealt with the heritage of the Nazi rule in different ways. Austria largely externalised Nazism by presenting itself as the first victim of Hitler's aggression. West Germany had claimed the status of juridical succession to the German Reich. As such it had accepted the Nazi period as part of its own history, which it had to address and come to terms with. Conversely, the GDR aimed to universalise German history. Ironically, the wall contained an ele-ment of universalisation. Berlin became the focal point, the symbol par excellence, for the 'universal' conflict that the Cold War constituted. East German writer Stefan Heym expressed such blind illusions retrospectively in this way:

> In the shadow of the anti-fascist protection wall one could have nice dreams about an intact and well settled socialist life in the GDR; the leaders of party and state closed their eyes and ears towards the thoughts and feelings of people in the country and insisted on their wrong methods and catchwords.
>
> (Heym 1990: 241)

The construction of a socialist nation required the engineering of historical facts but also, more importantly, a huge security apparatus, which would control the compliance of the population. For instance, conceptions of space in East Germany differed from the West. The boundaries of public space were wider and included

the economic life. Private spaces were demarcated more narrowly and less con-
spicuously. Public office and companies required *Passierscheine*, whilst private
buildings often were not locked. Fundamentally, however, the ideological claim
made by the party did not match social and economic realities. Already Marx
had observed that the superior development of productive forces constituted
an absolute necessity for communism, 'because without them scarcity becomes
generalised, that is with misery *(Notdurft)* would start again the conflict over the
necessary and the whole old shit . . .' (Marx 1971: 362).

Nevertheless, diplomacy and the common-sense approach of Willy Brandt's
Ostpolitik achieved small but significant steps in the normalisation of German–
German relations. During the period of détente, a series of treaties improved the
relations between the two German states. The FRG recognised existing post-war
borders in the treaties of Moscow and Warsaw, and thus renounced revisionism.
The Basic Treaty *(Grundlagenvertrag)* between the FRG and the GDR in 1972
then led to the recognition of two states, but without achieving recognition
according to international law. Thus the FRG's interpretation maintained its long-
term aim of peaceful achievement of German unification, while the GDR conceived
of a new 'two-nations theory' which it also enshrined in its 1974 constitution.
Likewise, while the West viewed the 1975 OSCE Helsinki Accord as a recognition of human rights by the communist states, SED chairman Erich Honecker
focused upon an interpretation of the Accords that recognised existing borders, and
consequently international legitimation of the wall.

The daunting task of legitimising a revolutionary system against all past experience could, quite paradoxically, not draw any other legitimacy than constantly
referring to the past. The gruesome reality of a wall cutting apart an organic life in
a city co-existed with an imaginary reality in which East German identity was fed
with a very selective perception of historical events. The GDR was bound to tie its
destiny to an inflexible, distorted and nevertheless backward-oriented version of
Germanhood. As Wolfgang Engler put it:

> Strange but true: As East Germans irrevocably extricated themselves from
> their involvement in the all-German pre-history, they became increasingly
> confronted with that history. They worked themselves out of the disaster in a
> way that irrevocably tied them back to it. Whilst in many ways they changed
> more quickly and more profoundly than West Germans, they carried the signs
> of their origin more clearly on their forehead than their Western counterparts.
> They only could become East Germans with being close to Germany, they
> only could remain Germans – in a way difficult to define – by becoming East
> Germans.
>
> (Engler 1999: 31)

The afterlives of the wall

The third layer of liminality concerns the wall's creativity in maintaining mutually contradictory imaginations of one people despite the undeniable fact that the

two Germanys had drifted apart. The ideological divide between communist East Germany and liberal-capitalist West Germany overshadowed the fact that Germanhood did not mean clear-cut identities on each side. The wall represented three different meanings to Germans. For citizens in East Germany it was a bulwark, a defence wall, standing representative for servitude and unfreedom. It was, secondly, a piece of architecture that symbolised the political division not only of a city, a country, but also of the world. Thirdly, from the West German side it was considered to be a monster, a wall of shame. And yet, throughout the 1970s, the wall not only had become a factor of normality but also an aesthetic focus for artists, turning it into the longest canvas in the world. Wall art was art that combined the violation of the border with messages that went beyond borders and used aesthetics to denounce the effect of deterrence of the wall. The repulsion the wall had attracted during its existence had gradually turned into a pop-star status after its collapse. People from all over the world sought souvenirs in the form of little pieces, which they proudly would expose but pay huge amounts to own.

Whilst its presence seemed overwhelming and without appeal, both its construction and its disappearance owed to unpredictability, surprise and utter confusion. With the exception of a total of 1.5 kilometres of remainders scattered around the city, practically all traces of the wall have disappeared. In spite of its iconic status as the 'end of the Cold War' in Europe, its collapse has neither become a national holiday nor has it reached a prominent status as a memory regime. In spite of its triumphant transformation from a symbol of servitude into an iconic symbol of freedom, the afterlives of the wall intimate perpetuated political identities of a divided nation.

The very end of the wall was shrouded in confusion and liminality. Nothing predicted the wall would fall following the reconstitution of the SED politbureau on 8 November. At a live press conference on 9 November politbureau member Günter Schabowski came out with the usual empty clichés. The spontaneous interjection by an Italian journalist regarding a draft law on travel increased the confusion. After some roundabout explanations Schabowski hinted at the future possibility of travel for citizens of the GDR. Confusion reigned not only in his facial expressions but also in the mimicry as can be seen on the film documents. Eventually, he reacted to further questioning by saying that the planned permission for private travel already could happen without any preconditions. And that the 'law actually is valid . . . as of now'. When the press conference ended at 7.54 p.m., the audience was stunned and journalists speculated whether this meant the opening of the wall. In a chain reaction, rumours became press-agency breaking news. This spiralling up entailed a wave of East Berliners moving towards the wall. There were met by completely confused policemen, who after letting people with passports through the gates, surrendered to the masses and opened the barriers. As a result, people danced on the wall throughout the night, giving rise to unprecedented scenes of happiness, joy, ecstasy and festivities. Many people grasped this happening in the words craziness or hallucination.

Did Germans in the West really consider the wall as the painful reminder of a torn apart nation? Was there an organic feeling of belonging in the sense of one nation? One may have legitimate doubts. West German and international claims about the shame and repression as being fundamental to the wall do not change the fact that the wall had a stabilising effect on inner-German relations and actually inaugurated the Ostpolitik. Whilst political elites had stressed the provisional character of the FRG, the reality of 40 years of division had actually produced a sociological centripetality regarding West German values that also affected political orientations. These were based on the idea of a cohesive strong narrative of democratic maturity, West integration, and values of freedom and justice. In terms of mentalities West Germans saw themselves rather as Europeans or citizens of the federal republic rather than as Germans. As historian Thomas Nipperdey once suggested it was a specific characteristic of West Germans to think that there was nothing special about being German. Conversely, East Germans were much more German than West Germans. As historian Christian Meier put it, West German society with its focus to the West (and the South) left the other Germans literally behind (Meier, 2010: 134).

Given the truly worldwide resonance of the collapse of the wall, it is at least surprising that 9 November has not become the cornerstone of a constitutive mythology in the guise of a national holiday. On 9 November 1989, it was literally a vote by the feet, which showed that it was not only the people but one people that gathered in the centre of Berlin. Yet, with the disappearance of the wall, divisions remained. Such divisions concern social, political and economic integration. Divisions also relate to the status of the collapse of the wall within German memory regimes in the twentieth century. The date of 9 November has an ambivalent meaning in recent German history. On 9 November 1918 the ceasefire in World War I was signed, whilst the revolution started in many German cities. On 9 November 1923 Hitler staged his putsch in Munich, and 9 November 1938 recalls the Night of Broken Glass (*Reichskristallnacht*), the first widespread anti-Jewish pogrom in Germany. More critically, West Germans were only onlookers of what happened on 9 November in Berlin. Spatially, West German society was not the actor of the drama and emancipatory carnival of November 1989. West Germans did not want the East Germans to become the heroes or founders of the new united Germany. Of course, the dates alone do not reflect the deeper narrative traditions, which have formed before 1989 and after. One key point concerns the fact that West Germany has drawn much of its political identity from a unified memory regime about the Nazi past such that it is difficult for other types of memory regimes to become salient parts of the mnemonic field at all (Art 2014). The politics of regret or the culture of contrition dominated the Bonn memory regime, and has established the narrative of Holocaust commemoration as a permanent duty for Germans.

Let us now come back to Willy Brandt's emphatic claim that 'now what belongs together will grow together'. My proposition has been to understand belonging in the two Germanys neither through the lenses of a continuous national identity after 1945 nor by means of a centripetality of two hermetically closed divided Germanys. Rather, I have sketched out the porous nature of the wall, characterised by the liminal fractures that preceded the construction of the wall as well as the liminality created by the wall itself. The wall created important centrifugal forces that did not start but only deepened Germany's paradoxical condition.

When Khrushchev gave the final green light to the construction of a border within Berlin, which would stop the bloodletting in 1961, he might have followed Karl Marx who argued that it is not consciousness that determines life but rather life that determines consciousness: '*Nicht das Bewusstsein bestimmt das Leben, sondern das Leben bestimmt das Bewußstsein.*' We have, however, to modify Marx's understanding of life. As Georg Simmel reminded us, processes of spatial boundaries have their roots in the psychological forces of the soul by which people in a given territory hold together a geographical space. 'The border is not a spatial fact with sociological consequences but rather a sociological fact that is shaping up spatially' (Simmel 1992: 697). Simmel also referred to the forces of the soul that constitute the forces of tension (*Spannkräfte*) which provoke the distributions of space. At the end of bordered entities there is always defensive and offensive; that is refusal and attraction. The political anthropology of the Berlin Wall undertaken in this chapter has suggested that the political imagination of belonging followed such forces of refusal and attraction. By cutting life worlds apart West Germans created a non-German identity in West Germany, whereas the East Germans could only remain Germans by isolating themselves. The wall as a cornerstone of East German identity is perhaps most succinctly understood by looking at the political subjectivity of those whose generational consciousness was most affected by the building of the wall. As Bärbel Bohley (born in 1945), a prominent political dissident in 1989, put it:

> Most formative for me was the fact that I am a postwar child . . . Then there were the events of 17 June (1953), the 1956 Hungarian uprising and Prague 1968. These were the factors that made me sympathetic to the building of the wall in 1961. I thought this might give us some peace, so that we could get on with creating a socialist state. It turned out in retrospect that this was an illusion.
>
> (Andrews, 2002: 83)

Such generational identities also dominated visions of Germany amongst citizens of the Federal Republic. When I gave my first ever academic paper in a conference on European identity in Pamplona in October 1990 just after reunification had been achieved on 3 October, I extensively commented on the imminent decision of the German Bundestag of whether the seat of government should remain in Bonn or move to Berlin, the new capital. I argued passionately for keeping it in Bonn. My main reasoning was twofold. On the one hand, the provisional character of Bonn as seat of government had suited West Germany very well; it had kept it integrated in Western institutions and prevented it from playing again a primary role in international politics; moreover, Berlin not only stood for the divided city that had upheld the thirst for freedom in difficult times but it also stood for Prussian militarism, the rise of Nazi power and, eventually, for the capital of the SED regime. On the other hand, moving the seat of government to Berlin would definitely change the character of the FRG, exposing it to the demands and problems of Eastern Europe. The vote in the Bundestag in June 1991 that decided on whether the seat of government would be Berlin was taken with a very narrow margin: 320 members of parliament voted for Bonn, 338 for Berlin. MPs from the north and east of Germany largely favoured Berlin, whereas most MPs from the west and south of Germany favoured Bonn.

It may be far-fetched to link the afterlives of the wall to broader questions of German foreign policy in the twenty-first century. Yet, I would suggest that the invisible afterlives of the wall continue having effects. In his speech on the occasion of the national holiday of German unity on 3 October 2017 German President Frank-Walter Steinmeier talked about the continuity of walls. Starting with the question 'Who is this actually – We, Germans', he said:

> The great wall across our country is gone . . . However: New walls rose, less visible, without barbed wire and death strip but walls that hamper our common 'We'. I mean the walls between our life worlds: between city and countryside, online and offline, poor and rich, old and young, walls behind which one does hardly notice what the other is doing. . . . And I mean the walls made of alienation, disappointment or anger that for some have become so solid that they become impermeable for arguments. Behind such walls deep suspicion is instigated against democracy and its representatives and against the so-called establishment.

Such suspicion had been articulated in the famous dictum of the walls in people's minds and hearts (*Mauer in den Köpfen*), which had characterised the attitudes of West Germans towards East Germans in the 1990s and beyond. Nearly 30 years after German unification much progress has been achieved without, however, making the mental rifts of the wall obsolete. This can also be sensed in Germany's foreign policy. Germany's place in Europe and in the world in 2017 is very different from 1989. In the wake of the financial crisis of 2007, the relative decline of French influence in the European Union, and the anti-liberal spasms of Brexit and the Trump election, prominent opinion makers such as the *New York Times* and the *Financial Times* have called for Germany to lead the free world. Beyond the lack of proper resources and capacities, especially in the military field, the united Germany continues lacking the proper identity for leadership. For a long time, it was a proper sign of West German identity to exhibit a non-German identity. The sea change that catapulted West Germany out of its cosiness of the FRG meant that life after 1989 would end the fracture created by the wall but it would also open up new fractures. Germans on both sides of the former division have still to come to terms with these challenges and will have to cope with the afterlives of the wall for quite a while to come.

Notes

1 This formula became famous as a marker of orientation in the early days after 9 November 1989. Brandt actually did not use this wording in his short speech before the town hall in Schöneberg on 10 November 1989. It was rather used in two interviews shortly after and became the motto of the SPD congress in December 1989. Whilst it was not as electrifying

as President Kennedy's '*Ich bin ein Berliner*' in 1963 or Governing Mayor Ernst Reuter's 'Peoples of the world, look at this city' of 1948, it was crucial for the immediate aftermath of the collapse of the wall.

2 www.chronik-der-mauer.de/material/178789/brief-des-regierenden-buergermeisters-von-west-berlin-willy-brandt-an-den-amerikanischen-praesidenten-john-f-kennedy-16-august-1961 (accessed 7 October 2017).

Bibliography

Andrews, Molly (2002) 'Generational Consciousness, Dialogue, and Political Engagement', in June Edmunds and Bryan S. Turner (eds), *Generational Consciousness, Narrative, and Politics,* Lanham: Rowman & Littlefield, pp. 75–88.

Art, David (2014) 'Making Room for November, 9? The Fall of the Berlin Wall in German Politics and Memory', in Jan Kubik and Michael Bernhard (eds), *Twenty Years after Communism*, Oxford: Oxford University Press, pp. 195–212.

Engler, Wolfgang (1999) *Die Ostdeutschen. Kunde von einem verlorenen Land*, Berlin: Aufbau-Verlag.

Heym, Stefan (1990) *Einmischung-Gespräche, Reden, Essays*, Gütersloh: Bertelsmann.

Krockow, Christian (1995) *Die Deutschen vor ihrer Zukunft*, Reinbek: Rowohlt.

Lepsius, Rainer (1989) 'Das Erbe des Nationalsozialismus und die politische Kultur der Nachfolgestaaten der "Grossdeutschen Reiches"', in Max Heller et al. (eds), *Kultur und Gesellschaft*, Frankfurt/Main: Campus.

Marx, Karl (1971) *Die Frühschriften*, ed. Siegfried Landshut, Stuttgart: Kröner.

Meier, Christian (2010) *Das Gebot zu vergessen und die Unabweisbarkeit des Erinnerns*, München: Siedler.

Münkler, Herfried (2010) *Die Deutschen und ihre Mythen*, Bonn: Bundeszentrale für politische Bildung.

Simmel, Georg (1992) *Soziologie*, Frankfurt/Main: Suhrkamp.

Voegelin, Eric (1999) *Hitler and the Germans*, trans., ed. and with an introduction by D. Clemens and B. Purcell, Columbia: University of Missouri Press.

Wolfrum, Edgar (2009) *Die Mauer: Geschichte einer Teilung*, München: Beck.

Wydra, Harald (2015) *Politics and the Sacred*, Cambridge: Cambridge University Press.

7 The Great Wall of China does not exist

Erik Ringmar[1]

Introduction

Walls are distinct, man-made features of an environment, and to the extent that they block our way or our vision they are impossible to ignore. As such they are inherently in need of an explanation. Yet walls can be built with many purposes in mind and serve several functions, and functions, moreover, are likely to vary over time. A tall, solid wall appears impassable in its concrete concreteness, yet walls, no matter how high, are never actually all that daunting. If we keep on moving, keep on exploring, we will sooner or later find a way around, across or under them; a gate will be found ajar, a tower unmanned or a guard who can be bribed (Lattimore 1962b: 486). Walls in the end are nothing in themselves and only something as a part of a tactic, but tactics often change – for technological, political or cultural reasons – and the walls, as a result, will be rendered obsolete and useless. Walls are not final conclusions as much as temporary statements awaiting refutation. As a result, walls will tell us a lot about the outlook of the societies that built them. Walls tell stories about presumptions and premonitions, fears and ambitions; about who we take ourselves to be and how we relate to others. Yet as far as storytellers go, they are annoyingly silent. Walls cannot talk; they stonewall us; and it does not help if we plead with, or wail before, them.

Take the case of the Great Wall of China (Waldron 1983; Waldron 1992; Lovell 2007; Huang 2012). As history textbooks explain, the Great Wall was built to keep the barbarians at bay. North of the wall, on the enormous steppes of inner Asia, was where the nomads lived with their grazing herds. It was here that Chinese-speaking peoples, sometime in prehistory, came to stop in their gradual northward expansion. The nomads were a constant threat to the new arrivals, and this, the textbooks tell us, was why the Great Wall was built. The wall would protect the crops and lives of the Chinese farmers, and it would protect their culture too. Culture is often said to require walls; culture, after all, refers to 'cultivation', to the 'tilling of the land'. Just as walls are built to protect crops, they are built to protect a culture from whatever comes towards it from the outside – foreign influences, barbarian hordes, the winds of change. This is how Chinese people always have defended themselves, the first European visitors to China concluded; the Chinese are inherently a wall-building people and the Great Wall is their 'pièce de résistance'. It was by limiting trade and keeping the country secure that the Chinese protected their wealth and their way of life. We have no use for Facebook and Twitter, as today's Chinese leaders explain when implementing the 'Golden Shield Project', intended to protect their culture, and their people, from the rest of the Internet. Appropriately enough, the policy is commonly referred to as the '*fánghuǒ chángchéng*', 'the Great Firewall of China'.[2]

This agricultural mind-set contrasts sharply with that of a commercial economy. As Adam Smith explained, a nation is wealthy not because it has gathered a lot of treasure but because of what it can produce. Productivity requires specialisation and specialisation requires exchange. The larger the market, and the more unimpeded the exchange, the more far-reaching the division of labour and, ceteris paribus, the more productive we become. Walls, from this point of view, are an abomination. Walls do not keep our wealth in but they keep exchange out; they limit the division of labour and they lower productivity. Moreover, walls block access to new ideas, to the latest technological advances, medical discoveries and scientific breakthroughs. Walls, in short, limit access to civilisation. Thus, while culture may require walls to be erected, civilisation requires walls to come down. As a result, a country that hides behind walls can never be civilised (Ringmar 2011b: 5–32). This is why China is so backward, Europeans came to conclude in the nineteenth century, once free-trade doctrines had become the official wisdom in Europe. This is why China's economy has stalled and why Chinese people are so ignorant, so secretive and so corrupt. And this is also why the country seemed to be perpetually stuck in the past tense. History, the Europeans pointed out, is a matter of progress, but since nothing in China ever changes, China, per definition, is history-less (Mill 1859: 413). The Great Wall was the perfect symbol of this stationary mind-set, and, what was particularly infuriating to the Europeans, the Chinese utterly failed to understand the nature of the predicament they were in. '[I]f they are ever to be further improved,' as John Stuart Mill concluded in *On Liberty* in 1859, referring to the Chinese, 'it must be by foreigners' (Mill 1859: 129). The assistance that China so urgently required was given in the First and the Second Opium Wars, 1839–42 and 1856–60, respectively. Positioning their rifled ordnance facing China's walls, the Chinese were forced to open up to the outside world (Ringmar 2011a: 273–98; Ringmar 2013). Soon European goods and ideas flooded in, spreading civilisation while destroying Chinese culture and uprooting its people.

Considering all that we think we know about the Great Wall of China, it is surprising to learn that there is no such thing. That's right – the Great Wall of China does not exist. There are certainly many walls scattered across the plains of northern China, and bits of walls, and remnants of former walls, but there is no 'Great Wall of China' understood as a unified project constructed at a particular time and with a particular object in mind. The Great Wall is not a physical as much as a social construction. Yet what is constructed can be deconstructed, and such deconstruction is what we will engage in here. As we will discover, the irony, and the tragedy, is that the Great Wall of China, and the wall-building mind-set of the Chinese, existed nowhere else but in the imagination of the Europeans. The Great Wall justified admiration as long as walls were admired, but once walls came to be seen as an abomination, it became a pretext for European imperialism.

Wall building in China

Despite its ethnic and linguistic diversity, the Chinese empire was always, officially at least, based on only one socio-economic model (Lattimore 1962b, 469–91). The subjects of the emperor were all farmers who worked on small plots of land, growing millet in the north and rice in the south. To compensate for the dearth of land, they supplied other factors of production; notably their own labour and that of their family members, but they also relied heavily on artificial irrigation and on fertilisers. The imperial state glorified the farmers while exploiting them for corvée labour and taxes. It is the farmers who feed us all, Confucian rhetoric proclaimed, and farming is the only truly productive occupation. Yet as each dynasty was acutely aware, their ability to maintain themselves in power depended more than anything on their ability to keep the farmers in their places.

There was an obvious geographical limit to the feasibility of this socio-economic model (Lattimore 1962b: 477–81). On the steppes of Eurasia – covering much of the landmass from north-west of Beijing all the way to Hungary – there was not enough rainfall to sustain agriculture, few large rivers and no means of irrigation. This was instead where the nomads lived. Although the climate was arid, there was plenty of grass on which their animals could feed and the nomads compensated for the lack of water by means of other factors of production – notably land, which was over-abundant. When the grass in one pasture had run out they simply moved to another pasture. The pastoral economy, to put it differently, was highly specialised. Since the nomads produced only what they were best at producing – meat, wool, horses – they required others to provide them with everything else that they needed (Khazanov 1994). That is, they had to trade, or failing that they reserved the right to raid their farming neighbours. The perennial problem of imperial Chinese history, from the third century BCE onwards, was how to deal with this recurring menace. There were three main options: to subdue the nomads by offensive military means; to concede to their demands and involve them in exchange; or to repel them by means of defensive arrangements, including walls (Waldron 1992: 55–6).

The first option, a military offensive, was never going to be easy. The terrain that separated the Chinese heartlands from the steppes was flat and open and difficult to defend. Moreover, the nomads were the vastly more efficient warriors. They only had cavalry, no infantry or supply train, and they were highly mobile. As a result, they could quickly assemble in force at a certain location, make a strike or a breech, and then just as quickly disperse again. Or they could outflank an enemy who came marching towards them and attack them from the rear. Moreover, since they had no particular territory to defend, the nomads did not differentiate between offensive and defence warfare. To retreat was not humiliating, but instead an opportunity to outrun, or ambush, any imperial soldiers who pursued them. The only way to defeat such an enemy, the Chinese eventually discovered, was to learn to fight in the same manner (Waldron 1992). But for this to be possible the Chinese needed a powerful, horse-based, army guided by entirely different tactics than previously and they needed knowledge of the steppe and its people. The Tang dynasty, 618–907 CE, was successful in this regard, but they were famously open to outside influences and foreign ideas (Lovell 2007: 138–47). The Yuan dynasty, 1271–1368 CE, and the Qing dynasty, 1644–1912, were also good at dealing with the nomads but the Yuan emperors were Mongols and the Qing emperors were Manchu – both peoples with their origin on the steppes.

The second option, trade, was much what the nomads themselves would have preferred, and this was also what they repeatedly requested (Waldron 1992: 178–82). In the eyes of the Chinese authorities, however, trade was not understood as an opportunity but instead as a concession. We have everything a person might require within our own borders, Confucian scholars argued, and therefore we never have to leave our country; foreigners, by contrast, come here since they have needs that cannot be fulfilled at home. The Chinese traded with these visitors, but above all out of a sense of magnanimity and in order to bring them into their own cultural sphere. Trade, the Chinese hoped, would transform the 'raw' barbarians into 'cooked' barbarians (Fiskesjö, 1999: 139–68). Such condescension was not appreciated by the peoples of the steppe and in any case, as they explained, they needed far more goods than the Chinese were prepared to supply (Waldron 1992: 176–7). Since the nomads were able to back up their demands with force, and the Chinese authorities were in a weak position, one concession would easily lead to another and before long the imperial authorities would be completely at the nomads' mercy. This, at least, is what Confucian hardliners at court argued. 'The situation of the empire may be described as like that of a person hanging upside down' (Memorial by Jia Yi of the Han dynasty, quoted in Waldron 1992: 41). Perversely, the nomads were on top and the Chinese were at the bottom.

The third, defensive, alternative, which included wall-building, was the fall-back option (Waldron 1992: 57–8). This is what you did if you were too weak or too timid to go on the offensive and too proud to trade. Defence was no one's favourite option but instead what you ended up doing when you did not know what to do. Although walls were unlikely to stop an invader, there was a variety of other roles they could play. In fact, from a military point of view, walls are best understood not as means of excluding an enemy as much as man-made obstacles that can help reshape the layout of a battlefield (Waldron 1992: 45; cf. Lovell 2007: 47–65). Walls are like speed bumps in a road, designed to slow down an enemy, and thereby structures along which armies can be organised. In this respect, they are more similar to ramparts or trenches. Moreover, in many cases walls were built mainly as a means of connecting already existing military installations to each other, making it possible to move troops securely from one position to the next. Or you could place your troops outside of the wall and use it as a way to protect your flank. In addition to these military uses, walls made powerful political statements. A wall, even a scalable one, is a manifestation of power. Powerful rulers have power-ful walls and the walls of the emperor of China had to be very impressive indeed – at least the walls built in places where people were most likely to see them. In addition, walls can be constructed as a way to stake out a claim; in order to let everyone know how far our imperial ambitions reach and what we one day would like to accomplish. And walls, quite obviously, can serve to keep people in – such as any oppressed Chinese peasants, tired of taxes and unpaid labour, who might consider taking up a freer life on the steppes (Lattimore 1962a: 340ff.; Lattimore 1962b: 484). As a result of this mix of military and political aims, walls can at the same time be part of a defensive and an offensive strategy.

It was for such a variety of reasons that walls came to be constructed in northern China already in the sixth century BCE, and why walls intermittently were constructed by any dynasty that failed to come up with other ways of dealing with the nomads. Qin Shihuang, the First Emperor, in the third century BCE, was one such wall-builder but his walls were made of mud and they quickly deteriorated (Waldron 1992: 195–202). Subsequent dynasties occasionally embarked on similar projects, but most of them did not. There were no walls to stop the Mongols from invading China in the 1270s and when Marco Polo returned to Venice in 1295, and started telling his stories of the wonders of the East, he said nothing about any walls. It was instead only in the latter part of the Ming dynasty, in the 1580s, that major wall construction begun in earnest (Waldron 1992: 140–64). The issue here concerned control over the Ordos, the land encircled by a vast loop in the Yellow River, strategically located just west of Beijing. Given its arid climate, the Ordos loop should really have belonged to the nomads, but the presence of the Yellow River meant that at least some of the region could be irrigated and thereby farmed and accessible to the Chinese socio-economic model. Moreover, holding this land was of a paramount military importance – the capital, after all, had to be defended from the nomadic threat (Lattimore 1962a: 462).

And yet, in the sixteenth century, the nomads moved into the Ordos. The imperial court reacted with alarm and an extensive discussion ensued among the emperor's advisors regarding what to do (Waldron 1992: 91–139). Some advocated an offensive military strategy, others advocated concessions and trade, and in the stalemate that ensued, the defensive, wall-building, strategy was agreed on. It was a compromise, a plan B, which had more to do with the internal politics of the court than with military expediency, and even now, during the late Ming, there was no concerted policy to build a 'Great Wall'. In the historical sources repeated references are instead made to the 'Nine Defence Areas', a series of nine heavily armed sectors spanning the strategic northern border (Farmer 2009: 463). In line with this policy walls were built at strategic locations such as at Badaling, north-west of Beijing, today the most popular location for visits to 'the Great Wall'. But walls were also constructed as a means of linking up already existing fortifications around the Ordos loop, although many of these were rampart made of mud. That these constructions were insufficient to provide protection was clear in 1644, if not before, when the assembly of walls was no match for the invading Manchus.

How the Great Wall was constructed

It was instead in Europe, not in China, that the Great Wall was constructed. It was built, beginning in the seventeenth century, in the minds of European readers of the letters which Jesuit missionaries had begun sending back (Mungello 1989; Porter 2002: 78–132). The Jesuits were in China to convert the Chinese to Christianity, but once they realised the impossibility of winning converts one by one, they decided instead to start at the top. By presenting themselves as purveyors of European knowledge – above all concerning astronomy, cartography and the arts – they managed to ingratiate themselves with the emperor. For some 150 years there were Jesuits stationed at the imperial court, and although they never managed to interest the emperor in their religion, they regularly sent letters back to Europe describing their strenuous efforts. Their strategy was to tap into well-established European conceptions regarding China as a land of endless wonders (Cf. Barrow 1804: 30–1). Given that China is such a rich and remarkable country, was the not-too-subtle subtext, our work, even if occasionally thwarted, will eventually be worth the while. One of the prime examples of wondrousness was what the Europeans came to refer to as 'the Great Wall'.

One of the first tasks the Jesuits embarked on was to make a map of the Chinese empire. The early eighteenth century was when European countries finally came to take on a definite geographical shape (Harley 2009: 129–48). From this time a state was more than anything a territorially bounded entity, its borders distinctly demarcated from others and clearly indicated on a map. China too, the Jesuits decided, should be portrayed in the same fashion, and between 1707 and 1717 a contingent of them embarked on a journey into the steppes of inner Asia in order to determine the location of China's northern borders (Elliott 2000: 621–4; Hostetler 2000: 651–8; cf. Huang 2012: 66). Following the assorted walls erected during the Ming dynasty, they decided that this constituted the frontier between China and Tartary. Where walls were confusing, running in parallel or off in the wrong direction, the border was clarified and simplified; where walls were entirely missing, the Jesuits' map readily supplied them. This was the Great Wall described already in the first chapter of Jean-Baptiste Du Halde's monumental *Description géographique, historique, chronologique, politique, et physique de l'empire de la Chine et de la Tartarie chinoise* (1736). 'This celebrated Wall was built by the famous Emperor Tsin Sh-whang, with a political view, 221 years before Christ', Du Halde explained. 'It bounds China on the north, and defends it against the neighboring Tartars' (Du Halde 1738, 1: 20). Du Halde's work was translated into English in 1738 and widely read across Europe, not least by the Enlightenment philosophers who had come to greatly admire the wisdom and rationality of China's government (Rowbotham 1932: 1052). Collaborating with Du Halde, Jean Baptiste Bourguignon d'Anville, Europe's leading cartographer at the time, published his *Nouvel atlas de la Chine, de la Tartarie chinoise et du Thibet* (1737), on which the Great Wall was depicted as a continuous, strong, fortified, northern border (Anville 1737).

This was not only a cartographical construction but also the way in which eighteenth-century Europeans imagined China. The Great Wall explained to everyone's satisfaction why China was so prosperous and so powerful. Wealth, according to the tenets of mercantilism, the dominant economic doctrine in Europe of the day, is created through protectionist measures. A country should accumulate resources – treasure, people, minerals, manufacturing industry, agricultural lands – while minimising foreign trade and restricting the outflow of precious metals. This was exactly what the Chinese empire had done and the Great Wall was one of the means to do it. As a result, 'It may be said, without exaggeration,' Du Halde concluded, 'that China is one of the most fruitful, as well as large and beautiful countries in the world' (Du Halde 1738, 1: 314).

Having read about the Great Wall, and having imagined it, the Europeans naturally wanted to see it, yet since China was closed to foreigners this feat could not easily be accomplished. There were only the lucky few – such as the members of a British diplomatic mission led by George Macartney who visited China in 1793 – who were given the opportunity. After having presented themselves at the court in Beijing, the Macartney mission followed the emperor to his summer retreat in Chengde, in Manchuria, north of the wall, and on their way, they were thrilled to visit the celebrated construction. 'If the other parts of it be similar to those which I have seen', Macartney concluded, 'it is certainly the most stupendous work of human hands', and he calculated that its combined volume was greater than that all other fortifications in the whole world and that the material used equivalent to that of all houses in England and Scotland (Macartney 1807: 243; Barrow 1804: 334). The Great Wall provided conclusive proof to European minds that China was a powerful empire and a wise and virtuous nation (Anderson 1797: 70; Staunton 1797, 2: 360).

The inordinate attention that the Macartney mission paid to the site seems to have puzzled the Chinese officials who accompanied them. 'They were astonished at our curiosity', Macartney reported, and 'appeared rather uneasy at the length of our stay upon it', and 'almost began to suspect us, I believe, of dangerous designs' (Macartney 1908: 294). The Chinese mandarins, it turned out, had themselves never visited the location. Yet this itself was hardly surprising. The Great Wall was not a 'sight' to be visited and in any case 'sightseeing' was a European, not a Chinese preoccupation. To educated European travellers, starting at the end of the eighteenth century, each city, each country, had its sights, carefully described in the guidebooks – the Colosseum in Rome, Notre Dame in Paris, Parthenon in Athens, and so on (Adler 1989: 7–29; Cf. Huang 2012: 74–7). Buildings such as these were what each country was famous for and the symbols by which they were recognised. Thanks to the indefatigable work of the Jesuits and the vivid imagination of European visitors, China now too had its representative symbol, and the Great Wall has been on the itinerary of visiting foreigners ever since. 'It's a great wall', as Richard Nixon observed after visiting the site on 24 February 1972, during his historic first trip to China (Frankel 1972: 14). 'It's majestic', as Barack Obama concluded on 18 November 2009. 'It reminds you of the sweep of history, and that our time here on earth is not that long, so we better make the best of it' (Higgins 2009).

How to batter down Chinese walls

In the decades around the turn of the nineteenth century, Europe's view of China changed dramatically. No longer the location for rational government and assorted wonders, China was, the Europeans now decided, a backward backwater plagued by Oriental despotism and the tyranny of outdated customs. Yet this radical transformation of European perceptions had next to nothing to do with China itself and instead everything to do with Europe. Above all, it was a result of a radical re-evaluation of the function of walls.

The problem with walls, European liberals now explained, is that they break up the world into a multitude of separate, non-communicating, compartments. If a wall is in the way, and if it is high enough, it is impossible to communicate with the people on the other side of it, or even to see who they are or what they are doing. In this way walls make the people on both sides more ignorant than they otherwise would be. What you cannot see you cannot inspect, scrutinise or verify, and walls as a result allow people to hide, to keep secrets and maintain unexamined prejudices. Walls block light, they block enlightenment; the 'Heim hides the heimlich'. And even if the wall does not constitute an absolute barrier, it is still the case that the authority that controls it can restrict and thereby shape the terms of the intercourse. Not surprisingly, walls are much relied on by people and institutions eager to limit their accountability. Since a political power which is hidden behind a wall is impossible to engage in conversation, it never has to explain itself nor provide reasons for its actions. In this way walls contribute to the sublime mystique of power but also, more prosaically, to political and economic corruption.

By destroying walls, nineteenth-century liberals were convinced, they would help spread civilisation. After all, exchange assures the free circulation not only of goods and services but of everything else which can be moved around – ideas, life-styles, institutions, fashions, dreams, desires and ambitions. By picking the best or the cheapest of what is on offer, we can improve our lives and develop our socie-ties. Compare the way the walls of the cities of Europe were being dismantled at this time, or the way economists, following Smith's lead, all railed against 'customs walls', 'tariffs walls' and 'walls of protection'. Free exchange, Lord Palmerston explained in the Corn Law debate in the British parliament in 1842, leads not only to an extension and diffusion of knowledge, to mutual benefits and kindly feelings, but it makes mankind 'happier, wise, better' (Palmerston 1842). 'This', he concluded, 'is the dispensation of Providence – this is the decree of that power which created and disposes the universe.'

The problem with China, Europeans now concluded, are the walls the Chinese have built around their country and their minds. The Chinese are inherently a wall-building people and there are walls everywhere – around natural resources such as forests and salt lakes; around every Chinese city, and inside the cities there are walls separating the Manchu and the Chinese sections, but also the members of professional guilds from each other or government officials from the rest of the population (Chang 1970: 63). Chinese houses are separated by walls and inside the houses walls divide family members from each other and inside the rooms themselves there are portable screens made of paper and wood. All these walls blocked exchange; they blocked access to new and cheaper products but also to new ideas, the latest technological advances, medical discoveries and scientific breakthroughs, and, European missionaries added, to the words of the Christian God (James 1862: 477–554).

Consider trade. In the nineteenth century British manufacturers were constantly on the lookout for export markets for the products that their factories kept spewing out. China, with an estimated population of some 350 million people, was an obvious target of these efforts. This 'third of mankind', British merchants imagined, were all waiting to be supplied with cotton cloth from Lancashire and cutlery from Newcastle. The problem was only that the imperial authorities in Beijing refused to grant access to foreign merchants. There was only one city – Guangzhou, 'Canton', in the south – where the Europeans could trade, and only during parts of the year, and even then they were not allowed to enter the city itself. The British demanded full access to all cities, all markets, all people, in all of China, and in addition to selling their British-made goods they insisted on the right to sell opium grown in British-held India. When the Chinese refused to make concessions and began blocking the opium trade, the British went to war in November 1839. Three years later a peace treaty was concluded in Nanjing which opened four more cities to the Europeans and turned the barren rocks of Hong Kong into a British colony. The British had wanted more, but they were still overjoyed. '[T]here is scarcely an article', Henry Pottinger, the first governor of Hong Kong, explained, 'that the manufacturers of England may not supply to them of a quality and at a price that will ensure an almost unlimited demand' (Gordon 1836: 6). It was inevitable, *The Times* commented, that 'an adventurous maritime people like the English should force themselves into connexion with a feeble and unprogressive race like the Chinese, inhabiting a rich country open to our trade' (*The Times* 1857). 'China is open! Hallelujah, China is open' (James 1862: 477).

To Karl Marx and Friedrich Engels, plotting a revolution back home in Europe, it was the opening up of China that constituted the best illustration of the world-transforming powers of capitalism. Once the search for profits has come to replace all other concerns, they argued in *The Communist Manifesto*, written six years after the signing of the Treaty of Nanjing, all aspects of life as we know it will be radically transformed. Capitalism shapes the world in its own image. The profit motive will destroy feudal relations and replace them with market relations; there will be constant revolutions, disturbances of all social conditions, uncertainty, and agitation. 'The cheap prices of its commodities are the heavy artillery with which it batters down all Chinese walls' (Marx and Engels 1906: 18). Engels knew very well what he was talking about here. After all, he fancied himself a military man. In a series of articles on the latest developments in military ordnance published in the *New-York Tribune*, he had discussed in great detail what form of military hardware was required to breach various kinds of walls (Engels 1957). Rifled guns, he had pointed out, constitute a 'real revolution' in battlefield tactics.

Yet Marx and Engels were wrong. Cheap prices were not the heavy artillery which in the end battered down the walls of China. Instead the walls of China were battered down by the heavy artillery of heavy artillery. Once the Treaty of Nanjing was signed and the Royal Navy returned home, the Chinese began dragging their feet. The imperial authorities, the British government decided, were not living up to their obligations, and besides, it was still the case that the British wanted all of China open. To do something about this unsatisfactory state of affairs, Lord Palmerston appointed John Bowring as the new governor of Hong Kong. Bowring was a disciple of Jeremy Bentham's, one of the original founders of the Anti-Corn Law League and an activist on behalf of various liberal causes (Todd 2008: 381–2). 'England has the highest and most noble of missions', Bowring had declared at a meeting of the League on 13 April 1843, which is 'to teach the world that commerce should be free – that all humble beings are made to love and help one another'.

> Freedom of commerce, I dare say it, is Christianity in action. It is the manifest-ation of this spirit of kindness, benevolence and love which everywhere seeks to distance itself from evil, and tries in all places to strengthen the good.
>
> (Bastiat 1862: 148)

Bowring hated walls – walls around countries, around cities, around prisons, and he regularly spoke out against the nefarious influence of quarantines. Coming to China he was immediately appalled by the ever-presence of its walls. Seizing on a pretext, he called on the Royal Marine to intervene, and in October 1856, a new war – the Second Opium War – had begun. Before long British gunships on the Pearl River were shelling the city walls of Guangzhou. Yet when news reached Britain regarding the renewed hostilities, Bowring was criticised in parliament and Palmerston's government was eventually forced to resign (Ringmar 2011b: 5–32). Lord Derby, a former Tory prime minister, was particularly incensed. He reacted strongly against Bowring's aggressive posture and defended the rights of the Chinese to their own way of life (Derby 1857). How would we like it, Derby asked, if the Chinese started attacking our institutions of government. Bowring had a 'monomaniacal obsessions' with the city walls of Guangzhou: 'I believe he dreams of the entrance into Canton, I believe he thinks of it first thing in the morning, the last thing at night, and in the middle of the night if he happen to awake' (Derby 1857: 1177).

Once again peace was concluded – the Treaty of Nanjing, 1858 – and this time around China was indeed forced to open up to foreign influences and trade. Once again defeated, China could no longer control its own borders. China's walls had finally come down, and British-made goods, and opium, began flooding in. 'The walls of Jericho have fallen flat to the ground', as an enthusiastic missionary put it. 'The fields are white unto the harvest. What is wanted? All that is wanted is, reapers to go and gather it in' (James 1862: 483). China was now for the first time able to receive the blessings of civilisation, even if its culture was destroyed in the process (Zeng 1887: 3). One of the reason why we need to build walls, Chinese folklore has always maintained, is that evil spirits only can move in straight lines. Walls will stop them. Chinese folklore may have been right about that, but in the 1850s their walls were too weak and the evil spirits too determined.

Life in the borderland

The Great Wall, we said, understood as a unified structure built for a given purpose, does not exist. There are many walls in China, and bits of walls, and remnants of former walls, but they were built for various reasons, at various times, and they were more than anything the result of political expediency. Instead the Great Wall is a social construction erected not in China itself but instead in the minds of Europeans who always claimed to know what China was. In early modern Europe, when China was admired for its wealth and its political stability, the Great Wall was the perfect symbol of the wisdom of mercantilism; in the nineteenth century, when China was mocked for its lack of progress, the destruction of all Chinese walls symbolised the wisdom of exchange. To the Europeans, it is the walling instinct of the Chinese that comes first and the Great Wall is only its most prominent expression. The Great Wall existed because the Europeans decided that it had to exist, and before long they had found it everywhere throughout the country. The walls that the Europeans went on to destroy in the nineteenth century were the ones they had created in the eighteenth century. The eventual result of this work of the imagination was an aggressive European posture and a policy of imperialism.

This is where the political anthropology of walls becomes a matter of some urgency. It is only by highlighting the varied functions of walls, and the reasons why they originally were constructed, that we can hope to influence the policies they justify (Ringmar 2018). No, we can say, this is not the way walls work; walls can never properly be controlled by the people who build them; walls always result in a number of unintended consequences. In particular, we can be critical of the idea that walls can protect a culture. On the contrary, as is obvious to all people living by a wall, it not only separates people but also unites them. Walls, that is, create a culture of their own. A border designates a borderland, an intermediate zone in which people on both sides may relate to each other far more intimately than they do to others. The border establishes a shared fate and a communality of interest (Lattimore 1962b: 484). The history of the walls of northern China provides an illustration. To be a Chinese border guard in a desolate fortress somewhere along the Ordos loop was to lead a sad existence. Fighting the Mongols was a hopeless task and it made far more sense to interact and to trade with them. This was also what the border guards ended up doing and there was nothing whatsoever that the officials back in Beijing could do about it (Waldron 1992: 150). In fact, the population living on both sides of the border were always far more heterogeneous than the official, Confucian, ideology acknowledged. There were plenty of Chinese people who took up a nomadic lifestyle and plenty of nomads who engaged in part-time farming. Moreover, the nomadic frontier was attractive to many ordinary Chinese since it allowed them to avoid the impositions of the state and gave them opportunities to make money from smuggling and trade.

As all nomadic people know, the agricultural metaphor is simply mistaken. A culture does not require walls to thrive. A culture does not require roots and it does not require a fixed location. Nomads have a culture of their own after all, a culture on-the-go that thrives in a shifting landscape. Nomads carry everything they need with them on a road that leads to somewhere else, and their culture is as mobile as their horses and as collapsible as their homes. In addition, nomads know a thing or two about civilisation. After all, it is only through exchange – voluntary if possible, if not forced – that their way of life becomes viable. Connecting societies is what nomads always have done – most spectacularly, no doubt, by the Mongols who maintained and protected the caravan routes – the 'Silk Road' – which connected China with India, India with Central Asia, and Central Asia with the Middle East and Europe. In this respect nomads are similar to the 'barbarian hordes' which today are said to 'overrun' Europe. Whenever we are forced to deal with the alien, we are forced to open up to the world and invited to see ourselves in the context of others (Horvath et al. 2015; Szakolczai 2017). The result, if the invitation is accepted, is civilising, but civilisation, we can conclude, does not equal the imposition of foreign solutions on a defenceless society. The formidable trading network that the Mongols created could be used by anyone, for whatever purpose, and it was by means of this bridge that Europe, in the Middle Ages, itself was civilised. A world without walls, the nomads will tell us, is not an abstract, formless, empty space; it is a world of paths, of places to discover and possibilities to explore.

Notes

1 I am grateful to James C. Scott for comments and suggestions.
2 The latest news on the official Chinese Internet policy is available at http://chinadigital times.net/china/internet-control/

Bibliography

Adler, Judith (1989) 'Origins of Sightseeing', *Annals of Tourism Research* 16, 1: 7–29.

Anderson, Æneas (1797) *Accurate Account of Lord Macartney's Embassy to China*, London: Vernor & Hood.

Anville, Jean Baptiste Bourguignon d' (1737) *Nouvel atlas de la Chine, de la Tartarie chinoise et du Thibet*, The Hague: Chez Henri Scheurleer.

Barrow, John (1804) *Travels in China, Containing Descriptions, Observations, and Comparisons, Made and Collected in the Course of a Short Residence at the Imperial Palace of Yuen-Min-Yuen, and on a Subsequent Journey Through the Country, from Peking to Canton*, London: T. Cadell & W. Davies.

Bastiat, Frédéric (1862) 'Meeting à Londres, 13 avril 1843: Discours du D. Bowring', in *Oeuvres complètes de Frédéric Bastiat*, 3: 145–53, Paris: Guillaumin.

Chang, Sen-Dou (1970) 'Some Observations on the Morphology of Chinese Walled Cities', *Annals of the Association of American Geographers* 60, 1: 63–91.

Derby, Edward Henry Stanley (1857) 'War with China', *Hansard*, House of Lords, 144 (February): 1155–245.

Du Halde, Jean-Baptiste (1738) *A Description of the Empire of China and Chinese-Tartary, Together with the Kingdoms of Korea, and Tibet: Containing the Geography and History*. Vol. 1. 2 vols, London: T. Gardner for E. Cave.

Elliott, Mark C. (2000) 'The Limits of Tartary: Manchuria in Imperial and National Geographies', *The Journal of Asian Studies* 59, 3: 603–46.

Engels, Friedrich (1957) 'Friedrich Engels on Rifled Cannon', edited by Morton Borden, *Military Affairs* 21, 2: 75–8.

Farmer, Edward L. (2009) 'The Hierarchy of Ming City Walls', in James D. Tracy (ed.) *City Walls: The Urban Enceinte in Global Perspective*, 461–87, New York: Cambridge University Press.

Fiskesjö, Magnus (1999) 'On the "Raw" and the "Cooked" Barbarians of Imperial China', *Inner Asia* 1, 2: 139–68.

Frankel, Max (1972) 'A Reporter's Notebook: The Great Wall Endures', *New York Times*, 25 February.

Gordon, G.J. (1836) *Address to the People of Great Britain: Explanatory of Our Commercial Relations with the Empire of China, and of the Course of Policy by Which It May Be Rendered an Almost Unbounded Field for British Commerce*, London: Smith, Elder & Co.

Harley, J. Brian (2009) 'Maps, Knowledge, and Power', in *Geographic Thought: A Praxis Perspective*, edited by George Henderson and Marvin Waterstone, 129–48, London: Routledge.

Higgins, Andrew (2009) 'Obama Weighs in on the Great Wall', *Washington Post*, 18 November.

Horvath, Agnes, Bjorn Thomassen and Harald Wydra (eds) (2015) *Breaking Boundaries: Varieties of Liminality*, New York: Berghahn Books.

Hostetler, Laura (2000) 'Qing Connections to the Early Modern World: Ethnography and Cartography in Eighteenth-Century China', *Modern Asian Studies* 34, 3: 623–62.

Huang, Chi Chi (2012) 'The Great Wall of China: The Jesuits' and British Encounters', *History in the Making* 1, 1: 65–78.

James, John Angell (1862) 'God's Voice from China to the British and Irish Churches, Both Established and Unestablished', in *The Works of John Angell James*, originally published in 1859, 16: 477–554, London: Hamilton, Adams & Co.

Khazanov, Anatoly (1994) *Nomads and the Outside World*, Madison: University of Wisconsin Press.

Lattimore, Owen (1962a) *Inner Asian Frontiers of China*, Boston: Beacon Press.

Lattimore, Owen (1962b) 'The Frontier in History', in *Studies in Frontier History: Collected Papers, 1928–1958*, 469–91, Oxford: Oxford University Press.

Lovell, Julia (2007) *The Great Wall: China against the World, 1000 BC–AD 2000*, New York: Grove Press.

Macartney, George (1807) *Some Account of the Public Life, and a Selection from the Unpublished Writings, of the Earl of Macartney*, edited by John Barrow, London: T. Cadell & W. Davies.

Macartney, George (1908) *Our First Ambassador to China: An Account of the Life of George, Earl of Macartney*, edited by Helen H. Robbins, London: John Murray.

Marx, Karl and Friedrich Engels (1906) 'Bourgeois and Proletarians', in *Manifesto of the Communist Party*, originally published in 1848, Chicago: Charles H. Kerr & Co.

Mill, James (1809) 'Review of M. de Guignes, Voyages à Peking, Manille, et l'Ile de France, Faits Dans L'intervalle Des Années 1784 à 1801', *The Edinburgh Review* 14 (July): 407–29.

Mill, John Stuart (1859) *On Liberty*, London: John W. Parker & Son.

Mungello, David E. (1989) *Curious Land: Jesuit Accommodation and the Origins of Sinology*, Honolulu: University of Hawaii Press.

Palmerston, Third Viscount (1842) 'Corn Laws, Ministerial Plan, Adjourned Proceedings (Third Day)', *Hansard*, House of Commons, February, 538–625.

Porter, David L (2002) *Ideographia: The Chinese Cipher in Early Modern Europe*, Stanford: Stanford University Press.

Ringmar, Erik (2011a) 'Malice in Wonderland: Dreams of the Orient and the Destruction of the Palace of the Emperor of China', *Journal of World History* 22, 2: 273–98.

Ringmar, Erik (2011b) 'Free Trade by Force: Civilization against Culture in the Great China Debate of 1857', in *Culture and External Relations: Europe and Beyond*, edited by Jozef Bátora and Monika Mokre, 5–32. Aldershot: Ashgate.

Ringmar, Erik (2013) *Liberal Barbarism: The European Destruction of the Palace of the Emperor of China*, New York: Palgrave.

Ringmar, Erik (2018) 'Order in a Borderless World: Nomads Confront Globalization', in *International Orders*, edited by Günther Hellman. Frankfurt: Campus.

Rowbotham, Arnold H. (1932) 'Voltaire, Sinophile', *PMLA* 47, 4: 1050–65.

Staunton, George (1797) *An Authentic Account of an Embassy from the King of Great Britain to the Emperor of China*. Vol. 2. 3 vols. London: G. Nicol.

Szakolczai, Arpad (2017) *Permanent Liminality and Modernity: Analysing the Sacrificial Carnival through Novels*. London: Routledge.

The Times (1857) 'In What Light Will These Debates on the Chinese . . .', 3 March 22618 edition, sec. editorial.

Todd, David (2008) 'John Bowring and the Global Dissemination of Free Trade', *The Historical Journal* 51, 2: 373–97.

Waldron, Arthur N. (1983) 'The Problem of The Great Wall of China', *Harvard Journal of Asiatic Studies* 43, 2: 643–63.

Waldron, Arthur N. (1992) *The Great Wall of China: From History to Myth*, Cambridge: Cambridge University Press.

Zeng, Jize (1887) 'China: The Sleep and the Awakening', *The Asiatic Quarterly Review*, January: 1–10.

8 Breaching Fortress Europe

The liminal consequences of the Greek migrant crisis

Manussos Marangudakis

Introduction

International borders, virtual walls par excellence, and the primary dividers and intensifiers of social interaction, recently have become a matter of contestation: the 'no-borders' international movement challenges their worthiness, blaming them for escalating global stratification, neo-colonial wars and destructive neo-liberal globalisation policies; thus, their demand to dissolve 'Fortress Europe' and allow migrants from the East and the South to enter the European Union (EU) at will.[1] This demand was 'met' in the period between March 2015 and March 2016 when more than a million migrants crossed the borders between Turkey and Greece and entered the EU (half a million through the island of Lesvos alone) in the hope of finding a new home. The actual event allows us to examine what exactly happens when – not as a consequence of warfare and conquest – international borders dissolve, even if only temporarily.

In theoretical terms, this 12-month period constitutes a 'liminal' condition. Liminality, as understood in sociological analysis, is the rupture of certainty and predictability caused by an overwhelming social crisis; it is also the loss of the taken-for-granted identity of social actors and the agonising search for meaning and purpose that this crisis generates (Eisenstadt 1995; Thomassen 2014; Horvath and Szakolczai 2018). Accordingly, social order is restored eventually, but the one that emerges out of the crisis is not identical to the ruptured one. Instead of being a restoration, what emerges out of a liminal situation is a new social order, defined by new marks of certainty and new societal contours. Due to this transformative effect, liminality is understood as a 'creative' process. This creative instance is called 'charismatic', in the Weberian sense, in that it constitutes a morally meaningful action that reorganises radically the basic orientations of the cosmological and ontological contours of social order, and subsequently the routinisation of the new charismatic vision into concrete social structures. Thus, liminality is understood as both a 'necessary' way by which a radical-charismatic mutation of a certain social configuration takes place, and a new moral social order is established through radical rearrangement of the basic structural components of a society.

Eisenstadt (1995) has offered us an exact theorisation of the process that occurs during a liminal process: due to the tensions inherited in any concrete social configuration, alternative definitions of the social order tend to form at the periphery of the major power configurations. During a systemic crisis these 'antinomian' and 'heterodox' discourses and orientations of protest take control of the public sphere in their effort to solve specific tensions of the social system. Three concrete themes of protest thereof are relevant to our subject: (1) the search to overcome the tension between the complexity and fragmentation of human relations; (2) the quest to suspend the tension in the model of the ideal society; and (3) the quest to suspend the tension between the personal and the autonomous self and the social role (Eisenstadt 1995: 314–15).

These are themes that touch upon specific aspects of the institutional order: the construction of boundaries between the collectivity and the personality, symbols of authority, and symbols of stratification and hierarchy. The celebration of the non-institutionalised and thus of the routinised and restricted forms of existence, such as expressions of subjectivism, of equality and communal solidarity, play a central role in these heterodox, antinomian and potentially rebellious orientations, and protests are staged in such a way as to contradict explicitly the concrete, 'profane', institutionalisation of social order. Yet, this liminal drive for authenticity is not unproblematic. Instead, the process is riddled with hypocrisy, strife and cynicism; and instead of heralding an original social system, more inclusive and 'functional' than the previous one, it might herald the perpetuation of uncertainty and strife – of perpetual liminality. Such is the case of the migrant in Greece. It started with the rupturing of the international borders between Greece and Turkey and the challenging of social identities that these borders sustain.

Breaching Fortress Europe[2]

For Europe, the time period 2015–16 is nothing less than a turning point. The one and a half million refugees and 'illegal' or 'irregular' immigrants ('migrants' hitherto) who crossed the Mediterranean Sea to enter the EU in their effort to reach the safe haven of north-western EU countries upset the institutional, political, social and cultural bearings and orientations of 'Fortress Europe' for the years to come. The rupturing of the virtual wall that divided the EU from the East and the hundreds of thousands of refugees and migrants crowding the Turkish borders, triggered a massive international humanitarian mobilisation to ease the pain of border-crossing, and initiated policies of friendly accommodation and incorporation of the incomers to the host countries (e.g. Germany, Austria, Scandinavian countries);[3] but it also strengthened the electoral power and political impact of xenophobic and isolationist parties across Europe, it divided communities over the issue of open borders and the limits of open society, raised worries about the 'Islamisation' of Europe, increased concern over Islamic terrorism, and instilled suspicion and ambivalence in the midst of European civil society and civil institutions (see Chapter 9 by Grišinas about the xenophobic and isolationist appeals of Europe).

Nowhere else in Europe was the immigrants' inflow more shocking, intense, traumatic and unsettling than in Greece – the country the vast majority of migrants chose to enter EU from. Here alone, 858,000 people crossed the sea borders with Turkey – mostly formally recognised as 'refugees' (780,000 from Syria, Iraq and Afghanistan) – in less than a year, compared with only 72,000 migrants who crossed the same borders in the previous year. Overall, since February 2015, roughly 1.3 million immigrants arrived in Greece.[4] Half of these people were washed off the coasts of Lesvos Island alone, while the rest landed on other Greek islands, located a few miles from the Turkish coast.[5] In terms of religion, most of them are Muslims. In terms of nationality, according to official estimations, more than 46 per cent are Syrian, 24 per cent Afghani, 15 per cent Iraqi, and the rest from other Muslim countries of Africa and the Middle East. Of these, 75 per cent are males and 25 per cent females, with the vast majority being young unmarried males – although many of these single males are members of kinship networks already residing in the EU. Only a small minority of migrants came as families. In these two years there were more than 300 incidents of drowning, and more than 150,000 people were rescued from the seas.[6]

The urgency of the problem, combined with both the structural inefficiencies and other shortcomings of the Greek state, invited the intervention of international organisations such as the UN High Commission for Refugees (UNHCR) and the International Organization for Migration (IOM), as well as of international human-itarian non-governmental organisations (NGOs), the international governmental organisations that turned Lesvos and a few other hard-pressed Aegean islands into zones of limited, or of multiple and overlapping, sovereignty. In effect, the Greek state surrendered its authority to the UNHCR which took over the task of manag-ing the migratory flows by coordinating the actions of the local authorities, the international and local NGOs, and the European border-patrolling agent Frontex.

In the months that followed the commencement of the migration crisis, these islands became the locus of a 'multiple governance' comprising all the institutional actors who contributed to the issue (the Greek government, international, national and local NGOs, the UNHCR, IOM, Frontex, etc.) organised in three virtual con-centric circles. The first one comprised a series of specialised and interconnected services and camps (rescue, reception, first-aid, food, sheltering, clothing, identific-ation, transition, families-only, unescorted youth-only, sickness, transportation, hotspot, etc.) dedicated, at least in principle, to serving the needs of the migrants and their organised flow to Germany and other receiving countries. The second concentric circle was made up of infrastructures and facilities supporting the aid workers and their services. And the third circle was made up of facilities and social networks erected to support the 'global observer': the international media and their reports which by and large shaped international attention and concern, as well as the humanitarian 'pilgrimage' network of famous visitors (e.g. Pope Francis and international artists, such as Angelina Jolie, Susan Sarandon, Vanessa Redgrave, Ai Weiwei) who in the following months paraded their concern and services to those in need.

Today, the flow of incoming immigrants has been decisively interrupted (20,000 in 2017, 17,000 so far in 2018) following the bilateral agreement between the EU and Turkey for the control of the borders (March 2016). The agreement, apparently, ended the '2015 migrant crisis', even though we are destined to live with its after-shocks in the years to come. There should be little doubt that the events constitute a liminal moment: border walls came crumbling down, the political power was effectively challenged from below, antinomian and heterodox movements imposed their presence – even their control – on the frontline of events, social structures were interrupted, routine symbols of trust, solidarity and power were challenged and replaced by heterodox ones, and the whole social fabric was challenged and undermined. In all, the liminality whose epicentre was the migrant crisis, could be analysed as two sides of the same coin: on the one hand as a 'primordial' cross-ethnic and cross-national cultural integration, as anti-structural performances and rituals, and as an egalitarian redefinition of trust, solidarity and power; on the other hand, as a schismogenic, divisive, process that traumatised both local communities and the Greek and European body politic. We start with the prior.

The antinomian suspension of social divisions

In the summer of 2015, the multiple governance scheme turned the island of Lesvos into a global symbol of suffering, compassion and solidarity. Accordingly, a com-prehensive discourse – a combination of social action, symbolic performances, and political promulgations – was developed, primarily but not exclusively in Greece, a discourse that was portraying the unfolding event as a 'humanitarian crisis' and a 'humanitarian response'. Accordingly, the event was conceptualised as a moral war between the forces of humanism and the forces of intolerance, racism and a callous international order. This discourse was initiated by the Greek government and soon was reinforced by images of helpless refugees and altruistic volunteers who were rescuing and sheltering dislocated victims of war. This discourse was indeed effec-tive, as it triggered a general shift of public perception and action: the migrants were not portrayed and were not described any more as dangerous 'illegal immigrants', but instead as suffering 'refugees'; and the hosts, portrayed by the same media, were not 'threatened' or 'invaded' anymore, as they were in the media before the crisis, but instead were 'compassionate fellow humans' who were doing their duty to help those in need.[7] This was a generalised shift of perception that no matter if it was instigated by the media, or indeed took place in the hearts and minds of the populace, cannot be overlooked. Until 2015 racist violence against migration in Greece was widespread, xenophobia was thriving and the issue of illegal immigration was on the political agenda. In fact, certainly the extreme right, and to a lesser extent, more mainstream politicians, were manipulating xenophobic reactions to real and imagined crime related to migration.

Indeed, the particularities of the 2015 migration wave made possible the dis-sociation of those migrants from xenophobic worries, and brought forward feelings of compassion and solidarity. Three factors made this perceptual shift possible (Papataxiarchis 2016): first, they were victims of wars (Syria, Iraq, Afghanistan) and were forced to abandon their homes to save their life; second, a significant portion of this wave were families with small children, a fact that triggered the paedocentric reflexes of the local populace; and third, and most important, they did not wish to settle down in Greece, but instead, they wished to pass from Greece to find a new home in other EU countries (primarily in Germany).

The fact that the distinction between refugee and (illegal) immigrant is ambiguous, and usually a matter of bureaucratic conceptualisations and definitions, makes shifting between the two terms a matter of moral voluntarism: a matter of choosing between a morally positive (e.g. a 'victim') or a negative (e.g. a 'parasite') connotation. Thus, the conceptual shift from calling the sum of migrants 'illegal immigrants' to 'refugees' is critical. It justifies all acts of compassion and condemns any hostility toward them. Papataxiarchis notes that this shift affected two qualities the term 'refugee' holds: 'irregularity' and 'otherness' (Papataxiarchis 2016: 13). In this context, irregularity lost its significance as attention shifted from the legality or illegality of the entry to particular aspects of the trip, such as the risks involved in crossing hostile borders and unwelcoming countries, and the rescuing of the travellers at the last leg of their arduous trip. As for the 'otherness', this was altered in two ways. First, the migrants, due both to their large numbers and their apparent moral worthiness, became visible, openly declaring their presence. Second, this visibility was not accompanied by concrete signs of identity (religion, ethnicity or class), but instead it was a visibility of the abstract presence of a 'human being'. This identification allowed the identification of the 'refugees' with the local populace who are descendants of refugees themselves. Thus, the presence of abstract categorisations allowed for the moral and emotive attachment of the hosts to the incomers:

> For many of the native inhabitants of the refugee settlement of Scala the historical consciousness of the 'Refugee' was activated during the crisis and contributed to an emotional stance with troubled travelers from Asia and Africa, which surpasses any suspensions their heterogeneity produces, and leads to some kind understanding of their plight. For many others, what played a catalytic role was the experience of refugee rescue and care. Especially through the 'rescue' the displaced travelers become recognizable above all through one general property, that of the 'human being'.
>
> (Papataxiarchis 2016: 14)

This certainly did not eradicate acts of violence against migrants or even racist attitudes, but the combination of sympathetic media and compassionate aid did prevent the legitimation of such discourses in the public sphere, and thus reduced the impact of racism, while at the same time it reinforced morally humanistic attitudes and rewarded compassionate practices (see Chapter 5 by Novikov in this volume on Kalighat, with regard to both the volunteers crossing boundaries as well as the ability of the victims to attain dignity in these situations to the extent they are embraced as possessive of human dignity). Soon, the two trends were combined, and under the authority of the Greek government, which was following an 'open-borders' policy toward the immigrants, they became the hegemonic discourse of solidarity.

If by solidarity we mean social organisations of horizontal power structures which incorporate migrant groups and networks in their organisational flow of information and resources, then indeed the 2015 crisis is characterised by an unprecedented number of grass-roots organisations and networks that were mobilised to offer 'solidarity' to the migrants. With the blessing and the encouragement of the government, these networks came to the fore, and in many cases found themselves in charge of the accommodation of migrants. These solidarity groups were to be found on the 'frontline' of first-aid camps, such as in Skala Sikamnias in Lesvos, in Athens, as well as in Eidomeni, in the vicinity of the borders with the former Yugoslav Republic of Macedonia (FYROM), where thousands of migrants were blocked from entering neighbouring countries after the quasi open-borders EU policy came to an end in March 2016.

This mobilisation of 'collectivities' ready to share power with the migrants, based upon the triptych of 'self-organisation', 'horizontal power structure' and 'emancipation', at least in principle, was nothing less but the counterattack of all these anarcho-autonomous political groups and organisations that for years were challenging and defying the conservative strategy of closed borders, detention centres and deportation/repatriation policies that the Greek governments were following in accordance with the Dublin Regulations.[8] Now, it was time to make the dream of solidarity come true. The way to do so was by replacing state agents and official policies as the semi-official hosts, protectors and stewards of the migrants. Symbolic action, such as occupying abandoned buildings, parks and squares, and organisational action, such as organising food and accommodation, medical aid and recreational activities for the migrants, became the way, according to this discourse, of actualising their political proclamations of a 'borderless' world.

The heterodox suspension of social structures

Yet, far from being an all-inclusive description of the events, this discourse leaves many aspects of the crisis unexplained, or ignored. In fact, accounts of people who do not belong to this 'humanitarian governance network' offer another reading of the events; a reading that presents a different reality; disheartening, despairing and bleak. It is a mirror image of the previous discourse, of confusion and selfishness, of self-gratification and cynicism. Below I quote from a letter published in *Kathimerini*, an authoritative conservative newspaper, by the well-known Greek painter Dimitris Geros, who spends several months a year in Mytilene, and who witnessed, first-hand, the events, narrates a very different story of uprooted refugees, desperate immigrants and some uncontrolled NGOs:

> The migrant issue, which troubles us lately, has made wealthy many Turkish traffickers, owners of plastic boats, diesel engine manufacturers, makers of deficient life jackets, hoteliers, restaurateurs, shop-owners and more. It has also made rich many Greeks who exploit the ignorance and urgent needs of the refugees and immigrants who start a long and dangerous journey without knowing any language other than their mother tongue, without knowing where to find on a map the countries they wish to settle, without any information

about the culture and the habits of the Europeans, without having any idea of the circumstances in which they will be forced to adapt. Even compatriots of theirs accommodate them in doghouses against a high rent, sell to them tickets two and three times higher than normal, issue them fake documents, rob them, even kidnap them for a few euros.

. . . Due to the refuge crisis, more than eighty NGOs made their appearance in Lesvos; NGOs that nobody knows where they come from, what is their mission, and who funds them. The Municipality of Mytilene and the police are not in a position to tell us how many such organizations exist, or of the number of people they employ . . . there are NGOs that are composed of opportunists and equally terrible exploiters of human pain who are here to make their dream holidays pretending to help, while they get lazy enjoying themselves while at the same time thousands of fellow human beings are being malnourished and sleep in the sludge. In fact, for their 'services', they even receive handsome salaries.

. . . The most basic help that their members offer is to sit on the beaches, gathered in groups, to enjoy the sunrise, often after all-night partying at the island's clubs, and when the boats arrive, they just tend the hand to help [the migrants] get out on land without having to, in most cases, wet their own shoes! 'Rescues' are usually done in this easy and safe way . . . NGOs always know when the boats will arrive and how many refugees will be arriving on them. The information is rumored to come from secret services that detect the mobile phones of refugees and immigrants. Depending on the number of boats, their rescuers also appear accordingly . . . There is a wide suspicion that theses NGOs work in co-operation with the Turkish traffickers . . . Based on what is heard and said against the paid members of some NGOs, but also on what I saw and photographed, the authorities in charge should have already intervened and taken appropriate measures against them. Yet, a large proportion of residents earn money out of this – a serious reason for the authorities to turn a blind eye.

I have been informed that hundreds of NGO workers receive salaries high enough to allow them to rent villas for 3,000 or 4,000 euros a month. Others stay in expensive hotels and use equally expensive cars. Of course they eat in good restaurants and they do not care if the poor migrants wait in the queue to get a paper cup with little, dubious quality and origin, soup or water-lipped rice along with just two small slices of bread and a banana . . . In the port of Mytilene – whose inhabitants are angry since due to the refugee crisis all cruises have been canceled for this year and hotel reservations have been reduced by 80%, right next to the municipal beach the authorities have allowed NGOs to build a miserable slum, visible to the passengers of the ships, supposedly in exchange for the organization's beneficial services to the multitude of refugees and immigrants.

When I asked two young people to tell me where they were from, they said they were 'citizens of the world'! So specifically! If someone told me they were drug users, I would have no reason not to believe them. Seeing them, one would think that Europe loaded on a boat any inhabitants it wanted to get rid of and sent them to Lesvos, where the authorities gave them public space, water and plenty of food to make their holidays carefree, debauched and undisturbed. On the tent of a shanty used as a kitchen, they had written in large red letters the word 'Revolution' and instead of a tone they had placed the anarchists' 'A' over the iota and at the end of the word they had added the red sickle and hammer . . . So I reasonably wonder, as I imagine the readers, if this is an NGO that came to help the poor people or came to propagate its views and the revolution. And what kind of revolution do they dream about, these European wastelanders in Mytilene? And what do the authorities do? In their kitchen I saw large quantities of raw materials for the preparation of regular food, but to which refugees and migrants had no access. At noon I visited the camp; there were more than thirty NGO staff and fewer than ten refugees or immigrants, mostly young North Africans. But I did not see any families . . .

The site of the camp at Moria was not enough to accommodate so many thousands of people, so small and large tents were set up outside the camp which is surrounded by olive groves. Because the ground was sloping and uneven, with very few flat surfaces, people were struggling to sleep. Because of the rainfall, the area was full of mud and so they were forced to stay constantly in the tents. Some were playing cards, others were asleep not to burn precious calories, which they could hardly replenish, while on a big tent I heard some people, keeping their courage, singing with enthusiasm . . . This is, in short, my reflections, which Sappho, Alcaeus and Elytis could never imagine happening today in Lesvos . . .[9]

The letter is informative in two respects. First, it reveals factual aspects of the crisis that went unnoticed, ignored or omitted by the hegemonic discourse. Second, it captures the bitterness and anger many felt at the suspension of social order, such as the absence of state services and of government officials; the parasitic aspects of the crisis economy; the dubious motivations, services and results of the NGOs' involvement; and the detrimental living conditions of the migrants after they landed on the Greek shores. To these I add here my own first-hand observations: the division that was erected between those inhabitants who supported and those who opposed the landing of the migrants;[10] the bitterness that many Greeks felt at the erosion of Greek sovereignty and the power-sharing with international organisations;[11] the horrendous living conditions without adequate provisions which led to the death of a few migrants;[12] the despair of refugees that were trapped in Greece when the borders with FYROM, Bulgaria and the Visegrad countries closed in March 2016;[13] the deep rifts that divided local communities, as much as the EU itself, concerning the proper treatment of these people;[14] and last, but not least, the extensive corruption that enfolded the management of EU aid given to the Greek government to deal with the crisis.[15]

In all, the developments that followed the virtual suspension of the borders between Greece and Turkey – suspension concerning the people who were washed of the Greek coasts – confused and challenged the given social order both symbolically and organisationally. Symbolic categories, such as 'neighbour–stranger', 'friend–foe' and 'co-patriot–foreigner', broke down; international agreements and state functions, such as 'security', 'European borders' and the Dublin Agreement, were ignored and bypassed; and ordering concepts such as 'refugee' vis-à-vis 'illegal immigrant' lost their importance. In this context, one million refugees managed, at last, to reach the Promised Land, racism receded, movements of protest reaffirmed their presence and purpose, and 'open-borders' supporters around Greece and the EU celebrated the dissolution of social structural barriers between migrants and Europeans. On the other hand, the same developments were confusing and painful, for the same reasons.[16] International relations were strained, fears of Islamic terrorism were heightened, neighbourhoods and families were divided, and xenophobic political parties made their presence felt across Europe. Furthermore, these liminal symbols of protest were contested and rejected; discourses of liberation were scorned and refuted; and noble intentions were deconstructed and scorned. Even today as we speak, due to this liminal moment, Europe is divided to its core.

The two discourses – the one concerning the suspension of social divisions and the other lamenting the suspension of certainty – are not contradictory; in fact they complete the picture of a liminal situation which developed in the first months of 2015, when the borders between Greece and Turkey were ruptured, taking both Greece and the EU by surprise. Together, the two discourses clearly point to the emergence of communitas, anti-structure (Turner 1969) and of primeval (literally as well as figuratively) solidarity, all being signs of a liminal condition. Equally vivid (though in contrasting terms) are also the symbols of protest, the unruly behaviour, as well as the very strong ambivalence to social and cultural order. This ambivalence and the strong emphasis on anti-structure or communitas, which were built in this kind of situation all over Greece are the mirror image of the social, structural and cultural order against which these counter-cultural patterns of behaviour rebel; that is, of the highly restrictive and bureaucratic way in which migrants were treated up until then.

Yet, as the very construction of social boundaries and of their institutional derivatives add an element of frustration to the human situation, and generate a strong ambivalence to social order that movements of protest exploit, so does the deconstruction of such boundaries. In other words, both the construction of a social order as well as its deconstruction necessarily impose severe limitations on creativity, and gives rise to an awareness of both the limitations and the affordances social structures and social boundaries offer. In 2015, Greece, and especially the island of Lesvos and its inhabitants, found themselves in the middle of a perfect liminal state, torn apart by the forces of ambivalence. In March 2016, the predicament was completed when FYROM and Bulgaria erected fences across their borders with Greece, effectively placing the migrants between a wall and the moat – the sea borders with Turkey.

The emergence of such a dramatic event begs the question: was it a circumstantial incident, or a historical contingency, impossible to prevent? Looking at the large picture, the condition of Greece and of the migrants crowded at the shores of Turkey, in 2015, this seems like a valid hypothesis. Both these conditions were intensely critical: the seemingly endless economic depression that hit Greece in 2011 had taken away the arrogance many Greeks had shown in the ante-crisis period, and had thrown them in a perpetual self-doubting condition, predisposing them to act in ways which would restore national pride and self-respect; as for the migrants, who in the previous months and years had assembled at the Turkish shores, in a state of insecurity and ambivalence, they were ready to follow guidance, instructions and aid from the various *in situ* humanitarian schemes.

This combination of crises can explain the psychological part of the equation, that is, the moods of the two populations; of how the anxieties and uncertainties of both parties, caused by the respective crises, while very dissimilar, were compatible. And the fact that the migrants, economic immigrants and refugees alike, had expressed their strong desire not to stay in Greece, reinforced the amicable feelings of both sides. The Greek population knew that these people were passengers, and thus not a threat to their ordinary life; and the migrants obliged themselves to be as polite as they could under these horrendous conditions. Indeed, considering the number of people washed on the shores of Greece in 2015, criminal behaviour toward the Greeks (but not inter-ethnic violence and sexual abuse inside the cramped camps) was negligible – mostly petty crimes related to the alleviation of immediate hardship. Both necessity and self-respect reinforced good behaviour.

But this 'fortunate' coincidence does not explain the almost complete absence of state structures, and in many cases blatant state indifference, which led to the dubious 'humanitarian governance' and spread anxiety, despair and frustration amongst Greeks, migrants and the EU. More important, it tells us nothing of the eruption of the crisis itself: of the sudden increase in the numbers of migrants who chose to enter Greece in 2015. The government did claim that the enormous numbers of incoming people in Greece are the result of the war in Syria and the conflicts in various Asian and African states. Yet, this rhetoric does not explain why Greece was preferred. Bulgaria, also a neighbouring country with Turkey, should have been equally pressured, as an equally safe, if not safer indeed, route to the desired destination of the vast majority of migrants, Germany.[17] Yet, in 2015 the flows to Bulgaria only increased by 20 per cent compared with 2014. In Greece the flows increased by 1,000 per cent.[18] What made migrants choose the dangerous sea crossing in the Aegean rather than to walk from Turkey to Bulgaria?

To account for this, we turn to a structural factor, the party that since 2015 holds power. It is not an ordinary party. On the contrary, it is a neo-communist, Marxist party, and self-declared enemy of the neo-liberal establishment, of the EU immigration policy and of 'globalisation'.

The Syriza government and its ambiguous political programme

The 'Greek migrant crisis' occurred five years after the commencing of the deep economic crisis that shook Greece to its core, whipping off 30 per cent of the country's wealth, impoverishing a third of the population and delegitimising the old, moderate yet corrupt, political order.[19] But it occurred only a couple of months after the Syriza Party assumed power in January 2015. Syriza, an until then marginal neo-Marxist party led by 'charismatic' Alexis Tsipras, came to power holding a strong moralistic, anti-systemic, anti-establishment, anti-liberal, anti-EU agenda (Kouvelakis 2016). While it is true that Syriza had risen to prominence due to its strong anti-memorandum agreement agenda,[20] which was promising to throw in jail those who stole the wealth of the Greeks, and force the 'troika' to take back those fiscal measures which, according to the party, were the cause rather than the consequence of the economic crisis, Syriza was *not* a protest, single-issue, party.[21] On the contrary, Syriza, which considers the Maduro regime of Venezuela to be its model, was challenging the liberal institutional contours of both the country and the EU. Interestingly enough, following the Jacobine tradition, it declared itself to be morally superior to its 'enemies', indeed to be charismatic. Claiming the halo of Greek communist heroes of the past, and to be the continuation of the leftist resistance to the authoritarian right, it successfully cultivated the public image of the defiant fighter for the people's rights. Equally interestingly, both the mass media and the agents of the public sphere accepted this claim, and treated the party members and particularly its leader, the young, vibrant and ruthless Alexis Tsipras, as the genuine carriers of the cosmological and ontological principles that define Greek populist civil religion (Marangudakis 2015).

One third of the Greek voters welcomed the defiant Syriza party as their saviour and avenger. Little did they notice (or care) that next to the political programme of 'tearing the memorandum apart' lay a radical left political programme concerning public matters other than the memorandum. Such were the political principles of the party concerning migration. These principles demanded an 'open-borders' policy in clear disagreement with Greece's international obligations. Specifically, the party declaration (14 July 2013) stated:

> We recognize that the migration issue in all its complexities is a humanitarian, class, and international issue. Large migratory flows are the result of neo-liberal capitalist globalization, which uproots people from their homes as it makes them victims of wars, or deprives the elementary means of survival. Economic and political migrants and refugees are the modern 'damned of the earth' . . . We are seeking a change in European immigration policy based upon the criteria of European co-responsibility and the prevention of pheno-mena of underpaid immigration work. The Dublin II and the Immigration Agreements must be abolished in order to release refugees and migrants who do not wish to remain (in Greece), humanize the institutional framework for legalization, granting asylum and conceding travel documents, regaining resi-dence permits and work for migrants and refugees who have been deprived of them by the delegalization processes of recent years. We also demand a new process of legalization of the immigrants 'without papers' and a new natural-ization process for those living and working for years in Greece, equal and fair treatment of migrant workers and the direct provision of citizenship to those children born in Greece. We will proceed with the abolition of the current inhuman detention centers for foreigners and the creation of decent open centers of living.[22]

Following this principle, the Ministry of Immigration Policy, in early March 2015, issued an order according to which no immigrant entering the country illegally would be held under police detention. This order changed everything. Until then, refugees from Syria were issued with papers (according to the Dublin Regulation) which allowed them to remain in the country free, with a six-month postponement of deportation that was automatically renewed until they were accepted in their new home country. On the other hand, economic migrants were taken to closed camps until they were returned to their country of origin. The returns were not very successful because it was extremely difficult to reach an agreement with the country of origin, but it was a deterrent. At the same time, all entrants were identified and fingerprinted and their data recorded in the European electronic fingerprint database, known as EURODAC.

As a new advocate of open borders, the government changed this policy in a rather radical way. Accordingly, economic migrants were equated with refugees. Everyone was free to continue their journey to the rest of the EU. The fingerprinting system of EURODAC entrants collapsed. European authorities claim that out of 455,000 immigrants who had entered the EU between January and early September 2015, only 755 were identified in Greece following the projected Schengen standards.[23] Furthermore, the Greek government publicly refuted the use of the term 'migrant' since, it argued, almost all the incoming migrants were refugees. The government even claimed that the Syrians, Afghans and Iraqis – by definition refugees – accounted for 90 per cent of all incoming migrants. However, the government concealed the fact that many economic migrants claimed that they were Syrians (or even Afghans) using fake documents issued in Turkey.[24] This hoax was revealed when tens of thousands of forged documents were identified when these people filed for asylum in Germany. Due to Internet and mobile phones, the new situation quickly became known to various stakeholders. While there were only 1,700 incomers in January, 31,000 arrived in June and 108,000 in August. And last, but not least, the 'open-borders' dogma of the government was not accompanied by policies of structurally incorporating the migrants into Greek society (as in other EU countries, such as Germany or Austria). In fact, the migrants were welcomed but then cynically ignored, a 'policy' in tune with the Jacobin political orientation of Syriza which recognises the body politic as an undifferentiated 'people', as a *communitas* which, in order to be revolutionary and pure, needs to remain deprived.[25]

Thus Greece, from being a country where the rules of the Schengen Agreement were broadly followed, was transformed into a bridge to be crossed by the migrants who were heading for the Central European countries. In fact, Greece was becoming an in-between country not only in matters of migration, but in all aspects of social structures. For the months to follow, Greece was neither an ordinary EU country, nor foreign to it; it was a country that opposed its EU, Schengen and Dublin Accord commitments, but did not wish to break its formal ties with them; the time when Greece's democratic regime was challenged by Prime Minister Tsipras who by deeds and proclamations tried to impose a populist regime not unlike the one imposed in Venezuela by President Maduro. And, last, but not least, it was a time when the future of Greece was on the line as Minister of Economics Yanis Varoufakis played a game of chicken with his counterparts in Brussels.

This is to say that in the liminal condition of Greece in 2015 it was not only the grass-roots protest, no-borders movements that challenged the rigidity of social structures that were antinomian and heterodox combined with the plight of the migrants. In 2015, antinomian to the political system, and heterodox in its ideology, was the political centre as well. And it was the political centre that, due to its political programme and its expressed neo-communist, Marxist ideology, placed Greece in ambivalence and insecurity concerning its strategic structural contours and orientations. In effect, Greece became a liminal country due to the systemic challenges the government initiated. In fact, being in between was the way Syriza conducted its governmental affairs: unleashing antinomian and heterodox social action in the midst of nomian and orthodox social structures.

The Syriza government challenged the social order by implementing two 'passive' policies. The first was to show excessive leniency to violent acts of far-leftists groups against civilian targets in Athens, acts that undermine the ordinary flow of social life, such as assaults against police and army personnel, and regular interruption of legal procedures, occupation of university buildings, interruption of academic procedures, and violent riots in the centre of Athens; recently, even the parliamentary procedures were interrupted by anarchists. Members of these groups usually are not arrested as the police are ordered not to interfere; the only exception so far concerns the assault of an anarchist group (the notorious 'Rubicon') on the Spanish embassy, and then only after the embassy had formally requested the prosecution of the perpetrators; 18 members of the group were prosecuted, and sentenced to six months imprisonment with probation.[26]

The second passive policy was to turn a blind eye to the migrants entering the country illegally. The international borders of Greece were a crucial symbolic and organisational landmark of the systemic social order. By turning a blind eye to the formal procedures of entry into the country, and actually encouraging such an entry, Syriza challenged the totality of the status quo and reaffirmed its commitment to radical egalitarianism: the dissolution of power, identity, and trust divisions and structures – both in Greece and the rest of the EU. In effect, the radical-left government not only initiated, but in fact perpetuated the migrant crisis as a way to impose liminality. If the government could not openly declare the exit of Greece from the 'neo-liberal', 'pro-globalisation' system, perhaps the migrant population, the 'modern damned of the earth', could challenge the established structures in Greece and the EU, according to the party's stated political proclamations, and initiate an order-transforming process. Interestingly enough, the government did not show any feelings of compassion towards them. No urgency was demonstrated in dealing with the numerous migrants seeking shelter and food. No far-leftist groups, vociferous until Syriza came to power, protested against the horrendous conditions of the camps in which these people were confined. And no apologies were expressed for the migrants who died in the camps while under the care of the state. As it was said bitterly, the far left recognises classes, not individuals and their ordeal.

Having said this, the order-transforming efforts of the Syriza government were partially successful. In organisational terms, the EU, and in particular and noticeably Germany and Austria, indeed opened its borders to more than a million migrants. In symbolic terms, the term migrant came to denote a 'damned of the earth' rather than a liminal person. But this liminality also led, as far as antinomian NGOs are concerned, to corruption, self-indulgence and arrogance; it mobilised and strengthened European political xenophobia; divided and traumatised local communities; caused immense pain and insecurity to migrants constrained in state-supervised camps and unable to continue their trip to their desired destination; and heightened fears of terrorist attacks instilling fear and insecurity in the public sphere. In effect, what Syriza achieved was to instil uncertainty and confrontation in the midst of the EU; to trigger schismogenic processes of unpredictable effectiveness or duration.

Discussion

While borders and the international law and agreements that accompany them are artificial, their presence enables the formation of a social order, and thus of certain marks of certainty and the normalisation of social interaction. Such social arrangements are both intended and unintended: the Schengen Treaty weakened the national borders of the EU countries, and strengthened the external borders of the EU vis-à-vis non-European countries, thus constructing the 'European citizen'. Less visibly, but equally significantly, the same Treaty 'constructed' the identity, and even the behaviour, of the 'international refugee' since it formulated and standardised the contact of the latter with *any* EU country and the procedures EU authorities should follow to grant 'refugee' or 'illegal immigrant' status. In a sense, it was the Schengen Treaty that prepared the ground for what followed in 2015, allowing a country-specific contingency (such as the rise of Syriza to power in Greece) to affect all of the EU countries.

It is the interplay between the loss of these marks of certainty and the suspension of the social tensions and contradictions this normalisation entails that decides the worth of existing borders' suspension. In the Greek migrant crisis case, the results are mixed: on the one hand, desolate people did find a new home, anti-systemic solidarity was materialised and fear of the foreigner did recede; on the other hand, social rifts traumatised local, national and international social institutions and structures; political xenophobia across Europe increased; and tens of thousands of migrants found themselves in a state of limbo: neither heading for the promised land, nor returning home.[27] Worst, of the four objectives that social services lay down concerning the treatment of refugees, namely empowerment, improvement of provisions, boosting dignity and self-esteem, and shifting perceptions, only the latter was met (Bar-On 2015).

The liminality of the migrant crisis allows us to dissociate and distinguish between Bateson's (1958) and Turner's (1969) predictable, tribal, 'ritualistic liminality', and 'structural liminality' found in differentiated social configurations, such as our case. The latter does not constitute a 'rite of passage' writ large; it does not include a 'master of ceremonies' to guarantee the happy conclusion of the event; and its outcome is not predictable and repeatable. In fact, structural liminality might not lead to any social transformation at all. Instead, as is our case, it might lead to a permanent state of insecurity, mistrust and conflict (Szakolczai, 2014, 2017).

The permanent liminality that was developed in our case indicates the following: first, the entry of charisma on the public stage does not *follow* the commencing of liminality, but instead 'charisma' sets off a liminal condition if its target is to undermine the social system itself; second, instead of catharsis and the emergence of a new social order we are faced with the presence of a series of long-term, simmering tensions in the midst of the social organisation and social symbolisation, tensions of schismogenetic nature and of unpredictable duration; and third, the selective affinity between the commencing of a liminal situation and the structure, the ideology, and symbols of political power of an anti-systemic charismatic political centre.

In such a circumstance, liminality is not only initiated by the antinomian and heterodox political centre, in our case Syriza, but is perpetuated by it as well, as a way to erode otherwise established systemic social structures, such as the liberal regimes of Greece and of the EU. This is a structural 'necessity': an anti-systemic party, such as Syriza, is structurally obliged to use eroding 'passive strategies' if it wishes to remain true to its principles without being rejected by the system. In this case tactical games that nurture insecurity, ambivalence, unpredictability and uncertainty become the means to breed liminality, while lip service to the system allows the party to retain systemic power. It is a condition that breeds schismogenetic phenomena, such as raptures in the body politic, and politicians-tricksters who have the unusual ability to manipulate both orthodox and heterodox networks of power for their own benefit. The dissolution of borders, and thus of the challenging of social boundaries and identities, is a first, and in fact a necessary, step towards the establishment of liminality.

In a nutshell, a fiscal crisis that was left unresolved for far too long drove a large proportion of Greek citizens into a liminal situation of uncertainty and despair, from which they were willing to embrace trickster-logic and anti-systemic parties. Anti-systemic social networks of power (such as a political party and the social organisations it controls), when moved to a delegitimised political centre, though not identical to a liminal state of affairs, *invite* liminal crises. Thus, while liminality, structurally speaking, *resembles* a crisis, it is not a crisis. To explain: crisis is the failure of routine action (that is, of structure) to deal with a new, external challenge, or encounter, and thus heralds the beginning of a search for a response which will satisfy the basic societal values, or cultural orientations, of the responding social order. This two-in-one meaning is reflected in that in Greek the word is used invariably to denote both emergency and judgement: 'crisis' assumes entry and exit from an emergency situation. Liminality is something else. It is a state of suspension without any guarantee of returning to structural predictability and certainty (Horvath 2013).

What is missing from the condition of liminality is the presence of a leadership able and willing to evaluate the situation and to decide to construct a new pattern of action, that is, a new social structure; in other words, the *absence* of charismatic leadership. Such an absence could have two causes: either the actors involved choose to postpone resolution, or are forbidden to do so. As in Kusturica's film *Underground* (1995), these eventualities could be interweaved: the 'leader' of the group could maintain the agonising suspension of ordinary life for personal gain. Just as Marko manipulates the group of people hidden in the cellar telling them that the war against the Germans still goes on, long after the war is over, someone's liminality could be someone else's power game and gain. Thus, liminality could be caused by a leadership that takes advantage of a crisis and postpones resolution for its own benefit. In such a case, charisma is not constructive, but destructive (Eisenstadt 1995: 314), and the leader is the mirror image of a charismatic leader: he is a trickster (Hyde 1998; Horvath 2008; Armbrust 2013). This is to say that in contrast to a crisis, which, in retrospective, involves evaluation, decision-making and original action, liminality involves manipulation and trickery.

In this vein, in the framework of modernity and in terms of the institutionalisation of the charismatic vision, we could argue that liminality is not a crisis as such, but the *artificial perpetuation* of crisis. Such a postponement means that the process of institutionalising a charismatic vision to concrete social structures allows anti-nomian and heterodox visions of cosmic and socio-political order time and space to flourish beyond the ordinary span a crisis allows them to do so. Thus, post-ponement of the very process of the construction of social and cultural order nourishes the destructive aspects of charisma, that is, of trickster-logic; of protests that deny not only a concrete social order, but indeed the institutionalisation of communication, and thus of the social structures this institutionalisation entails.

Instead of being the transitory stage of a progressive breakthrough, the means by which charisma transforms and renews social structures, liminality could be a permanent state of insecurity, ambivalence and schismogenesis. And public space, instead of being a neutral open ground wherein trustful public debates unfold, could be a treacherous arena of strife, deception and pretence. Suspension of esta-blished boundaries/walls by institutional macro-actors are more likely to create confusion and uncertainty than not; and this confusion and uncertainty invite the establishment of new ambivalent boundaries and walls which perpetuate insecurity and absence of clear social identities; which in turn invite authoritative power and tyranny as a means to impose arbitrary boundaries of friend and foe, of access to power and of membership criteria, if any social order is to be achieved.

Notes

1 For example, see: www.migreurop.org/?lang=fr; http://www.contested-borderscapes. net/.
2 *The Penguin Companion to European Union* (2012) https://penguincompaniontoeu. com/additional_entries/fortress-europe/.
3 'More than One Million Refugees Travel to Greece Since 2015': www.unhcr.org/news/ latest/2016/3/56e9821b6/million-refugees-travel-greece-since-2015.html.
4 'Number of Refugees and Migrants Arriving in Greece Soars 750 Per Cent Over 2014': www.unhcr.org/news/latest/2015/8/55c4d1fc2/number-refugees-migrants-arriving-greece-soars-750-cent-2014.html.

5 'A Tragedy Unfolds on Lesvos': www.newyorker.com/culture/photo-booth/a-tragedy-unfolds-on-lesvos.

6 'Since Alan Kurdi Drowned, Mediterranean Deaths Have Soared': www.unhcr.org/news/latest/2016/9/57c9549e4/since-alan-kurdi-drowned-mediterranean-deaths-soared.html.

7 For an analysis of the racist perception, see Xristina Pantzou, 'Immigration and Racist Discourse on Mass Media': http://tvxs.gr/news/egrapsan-eipan/i-xameni-nifaliotita-metanasteysi-kai-ratsistikos-logos-sta-mme-tis-xr-pantzoy.

8 http://eur-lex.europa.eu/legal-content/EN/ALL/;jsessionid=jHNlTp3HLjqw8mqGbQ SpZh1VWpjCyVQq14Hgcztw4pbfSQZffnrn!557467765?uri=CELEX:32013R0604.

9 'The Island of Lesvos, the Refugees, and Many Questions': *Kathimerini* newspaper, 28 March 2016 (translated by M. Marangudakis): www.kathimerini.gr/854585/gallery/epikairothta/ellada/h-lesvos-oi-prosfyges-kai-polla-erwthmata.

10 Προσφυγικό: Διχασμένοι οι κάτοικοι των νησιών (Refugee Crisis: The inhabitants of the island are divided over refugees): www.kathimerini.gr/931482/article/epikairothta/ellada/prosfygiko-dixasmenoi-oi-katoikoi-twn-nhsiwn.

11 «Ξέφραγο αμπέλι» η χώρα (The country is like a 'fenceless field'): www.eleftherostypos. gr/ellada/128651-ksefrago-ampeli-i-xora-pano-apo-2-400-prosfyges-kai-metanastes-apo-tin-1i-septembrioy-sto-aigaio/.

12 'Greece: Anti-Torture Committee Criticises Treatment of Irregular Migrants and the Continued Detention of Migrant Children': www.coe.int/en/web/cpt/greece?desktop=true.

13 'Macedonia Closes Its Border "Completely" to Migrants': www.telegraph.co.uk/news/worldnews/europe/macedonia/12188826/Macedonia-closes-its-border-completely-to-migrants.html; 'Europe: United Against Refugees': https://newint.org/blog/2016/10/13/europe-united-against-refugees.

14 'Greece: Between Deterrence and Integration': http://issues.newsdeeply.com/greece-between-deterrence-and-integration; 'EU Solidarity Damaged by Splits on Migrants and Greece': www.bbc.com/news/world-europe-33152890.

15 'Where Did the Money Go? How Greece Fumbled the Refugee Crisis': www.theguardian.com/world/2017/mar/09/how-greece-fumbled-refugee-crisis.

16 Racism became a partial exception, since people who saw the opening of the borders as a negative development, were divided over the prospect of migrants' incorporation into local social structures.

17 'Number of Refugees to Europe Surges to Record 1.3 Million in 2015': www.pewglobal.org/2016/08/02/number-of-refugees-to-europe-surges-to-record-1-3-million-in-2015/.

18 'Migration and Migrant Population Statistics': http://ec.europa.eu/eurostat/statistics-explained/index.php/Migration_and_migrant_population_statistics.

19 'The Origins of Greece's Debt Crisis': www.investopedia.com/articles/personal-finance/061115/origins-greeces-debt-crisis.asp; also 'The Greek Debt Crisis: Overview and Implications for the United States': https://fas.org/sgp/crs/row/R44155.pdf.

20 'Memorandum' (of understanding): The agreement between Greece and the Troika (the EU Commission, the European Central Bank and the IMF) concerning structural and fiscal adjustments of the Greek economy in return for financial aid. Its implementation (a series of sudden reforms and austerity measures) led to impoverishment and loss of income and property, as well as a small-scale humanitarian crisis. See 'Financial assistance to Greece': https://ec.europa.eu/info/business-economy-euro/economic-and-fiscal-policy-coordination/eu-financial-assistance/which-eu-countries-have-received-assistance/financial-assistance-greece_en.

21 The term refers to the presence of the European Commission, European Central Bank and International Monetary Fund in Greece since 2010 and the financial measures that these institutions have taken to support the structural readjustments of Greek economy.

22 www.syriza.gr/pdfs/politiki_apofasi_idrytikou_synedriou_syriza.pdf in http://www.viadiplomacy.gr/pia-politiki-protini-o-siriza-gia-metanasteftiko-tou-gianni-kolovou/.

23 Aggelos Sirigos, 'Where and How Control Was Lost Over the Migrants' Issue': www. kathimerini.gr/843088/article/epikairothta/ellada/poy-kai-pws-xa8hke-o-elegxos-sto-metanasteytiko.
24 Ibid.
25 'Greece: Refugees Living in Limbo': www.dw.com/en/greece-refugees-living-in-limbo/a-40035203. See also http://donors.unhcr.gr/relocation/el/home_gr/. The de-bourgeoisement of the Greek middle classes by heavy taxation is another application of the same political philosophy: www.imegsevee.gr/dtimegsevee/1127-dteisodima2016; www.iefimerida.gr/news/315011/ereyna-gsevee-stoiheia-sok-gia-ti-ftohopoiisi-tis-mesaias-taxis-stin-ellada.
26 'Unchecked, Greek Anarchist Groups Terrify in Violent Spree': www.thenational herald.com/179830/unchecked-greek-anarchist-groups-terrify-violent-spree/; 'Spain Ambassador "Shocked" After Anarchists Storm Embassy in Athens': http://greece. greekreporter.com/2017/10/11/spain-ambassador-shocked-after-anarchists-storm-embassy-in-athens/.
27 'Refugee Crisis: Majority of Europeans Believe Increased Migration Raises Terror Threat, Survey Says': www.independent.co.uk/news/world/europe/refugee-crisis-asylum-seekers-europe-terrorism-terror-threat-brexit-immigration-migrants-a7132256.html; 'Greece in 2016: Vulnerable People Left Behind': www.msf.org/en/article/greece-2016-vulnerable-people-left-behind.

Bibliography

Alexander, Jeffrey (2006) 'Cultural Pragmatics: Social Performance between Ritual and Strategy', in Jeffrey Alexander, Bernhard Giesen and Jason Mast (eds), *Social Performance: Symbolic Action, Cultural Pragmatics and Ritual*. New York: Cambridge University Press, pp. 29–90.

Armbrust, Walter (2013) 'The Trickster in Egypt's January 25th Revolution', *Comparative Studies in Society and History* 55, 4: 834–64.

Bar-On, Arnon (2015) 'Indigenous Knowledge: Ends or Means?', *International Social Work* 58, 6: 780–9.

Bateson, Gregory (1958) *Naven*, Stanford: Stanford University Press.

Eisenstadt, Shmuel (1995) 'The Order-maintaining and Order-transforming Dimensions of Culture', in *Power, Trust, and Meaning*, Chicago: The University of Chicago Press.

Horvath, Agnes (2008) 'Mythology and the Trickster: Interpreting Communism', in Alexander Wöll and Harald Wydra (eds), *Democracy and Myth in Russia and Eastern Europe*, London: Routledge, pp. 27–44.

Horvath, Agnes (2013) *Modernism and Charisma*, Basingstoke: Palgrave Macmillan.

Horvath, Agnes and Arpad Szakolczai (2018) 'Political Anthropology', in W. Outhwaite and S. Turner (eds), *The Sage Handbook of Political Sociology*, London: Sage.

Hyde, Lewis (1998) *Trickster Makes this World*, New York: North Point Press.

Kouvelakis, Stathis (2016) 'Syriza's Rise and Fall', *New Left Review* 97, 1: 75–90.

Marangudakis, Manussos (2015) 'Civil Religion in Greece: A Study in the Theory of Multiple Modernities', *Protosociology* 32: 5–30.

Nelson, R.M., P. Belkin and J. Jackson (2017) *The Greek Debt Crisis: Overview and Implications for the United States*, Congressional Research Service.

Papataxiarchis, Evthymios (2016) 'Μία μεγάλη ανατροπή: Η «ευρωπαϊκή προσφυγική κρίση» και ο νέος πατριωτισμός της «αλληλεγγύης»' ['A Major Overthrow: The "European Refugee Crisis" and the New Patriotism of 'Solidarity"'] *Σύγχρονα Θέματα* 132–3: 7–28.

Szakolczai, Arpad (2014) 'Living Permanent Liminality: The Recent Transition Experience in Ireland', *Irish Journal of Sociology* 22, 1: 28–50.

Szakolczai, Arpad (2017) *Permanent Liminality and Modernity: Analysing the Sacrificial Carnival Through Novels*, London: Routledge.

Thomassen, Bjørn (2014) *Liminality, Change and Transition: Living through the In-between*, Farnham: Ashgate.

Turner, Victor (1969) *The Ritual Process*, London: Routledge.

9   Imaginary walls and the paradox of strength

Arvydas Grišinas

Introduction

In many respects, 2015–16 was a critical year for the Western world. It was marked by unprecedented events, such as Brexit and Donald Trump's election, and we have entered a process that seems like a rapid return to nationalist, or perhaps post-liberal rhetoric and practice. A certain critical point has been reached where the cultural open-border narrative seems to have given way to a stricter and less inclusive political thinking. It still is early to say whether what we are experiencing is an epochal shift or just an opportunity for the liberally structured West to readjust its (at least) ideological axis. It is certain, however, that this crisis coincides with the emergence of different walls, both physical and figurative, around the borders of the Western liberal world.

This chapter focuses on the rhetoric and logic of this 'wall-building' in an effort to understand the emergence of these walls and its relation to the contemporary epochal crisis. It explores the related public media and seeks to uncover the imaginary structure underlying these narratives. Several recent wall-building cases in Western politics are discussed: Brexit, understood as putting up a political wall between Britain and the European Union, and Donald Trump's electoral campaign, supported by a very explicit image of a US–Mexico wall-to-be-built. Yet it is also critical to recognise walling within Eastern Europe: the pro-Western Ukraine and its defensive wall project against Russian aggression as well as Hungary, which built a wall dividing it from Serbia in anticipation of the Syrian refugee influx.

It is argued that political walls currently emerging are less important in terms of physical than symbolic presence. The chapter discusses the function and purpose of political images in crisis situations, arguing that images have the power to give perceived form to often ambiguous or unarticulated political phenomena. It will be concluded that the different processes of walling that the West now witnesses are a symptomatic indication of the abovementioned crisis. The walls that are being built are physical, symbolic and imaginary limits that encourage the formation of new identities, conceptualisations and power relations. Not only do they give new meaning to political space – they also have defensive and directive functions. They bring about rupture in space, creating antagonistic and non-reflective identities on both sides of the wall, which is the main danger in the contemporary politics 'on the margins'.

In recent years, both Europe and the United States have experienced the resurgence of wall-building projects. Some of these walls are physical, either already built or in progress of construction. Some are symbolic, countering the liberal tendencies towards political, cultural and social openness of the last two decades. Building a US–Mexico wall was one of the most well-known promises that Donald Trump made during his election campaign. Brexit can also be understood as a symbolic wall with the EU. In response to the Syrian refugee crisis in 2015 Hungary built a fenced wall with Serbia to stop the influx of refugees into the country (Browne 2015). Finally, after Russia's aggression against Ukraine, the latter also initiated an unfinished wall-building project on the border between the two countries (Pike 2017). The multitude of such walls emerging within a span of just a couple of years raises a question whether this is a mere coincidence or a part of greater dynamics. I will discuss the patterns in motivation, unifying the cases and possibly pointing to some broader factors that facilitate such political dynamics.

The Great Wall of Mexico

Donald Trump's election as President of the United States was one of the biggest international news stories of 2016. This suggests that it was the values and policies he represented and promised, rather than his political competence and experience, that secured his victory, despite his being among the most unpopular winning presidents in America's history (Leatherby 2017). Among the most renowned electoral promises Trump made was an initiative to build a US–Mexico wall which he compared in his speeches to the Great Wall of China (Schwartz 2015). This controversial comparison unveils the underlying political imaginary. The implication behind the comparison is building a wall that would stop illegal immigration, which was framed as a security threat, in a similar way that the Chinese wall was supposed to stop the nomadic tribes from the north. The interesting reality, however, as argued by Erik Ringmar in Chapter 7, is that the Great Wall of China is itself a construct of Western imagination rather than an intentional and unified piece of Chinese engineering.

During his public speeches, Trump's tactics was to depict the US in paradoxical terms. On the one hand, it was suffering from social, economic and political issues, mostly induced by foreign forces, which he promised to solve (Campbell 2015). On the other hand, the famous 'Make America great again' slogan refers back to the centre-of-the-world mind-set which, although 'lost', is to be recovered. 'Donald Trump, in other words, is the first person to run openly and without apology on a platform of American decline' (Engelhardt 2016). The perception of immigrants refers to the uncontrolled and alien force threatening the US, which parallels the Great Wall in China's medieval self-image as the centre of the civilised world securing itself against barbarians.

Another aspect of 'making America great again' rhetoric is its narrative retrospection. Instead of pushing the boundaries and seeking a progressive outward teleology, Trump used its opposite. While there is nothing wrong with such disposition per se, as Joan Davison argues in Chapter 10, the idea of a walled-in America is both politically and symbolically anti-American. Furthermore, it is important to note that the greatness once had and lost, which is indicated by the word 'again' in Trump's slogan, resides in an obscure and unclear mythological time. The symbolism of the wall put in front of the Americans urges them to return to this 'Golden Age'. It could refer to Lincoln's America, to the undiscovered Native America, to America of the 1950s or pre-9/11 America – it did not even matter. Several polls inquiring into the exact year of America's greatness showed a widely varying results (Sanger-Katz 2016). The fact that this image of returning to the Golden Age is so non-particular and non-factual paradoxically makes it very inclusive, appealing to a broad electorate. The mythological character of this image justified the existence of the wall, and directed the movement of the rhetorical 'us' 'backwards' into said greatness.

Finally, the Great Wall of Mexico is supposed to be a protective structure. The prototypes built in 2017 are '30-foot-tall concrete and steel sample barriers – some with extra-stout reinforced bases, others topped with metal spikes' (Partlow 2017). This depicts the US as being under threat from external powers, namely, from uncontrolled immigration from Mexico, Islamic countries, global economic outreach, and so on. The wall here represents at the same time the greatness and the taming, the firm and radical limit, imposed forcefully, to structure the perceived chaotic present situation. To many, the 2016 election result came as a shock, and to some, as a tragedy, yet to others it was the desired outcome. Donald Trump was elected President of the United States, which shows that a large portion of voters, particularly in geographical middle America, could identify with a set of images that Trump's campaign offered, and therefore could share his vision of the American present and future. It also needs to be noted that many votes were against the alternative of Hillary Clinton who in the eyes of many represented the established status quo in the American power structure (Cillizza 2016).

The symbolic wall of Brexit

Brexit, or, UK's project to leave the EU, also struck many as a surprise (Durando 2016). The outcome not only shook the EU, but also revealed the gap in political positions between London, Scotland, Northern Ireland and Wales as well as England beyond London (BBC 2016c). The ruling Conservative Party called a referendum on staying in or leaving the EU, partly to mollify its Eurosceptic MPs and partly to prevent its supporters from switching allegiance to the United Kingdom Independence Party (UKIP). The latter campaigned hard for Brexit. According to Sascha O. Becker, Thiemo Fetzer and Dennis Novy, there was a statistical connection between the UKIP and Brexit supporter (Becker et al. 2016). Their involvement manifested politically another, almost underground set of dispositions and anxieties previously only whispered about, although encouraged by some political powers. Eric Kaufmann (2016) argues that the Brexit vote outcome relied heavily on personal values of voters, demonstrating a revealing correlation with such factors as the 'order-openness divide' and a disposition towards the death penalty, among others. This suggests a more complex dynamic than the mere response to globalisation (Betts 2016).

The rhetoric that this campaign pursued shares the semblance of Trump's campaign. First, the main argument for Brexit was the division between 'us', the 'real' Britain, and 'them', the immigrants from Europe (and elsewhere), who take people's jobs, and for whom the UK drags the economic burden. The '£350 million a week' bus advertising campaign, which promised this amount of money to be spent weekly on the National Health Service once the contributions to the EU stop, was based precisely on this sentiment (Morgan and McCann 2016). There is no doubt that in the British narrative there always has been a division or a limit between the UK and Europe. Britain never fully identified itself with its continental neighbour. However, after Europe commonly and strongly associated with the EU, Brexit necessarily offered a different symbolic dynamic. Instead of a mere declaration of border, which was already there, it became a wall-building project.

Secondly, with this 'wall' under construction, the natural political dynamic is bound to turn backwards and inwards. No doubt, there will be a need for greater self-reliance, yet what form will it take? There are talks about rebuilding closer ties with the Commonwealth, which has both its supporters and critics (Blitz 2017). The result of the 'soft' or 'hard' Brexit deal will influence the relationship with the EU. Regardless of the outcome, the overall direction that the situation is headed is at the same time less progressive and inclusive than conservative, reserved and defensive.

The Brexit campaign was strongly motivated by various anxieties brewing within the British but also Western society in general. It symbolically articulated the social and economic crisis in the country, and blamed external factors as causes for the crisis. Among the external factors, outflow of British money, immigration and constraints on sovereignty were the most popular arguments used (Bennett 2017). Therefore, the 'Brexit wall' is supposed to serve as the defensive political and symbolic structure against these threats.

The refugee wall

A controversial wall was raised in Hungary during the summer of 2015 in response to the refugees from the Middle East and North Africa fleeing wars and hardships. In Hungary, the explicitly nationalist political government erected a wall on the border with Serbia to prevent the influx of illegal immigrants. Regardless, according to Eurostat with a record 1.5 million asylum seekers in the EU in 2015 Hungary received the highest number per capita of almost 18,000 applications per million inhabitants (Europa 2016). Not all of these migrants were actual refugees. Some immigrants departed places such as Kosovo, Pakistan or Bangladesh, which were tense and perhaps unstable, but not at war. Therefore, Viktor Orbán's initiative to build an anti-immigrant wall was cheered in Hungary, as the popularity of his political stance enjoyed substantial support. Among the main arguments that Orbán used to justify his political agenda was the protection of Hungary's European Christian heritage from the predominantly Muslim influx (Reuters 2015). This resonated with Hungary's historical tensions with the Muslim world since it had been under the Ottoman imperial rule. The wall (or in this case – the fence) was once again seen as a means of structuring the chaotic situation.

The wall served to direct the refugees towards different routes, along the wall. Refugees have sought new paths to enter Europe (Vasovic and Novak 2015). Meanwhile in 2016, the EU quota of minimum refugee intake was almost refuted, but in each case fell short. First in the referendum 98 per cent of ballots cast opposed the refugee settlement quotas, but the total vote cast failed to reach the 50 per cent threshold of all eligible voters. Next, the legislative effort failed due to disagreements inside Hungary's political right regarding how tough to be on immigration (BBC 2016e). Subsequently, in 2017 the country opened detention centres for refugees, keeping them in shipping containers, where they could wait and apply for asylum with little hope for success, or return to Serbia (DW.COM 2017).

The influx of immigrants with different cultural and religious backgrounds is and must be a serious puzzle from an ethical point of view. On the one hand, the wish to help others and basic human solidarity invokes compassion. The EU open-door policy as well as the Turkish support for the refugees demonstrated just that sentiment. On the other hand, the influx of refugees appears dangerous given jihadist activity, as well as the inevitable conflicts between the newcomers and locals (BBC 2016d). It appears that, unlike Germany or Sweden, Hungary has chosen the latter attitude – to treat immigration as a threat or, as Orbán expressed, as 'poison', with the wall standing to help defend against it (DW.COM 2017).

The European Wall

The Ukrainian crisis in 2014 was a breaking point in Russia's relations with the West. Previous accusations towards Russia regarding different human rights violations, including those of the Russia's LGBT minority before Ukraine's Maidan protests in 2013–14, were relatively mild in comparison with the tensions after the occupation of Crimea and the initiation of the war in the country's east. As a result, the stand-off with the West in the form of economic sanctions, rapid militarisation and an intense information war spread beyond the region. However, the war in Ukraine is still ongoing, as of 2018, and the eastern part of the country is still stuck in a simmering conflict. As a result, Ukraine initiated the building of 'The Wall', or, as it has symbolically been called, the 'European Wall', along the border with Russia. The project stalled in 2017 due to its scale (almost 2000 km), inadequate funds and rampant corruption, but is supposed to be due for completion in 2018 (UNIAN 2017).

The 'brotherhood' between Ukraine and Russia has deep historical roots, dating back as far as the early medieval Kiev Rus. The conflict, however, has put a wedge not only in their relationship, but also inside Ukraine itself. Indeed, the Ukrainian society has a complex ethnic composition. Centuries of close relations between the two countries as well as the colonialist demographic policy in the Russian Empire and the Soviet Union makes the clear definition of who is or is not Ukrainian or Russian particularly complex. 'The fact that nearly half of Ukraine's people speak Russian as their primary language doesn't necessarily make them any more loyal to Mr. Putin than English binds the Irish to the British crown' (Fomina 2014).

> Since 2014, a Ukrainian national identity has taken hold. It includes a strong anti-Russian animus. In an April 2017 public opinion survey conducted by Rating Group Ukraine, 57 percent of Ukrainians polled expressed a very cold or cold attitude toward Russia, as opposed to only 17 percent who expressed a very warm or warm attitude.
>
> (Pifer 2017)

This was certainly articulated at the political level, which is why the wall-building project started in the first place.

The divorce with Russia first of all meant a divorce with the Soviet past, which has probably stirred no less emotion and historical sentiment. A good example of this symbolic aspect was the 'Leninopad' or the massive toppling of Lenin's statues all around Ukraine (Alfred 2017). The titles of 'Euromaidan' and 'European Wall', on the other hand, also indicate the clear symbolic political teleology. The initiative to build a wall on Ukraine's Russian border implies a symbolic and political march 'back to the West' – a step that has been very common in the post-Soviet world.

The wall is supposed to protect Ukraine against a possible Russian invasion as well as against Russian assistance to separatists (Pike 2017). Although the effectiveness of this wall in the case of a serious Russian military advance is questionable, it does provide a sense of security from the unwanted outside attention from the East. In this sense, once again, the wall would play an important protective symbolic role (DW.COM 2016b).

The three functions of political walls

Some generalisations can now be drawn about the inner motivation behind the recent cases of political wall-building. Let me point out three aspects. First, all recent cases of political wall-building have a *discriminative* or *articulative* function. They divide space, splitting it in two, often creating new dialectics between the inner side and the outer side, the orderly and the chaotic, the 'us' and 'others'. In all cases, the walls emerged in the face of an increased influx of 'others'. This encounter not only with the unknown, but also with the prospect of rapid uncontrolled changes within 'ourselves' evokes a logical reaction of blocking the influx. The cases of Germany and Scandinavia are exceptions where a paradoxical choice of acceptance is made, but whether this is a result of wise and insightful decision-making or ideologically driven short-sightedness is still to be seen.

Walls also limit movement by channelling it along their line or away from it, and in this way possess a *directive* or *normative* function. This function affects both sides. Prior to the walling, free interaction existed, progressing the relationship (be it positive or negative). Now a backward-looking disposition prevails, referring the political process the other way. In some cases, it implies the return to the image of the 'self' in the past, in others – it projects a new identity and path for both sides. In either outcome, a wall at least symbolically negates the prospect and willingness to fully engage with the other side.

Finally, if walls are built to hold a roof, to shelter someone from the outside – climate, predators or ill will of others – they attain a *protective* or *sheltering* function. This happens in all cases when the 'other', the exterior, is perceived as a threat. The lack of engagement confirms the disposition and entrenches the defensive stance. In this way a new radical binary articulation of the situation emerges, 'protecting' one side from the other but also abolishing any normal exchange between the two. The best and most-articulated historical example of such political dynamics is the Berlin Wall and the Cold War, as discussed by Harald Wydra in Chapter 6. Chapter 4 by Glenn Bowman also provides an analysis of such a process in the case of the *encystation* of the Palestinian communities in the Gaza region.

The sudden, increased need to build walls, this quite drastic structuring impulse, points to a certain crisis in which the need for articulation, normativity and protection are heightened. In addition to this, however, one needs to recognise that these walls in themselves are hardly a solution to the crisis; at least their structural function is not as important as their symbolic imagery. The walls discussed above function much more strongly as symbols than actual structures. In order to understand why that is important, let us discuss the role of political images in crisis situations.

Imaginary walls and the political crisis

Political power is something conceived by people's minds and shaped by their weakness as a compensation. Human reasons motivate policies that tend to their needs and intrinsically reflect their conditions. Therefore, this 'filling' of human worldview, allegorically speaking, is the 'cement' that constitutes all walls in politics. It also provides the basis for identity, prejudice, narrative symbolism and other a-rational (or pre-rational), yet inevitable political realities.

In times of internet trolling, virtual reality and 'post-truth', political will-infused, abbreviated exaggerated or otherwise distorted narratives became an integral part of the public sphere. Myths or half-truths are often used as a means to directly influence politics, be it public opinion, election results or even public support for military action. They also have a mythological character in that they incorporate both fact and fiction, and are symbolic. It was under the influence of these recent shifts in political discourse that Washington University has offered a module on 'Calling bullshit' as an introduction to coping with the abundant (dis-)information (Bergstrom and West 2017). However, understanding the nature of these a-rational political factors can also be conductive to our inquiry.

The a-rational side of wall-building

The associative and particularly – emotional elements were clearly and brashly abused during the US election. Early in Donald Trump's election campaign, he described the Mexican immigrants as drug dealers, criminals and rapists (BBC 2016a). Along with the many other heavy-handed statements he made, this one was quite clearly not intended to state the factual truth, but to incite associative emotional reaction and raise support (Ruinard 2015). Kellyanne Conway later tried to defend such manipulative language when she introduced the notion of 'alternative facts' to defend her description of the reported attendance at Trump's presidential inauguration ceremony (Bradner 2017). Yet the intent of such myths and half-truths seemed to be particularly affective and leave an emotional impact. As a result, 2016 was called the start of the 'post-truth' epoch after the term was declared the word of the year by the *Oxford English Dictionary* (Tsipursky 2017). It therefore can be said that the tactics succeeded in a way in legitimising such language, which was previously reserved to the villain character Putin, within the Western public discourse. It is in such a context that symbolism and emotional association emerges as primary before factuality and rationality, and it is from this perspective that one needs to approach the question of the 'Mexican wall' as well. Regardless of the practical usefulness, the factual height or width of the structure itself, the important element in structuring the political imagination is its emotional weight and the human needs that the image of the wall responded to.

The Brexit campaign was thoroughly infused with evocative images of foreigners taking away British jobs, swarms of immigrants and distorted Britishness (Stewart and Mason 2016). Such images justified the Brexit campaign response: calls to taking back control of the country, dire warnings of political powerlessness and concern about some kind of paralysis. 'The three phases of Brexit – campaign, referendum, aftermath – have revealed three urgent problems. First, the lack of public faith in establishment politics. Second, the emotional deficit of the EU. Third, the return of a particularly ugly English nationalism' (Foster 2016). For clarity's sake it needs to be mentioned that the nationalist sentiment that Foster refers to is the kind that motivated the multiple post-Brexit attacks on non-English communities, originating from both inside and outside of Europe. It was these elements – faith, emotion and angry pride – that according to Russell Foster swayed the majority's vote. It should not be forgotten that, paradoxically, a large number of Brits were researching what the EU is on Google.com the morning after voting at the referendum. This illustrates the impulsive and a-rational rather than reflexive motivations behind the vote (Fung 2016). Some British citizens voted not for what they knew or thought, or estimated, but for what images of Europe, Britishness and the rest of their political cosmology were reciprocated and held as truth.

In the case of Hungary, the refugee crisis cannot be fully comprehended without understanding such human sensitivities as compassion from one side and fear and resentment from another. It was these sentiments, along with the realisation and imagination of the problem, that were framing the entire situation. There were volunteers helping the immigrants trapped at the Hungarian–Serbian wall and in the Budapest Keleti train station with food and other provisions, pertaining to the empathic solidarity narrative. They acted on the basis of pity for their suffering fellow humans (McLaughlin 2015). At the same time there were those, and a large majority of them, who saw the wave of foreign 'others' as a threat to be defended against and acted out of concern and fear (Toth 2015). From the perspective of immigrants and their dreams, the intent to reach the prosperous 'dreamland' met disappointing reality at the Hungarian border, inciting the political tensions that resonated throughout the West (Hartocollis 2015). We can thus observe a meeting of different interpretations and experiential contexts, fostered by different human faculties: compassion, sense of danger and imaginary expectation. The tensions with refugee walls in Hungary, this political problem as a phenomenon and social tragedy, would simply not have happened without these human experiences.

As for Ukraine, its conflicts were from the very beginning embedded in symbolical, emotional and narrative contexts. Scores of Ukrainians who went to the streets in late 2013 were not only protesting against the legal or economic policy of the Ukrainian government. They were protesting against interconnected myriad associative and contextual meanings that the government represented. It included the attachment to the Soviet past, the dependency on Russia, the post-Soviet corrupt political existence, the counter-posed dreams of imagined 'Western' life, transparent European political standards and, of course, economic prosperity (Snyder 2014). Arguably, it was this attack against political and historical images that also motivated the Russian information war, its further aggression against Ukraine and the consequential falling out with the liberal West. As such, Ukraine's unfinished 'European Wall' represents the westward-leaning aspirations and the rupture with Russia, naturally perceived as the dangerous 'other'. It also pertains to the country's liminal situation, halfway between war and peace, Soviet hangovers and post-Soviet development.

Political crisis and the search for the rational

Raoul Girardet argues that political myths come into prominence at times of crisis and are leaned upon to structure the experienced world.

> All mythological systems, without exception, are directly related to crisis phenomena: sudden acceleration of historical evolution, unexpected ruptures of cultural or social environment, disintegration of the mechanisms regulating the replenishment and solidarity within the life of a collective.
>
> (Girardet 2007: 241)

All the cases discussed above were encountering some form of destabilisation – be it due to external, or internal factors. In the US, the brooding disenchantment with the mainstream politics found an outlet in the presidential election. In the UK, the internal divide in the Conservative Party was hijacked and abused by the populists. Hungary found itself at the bulwark of the Syrian refugee crisis. As for Ukraine, its shift in political teleology was corrupted by Russia's attacks.

So how does one approach such an a-rational side of politics in crisis? The human impulse of associative thinking and symbolic motivation cannot be called foolish or insignificant, or even irrational. The wall-building projects discussed were not based only on mere emotionalism, and as discussed above they were structured and had their own logics. The answer to the question rather lies in understanding the symbolic role that political walls play in crisis situations. According to Charles Taylor, societies dwell in a certain pre-reflective network of expectations, norms and conceptions, the social imaginaries, which they use to articulate the surrounding social and political reality. They establish pre-reflective, taken for granted and heuristic notions of how members of societies imagine their surrounding world as well as themselves (Taylor 2007). People orient themselves within the social and political reality through contextual networks of commonly recognised images, which establish the mode of social co-existence, what behaviour and social or political choices are expected and appropriate. In some sense, therefore, *images delineate normality*.

At the same time, they reassure, create a sense – be it real or imaginary – of epistemological security and clarity as well as establish political identities. This way they give form to political reality that is otherwise chaotic, multi-faceted and even paradoxical. They provide political events with meaning and recognisable structure. A national flag or a monument for an unknown soldier, a logo of a political party or a stereotype of a foreigner present a simplified and easily conceivable version of political and experiential reality. During the crisis situations, when political reality is shifting rapidly and therefore becomes hardly rationally describable and overtly complex, such symbolic denominators and radical distinctions become particularly popular precisely due to their ability to label things. This is due to them being heuristic, emblematic, associative and able to transcend their direct meanings. Just like the abovementioned image of 'America's greatness', they can represent many things while pointing to nothing or no one, and speak to different audiences at the same time. Political images convey power, establish identity, structure political reality and mobilise political will. Apparently, the West is desperately grasping precisely for this kind of certainty, for the rational, which in this case should be understood in a classical sense, as related to a Latin word *ratio*, proportion or form (Szakolczai 2016: 84). This order and structure is thus sought in past experiences as well as historical and mythological narratives.

Walling in the weak and the paradox of strength

When discussing these cases, I noted that political walls tend to serve at least three purposes. First, they impose identities and associative definitions between the inner side, or 'us', and the outer side, or 'them'. Second, they also impact social dynamism, directing the public's attention and mobility away from the wall or along its borders. Third, they have a protective function, to a greater or lesser extent defending the inner side from the dangers, whether real or perceived, on the 'outside'. In terms of human experience, walls as images therefore tend to emanate stability and control, but most importantly – clarity. The contemporary walls we observe today are built not only to bar something or someone outside, but also to provide name, form and clarity to something that is inside. This way, political walls provide distinctions, identities and a directing sense of security to those who build them, at least during the period of their construction. Harald Wydra explains the retrospective intentionality of political mythology:

> The extraordinary is not bound to the chronological time. Profane time is chronological and irreversible. Conversely there is a mythical time of dreams and of apocalypse. In temporal matrix, the present thus becomes a constitutive and permanent reversal of past into future.
>
> (Wydra, 2015: 20)

Therefore, bringing the past, the 'good old times' or the image thereof, when the present crisis did not exist to solve the contemporary situations, to some degree appears reasonable and desirable. The articulative, retrospective and defensive role of political walls cater precisely to these needs.

Even though there is a certain logic to building these walls-as-images, they paradoxically indicate anxiety and fragility of that which is being walled in. Building a wall is not a demonstration of power and nationalist bravado, but of weakness and concern. It is a natural response from someone whose status quo is threatened and unable to withhold. As demonstrated by the newly forming alt-right movements in the US, it is precisely these sentiments that predominate their rhetoric (Khazan 2017). Different political and social images that comprise such imaginaries are capable of shaping politics, motivating political action and moving the masses, whose worries they cater to. Agnes Horvath's analysis of the trickster figure in politics shows how these imaginaries can be manipulated to push political life out of boundaries of normality (Horvath 2010). Building impassable barriers, be they physical or symbolic, generates binary identities, ordered in opposition to each other, and this way perpetuating the threat and therefore – the crisis, on which the victimhood narrative thrives.

Even though the intent to build walls often comes with a rhetoric of stability, strength and justice, increased emphasis on national pride, as well as an effort to make something great again, indicates the very opposite of these virtues. The West, surrounded by walls, becomes the vulnerable West, and this vulnerability is self-perpetuated. It is assimilated into the sense of the 'self' and becomes the generative factor in defensive identity and policy formation, as was the case with the Soviet Union during the Cold War. The wall-building projects therefore comprise both rational intention to structure and limit the collapsing reality, and the division of the lived and experienced space, leading to schismogenesis and artificially generated alienation. Aggression, which political walls undoubtedly represent, be it passive, reactive or proactive, invokes aggressive response, and thus perpetuates the crisis.

On the other hand, and quite paradoxically, *not* building walls, not structuring the world according to clichés, prejudices, pre-established images, requires strength, wisdom and immunity (though of course not apathy). But these are commendable and rare virtues rather than norms. Such qualities most often reflect in personalities rather than masses. This is because first they require wisdom to grasp the paradoxical nature of the matter. The second requirement is the determination to withstand,

and persevere through, the crisis in a reconstructive rather than defensive manner, which demands strong self-governance and moral constitution. Third, the physical capacity to do so is required, which in many cases is lacking within a society, which is precisely why the crisis ensues in the first place.

The cases discussed in this chapter vary in terms of exact conditions, under which the wall-building processes were initiated. However, they all share a similar pattern. First, they feature a conflictual encounter with a destabilising force – be it internal or external. Second, they all demonstrate similar reaction of establishing radical limits in efforts for stabilisation. Finally, they encounter the repercussion of such moves through increased activity of the radical, alienating and corrosive internal force, which threatens to transform the very foundation of the polity.

Yet, the determining factor is not the fact of wall-building and radicalisation per se. It's the society's resilience and ability to stabilise itself under crisis circumstances in such a way that epistemic crutches of political walls are no longer required. Perhaps Gandhi's refusal of violence, and humanist civil movements inside the former Socialist Bloc like Charter 77 in Czechoslovakia, Solidarność in Poland and Sąjūdis in Lithuania, or maybe Japan's path to recuperation after numerous nuclear disasters can provide inspiration for such policy. Yet no recipe or method will substitute for the inner determination within the society itself.

Conclusion

This chapter has discussed the public rhetoric behind four contemporary political wall-building projects on the geographical margins of the liberal Western world, specifically the US, UK, Hungary and Ukraine. It was observed that all these cases have certain functions in common: the articulative, the directive and the protective. Political walls provide a simplified identity binary between 'us' and 'them', the 'civilised status quo' and the 'invading barbarian'. Second, they provide political direction and orientation, mostly backwards, towards the imagined or symbolic 'Golden Age', but also away from the 'other'. Finally, they provide a sense of assuredness, a kind of protection, both in political and epistemological terms.

The chapter also noted that the symbolic role that the emerging political walls play are more important than the physical. The human factor is a very important element in contemporary politics, and it needs to be properly accounted for when approaching the issue at hand. The public need for political structures, like culture-defending walls, indicates a crisis that is not only factual and physical, but more importantly – symbolic. In many cases, the representation of these walls rendered these symbolic and emotionally associative images a considerable political force. The chapter demonstrated how the human factor influenced the wall-building projects at hand. These political walls represent human fears and aspirations, although their exact definitions may be blurred, mythological or imaginary.

To better understand this 'soft' and ambiguous question of the human factor in contemporary politics, I argued that particularly during political crises, images function as means of structuring the ambiguous reality. Therefore, instead of brushing them away as mythological or not real, we should understand them, because they can tell us a lot about the inner motivations behind the straightforward policy. Political images become particularly important as measures to control, structure and articulate the otherwise fluctuating and ambiguous reality under unstable political circumstances. However, oftentimes, instead of clarification of the experienced reality, the political image-making or wall-building maps the psychological structure of the narrative that is creating these images.

Through their very presence, these walls signify the crisis state that society finds itself in. They represent the vulnerable condition of the wall-builder. On the other hand, this process perpetuates wall-building, as it reproduces binary identities that the divisions by walls establish. In this sense, walls become both a cause and a result of the crisis, locking the process in a self-perpetuating cycle. The way out of this situation seems to be through withstanding the crisis instead of blocking it. However, this process requires wisdom, leadership and strength within the society to re-establish structure in an integrated and balanced manner.

Bibliography

Alfred, Charlotte. 2014. 'Leninopad, Ukraine's Falling Lenin Statues, Celebrated as Soviet Symbols Toppled Nationwide (VIDEOS, PHOTOS).' *The Huffington Post*, 24 February 2014. Available at www.huffingtonpost.com/2014/02/24/leninopad-falling-lenins-statues-ukraine_n_4847364.html. (Accessed 21 April 2017.)

BBC 2016a. 'Drug Dealers, Criminals, Rapists: What Trump Thinks of Mexicans.' 31 April. Available at www.bbc.com/news/av/world-us-canada-37230916/what-trump-has-said-about-mexicans. (Accessed 27 April 2017.)

BBC. 2016b. 'Eight Reasons Leave Won the UK's Referendum on the EU.' 24 June. Available at www.bbc.com/news/uk-politics-eu-referendum-36574526. (Accessed 19 April 2017.)

BBC. 2016c. 'EU Referendum: The Result in Maps and Charts.' 24 June. Available at www.bbc.com/news/uk-politics-36616028. (Accessed 5 February 2017.)

BBC. 2016d. 'Germany Attacks: What Is Going On?' 20 December. Available at www.bbc.com/news/world-europe-36882445. (Accessed 20 April 2017.)

BBC. 2016e. 'Migrant Crisis: Hungary MPs Reject Orban Anti-Refugee Bill.' 8 November. Available at www.bbc.com/news/world-europe-37903194. (Accessed 20 April 2017.)

Becker, Sasha O., Thiemo Fetzer and Dennis Novy. 2016. 'The Fundamental Factors behind the Brexit Vote.' VOX, CEPR's Policy Portal. 31 October. Available at http://voxeu.org/article/fundamental-factors-behind-brexit-vote. (Accessed 18 April 2017.)

Bennett, Asa. 2017. 'What Will Brexit Mean for British Expats?' *The Telegraph*. 24 February. Available at www.telegraph.co.uk/news/0/eu-facts-what-would-leaving-the-eu-mean-for-expats/. (Accessed 19 April 2017.)

Bergstrom, Carl, and Jevin West. 2017. 'Calling Bullshit in the Age of Big Data.' *Calling Bullshit*. Available at http://callingbullshit.org/. (Accessed 24 April 2017.)

Betts, Alexander 2016. 'Why Brexit Happened – And What to Do Next.' TED Talk, TED. com. June. Available at www.ted.com/talks/alexander_betts_why_brexit_happened_and_what_to_do_next?language=en#t-430593. (Accessed 18 April 2017.)

Blitz, James. 2017. *Financial Times*. 7 March. www.ft.com/content/bc29987e-034e-11e7-ace0-1ce02ef0def9. (Accessed 19 April 2017.)

Bradner, Eric. 2017. 'Conway: Trump White House Offered 'Alternative Facts' on Crowd Size.' *CNN*. 23 January. Available at http://edition.cnn.com/2017/01/22/politics/kellyanne-conway-alternative-facts/. (Accessed 27 April 2017.)

Browne, Rachel. 2015. 'Hungary Is Building a Wall Along the Serbian Border to Keep Migrants Out.' *VICE News*. Available at https://news.vice.com/article/hungary-is-building-a-wall-along-the-serbian-border-to-keep-migrants-out. (Accessed 18 December 2017.)

Campbell, Colin. 2015. 'Here Are the Big Ideas in Donald Trump's Presidential Campaign.' *Business Insider*. 16 June. Available at www.businessinsider.com/donald-trumps-2016-campaign-ideas-2015-6. (Accessed 12 January 2017.)

Cillizza, Chris. 2016. 'One of Hillary Clinton's Top Aides Nailed Exactly Why She Lost.' *The Washington Post*. 14 November. Available at www.washingtonpost.com/news/the-fix/wp/2016/11/14/one-of-hillary-clintons-top-aides-nailed-exactly-why-she-lost/?utm_term=.c2fc752bbf17. (Accessed 18 April 2017.)

Durando, Jessica. 2016. 'Global Reaction Pours in over 'Brexit' Result.' *USA Today*. 24 June. Available at www.usatoday.com/story/news/world/2016/06/24/global-reaction-united-kingdom-european-union-referendum/86322884/. (Accessed 24 April 2017.)

DW.COM. 2016a. 'Referendum in Hungary: Orban Has Already Achieved His Goal.' 2 October. Available at www.dw.com/en/referendum-in-hungary-orban-has-already-achieved-his-goal/a-35937072. (Accessed 20 April 2017.)

DW.COM. 2016b. 'Ukraine: A Wall along the Russian Border.' 16 March. Available at www.dw.com/en/ukraine-a-wall-along-the-russian-border/av-19121496. (Accessed 21 April 2017.)

DW.COM. 2017. 'Hungary Opens Shipping Container Camp for Refugees.' 28 March. Available at www.dw.com/en/hungary-opens-shipping-container-camp-for-refugees/a-38152515. (Accessed 20 April 2017.)

Englehardt, Tom. 2016. 'What Trump Really Means When He Says He'll Make America Great Again.' *The Nation*. 26 April. Available at www.thenation.com/article/what-trump-really-means-when-he-says-hell-make-america-great-again/. (Accessed 19 April 2017.)

Europa.eu. 2016. 'Record Number of over 1.2 Million First Time Asylum Seekers Registered in 2015.' 4 March. Available at http://ec.europa.eu/eurostat/documents/2995521/7203832/3-04032016-AP-EN.pdf/790eba01-381c-4163-bcd2-a54959b99ed6. (Accessed 19 March 2017.)

Fomina, Joanna. 2014. *Language, Identity, Politics – the Myth of Two Ukraines*. Warsaw: Institute of Public Affairs. 1 April. Available at www.bertelsmann-stiftung.de/fileadmin//files/Projekte/88_Europa_staerken_und_verbinden/POLICY_BRIEF_Language_Identity_Politics_the_Myth_of_Two_Ukraines.pdf. (Accessed 27 February 2017.)

Foster, Russell. 2016. '"I Want My Country Back": The Resurgence of English Nationalism.' LSE BREXIT. 3 September. Available at http://blogs.lse.ac.uk/brexit/2016/09/06/i-want-my-country-back-the-resurgence-of-english-nationalism/. (Accessed 24 April 2017.)

Fung, Brian. 2016. 'The British Are Frantically Googling What the E.U. Is, Hours after Voting to Leave It.' *The Washington Post*. 24 June. Available at www.washingtonpost.com/news/the-switch/wp/2016/06/24/the-british-are-frantically-googling-what-the-eu-is-hours-after-voting-to-leave-it/?postshare=8141466778634681&tid=ss_tw&utm_term=.f56e718b054e. (Accessed 5 February 2017.)

Girardet, Raoul. 2007. *Politiniai mitai ir mitologijos*. Vilnius: Apostrofa.

Hartocollis, Anemona. 2015. 'Why Migrants Don't Want to Stay in Hungary.' *The New York Times*. 5 September. Available at www.nytimes.com/interactive/projects/cp/reporters-notebook/migrants/hungary-treatment-refugees. (Accessed 24 April 2017.)

Horvath, Agnes. 2010. 'Pulcinella, or the Metaphysics of the Nulla: In Between Politics and Theatre.' *History of the Human Sciences* 23, 2: 47–67.

Horvath, Agnes. 2013. *Modernism and Charisma*. Basingstoke: Palgrave Macmillan.

Kaufmann, Eric. 2016. 'It's NOT the Economy, Stupid: Brexit as a Story of Personal Values.' *British Politics and Policy at LSE*. 14 July. Available at http://blogs.lse.ac.uk/politicsandpolicy/personal-values-brexit-vote/. (Accessed 5 February 2017.)

Khazan, Olga. 2017 'How White Supremacists Use Victimhood to Recruit.' *The Atlantic*. 15 August. Available at www.theatlantic.com/science/archive/2017/08/the-worlds-worst-support-group/536850/. (Accessed 1 December 2017.)

Leatherby, Lauren. 2017. 'Trump is Least Popular Incoming President since 1940s.' *Financial Times*. 20 January. Available at www.ft.com/content/3e843ab8-de9c-11e6-9d7c-be108f1c1dce. (Accessed 18 April 2017.)

McLaughlin, Dan. 2015. 'Volunteers Defy Hostile Leaders to Welcome Refugees to Europe.' *Al Jazeera America*. 5 September. Available at http://america.aljazeera.com/articles/2015/9/5/volunteers-defy-hostile-leaders-to-welcome-refugees-to-europe.html. (Accessed 18 April 2018.)

Morgan, Kate and McCann, Tom. 2016. 'Nigel Farage: £350 Million Pledge to Fund the NHS Was "a Mistake".' *The Telegraph*. 24 June. Available at www.telegraph.co.uk/news/2016/06/24/nigel-farage-350-million-pledge-to-fund-the-nhs-was-a-mistake/. (Accessed 18 April 2017.)

Partlow, Joshua. 2017. 'Mexicans See Models of Trump's 'Impenetrable' Wall, and They're Not Impressed'. *The Washington Post*. Available at www.washingtonpost.com/world/the_americas/mexicans-see-models-of-trumps-impenetrable-wall-and-theyre-not-impressed/2017/10/16/4f54bdb8-ad22-11e7-9b93-b97043e57a22_story.html?utm_term=.1e3467b21dc9. (Accessed 18 December 2017.)

Pifer, Steven. 2017. 'How Ukraine Views Russia and the West.' *Brookings*. Available at: www.brookings.edu/blog/order-from-chaos/2017/10/18/how-ukraine-views-russia-and-the-west/ (Accessed 18 December 2017.)

Pike, John. 2017. 'Military: Ukraine – Ukraine–Russia Border Fence/European Bulwark.' Available at www.globalsecurity.org/military/world/ukraine/border-fence.htm. (Accessed 21 April 2017.)

Reuters. 2015. 'Refugees Threaten Europe's Christian Roots, Says Hungary's Orban.' 3 September. Available at www.reuters.com/article/us-europe-migrants-orban-idUSKCN0R30J220150903. (Accessed 20 April 2017.)

Ruinard, Ken. 2015. 'Donald Trump's Tactics and Tricks.' *The Boston Globe*. 21 October. Available at www.bostonglobe.com/opinion/2015/10/20/donald-trump-tactics-and-tricks/tD9vC36BC7g0LaP8Q4YmSP/story.html#comments. (Accessed 24 April 2017.)

Sanger-Katz, Margot. 2016. 'When Was America Greatest?' *The New York Times*. 26 April. Available at www.nytimes.com/2016/04/26/upshot/when-was-america-greatest.html. (Accessed 18 April 2017.)

Schwartz, Ian. 2015. 'Trump on Border: We'll Call It "The Great Wall of Trump".' *RealClearPolitics*. 20 August. Available at www.realclearpolitics.com/video/2015/08/20/trump_on_border_well_call_it_the_great_wall_of_trump.html. (Accessed 12 January 2017.)

Snyder, Timothy. 2014. 'Fascism, Russia, and Ukraine.' *The New York Review of Books*. 20 March. Available at www.nybooks.com/articles/2014/03/20/fascism-russia-and-ukraine/. (Accessed 24 April 2017.)

Sprudis, Andris, Anda Rožukalne, Klavs Sedlenieks, Martins Daugulis, Diana Potjomkina, Beatrix Tölgiesi and Ilvija Bruge. 2017. 'Internet Trolling as a Hybrid Warfare Tool: The

Case of Latvia.' *StratCom*. Available at www.stratcomcoe.org/internet-trolling-hybrid-warfare-tool-case-latvia-0 (Accessed 24 April 2017.)

Stewart, H. and Mason, R. 2016. 'Nigel Farage's Anti-Migrant Poster Reported to Police.' *Guardian*. Available at www.theguardian.com/politics/2016/jun/16/nigel-farage-defends-ukip-breaking-point-poster-queue-of-migrants (Accessed 18 December 2017.)

Szakolczai, Árpád. 2016. *Novels and the Sociology of the Contemporary*. London: Routledge.

Taylor, Charles. 2007. *Modern Social Imaginaries*. Durham: Duke University Press.

Toth, Csaba Tibor. 2015. 'Volunteers and Vigilantes Watch Over Refugees in Hungary.' DW.COM. 28 August. Available at www.dw.com/en/volunteers-and-vigilantes-watch-over-refugees-in-hungary/a-18677868. (Accessed 18 April 2017.)

Tsipursky, Gleb. 2017. 'Towards a Post-Lies Future Fighting "Alternative Facts" and "Post-Truth" Politics.' *The Huffington Post*. 28 February. Available at www.huffingtonpost.com/entry/towards-a-post-lies-future-fighting-alternative-facts_us_58b42dd9e4b02f3f81e449fa. (Accessed 24 April 2017.)

UNIAN. 2017. 'В Харьковской области приостановлено строительство 'Стены' на границе с Россией' [The Building of the 'Wall' on the Border with Russia Stopped in Kharkov Oblast]. 19 January. Available at www.unian.net/society/1732877-v-harkovskoy-oblasti-priostanovleno-stroitelstvo-stenyi-na-granitse-s-rossiey.html. (Accessed 21 April 2017.)

Vasovic, Aleksandar and Marja Novak. 2015. 'Migrants Diverted to New Routes after Hungary Shuts Border.' *The Huffington Post*. 17 October. Available at www.huffingtonpost.com/entry/migrants-diverted-to-new-routes-after-hungary-shuts-border_us_5622bf90e4b08589ef47b665. (Accessed 20 April 2017.)

Wydra, Harald. 2015. *Politics and the Sacred*. Cambridge: Cambridge University Press.

10 Identities frozen, societies betrayed, communities divided

The US–Mexican Wall

Joan Davison

Walls: barriers to freedom or foundations of security

While borders and immigration controls exist as normalised, constitutive elements of the modern state, as a candidate and then president Donald Trump moved the United States' border policy from the rationalised arena of bureaucracies to the theatrical circus of a permanent campaign, introducing a level of rancour and scapegoating consistent with liminality and tricksters (Girard 1977, 1989; Horvath 2010; Horvath and Thomassen 2008; Szakolczai 2013, 2014, 2017; Turner 1982). Chapter 9 by Grišinas elaborates upon Trump's specific use of emotional rhetoric and myth, and highlights the importance of images and limits for electorates dissatisfied with the outcomes of liberalism. Indeed, Trump clamoured for an enhanced, fortified defence to provide the security essential to reclaim a mythical 'American' identity and its associated greatness, deemed lost in a liberal age. The proposed wall and other border controls became powerful symbols of a promise to rescue society. As such, Trump's slogan and proposals imitate recent other efforts, most notably in Israel, to achieve a security that protects a particular mythical identity of a bounded nation-state. Trump has even suggested contracting with Magal Security Systems, the construction firm building the walls to contain Palestinians within Gaza and the West Bank.

From the perspective of Trump and his supporters, a wall provides the fortification to secure the United States' identity and prosperity from outsiders, who based upon their intrinsic outsider identity threaten the United States. Trump thereby refocuses the paradigm of making America great, rejecting an emphasis on internationalism. He preaches a cathartic walling of the population and retreat into fortified space. Within the walls, the apple-pie culture of American identity – its homogeneity, purity and goodness – can be nurtured, socialised and restored. As both Bowman and Horvath discuss (in Chapters 4 and 1, respectively), the walled area – cyst or womb – might be perceived as a source of protection, but to the extent it quarantines and transforms, it also functions as a space of fears and limits. So too, Trump's walling process will transform linear space and freeze history, trapping individuals in an unreal vacuum of an ostensibly purified communitas (Turner 1969; Turner and Turner 1978). The character of the 'American' communitas within this liminality, however, will grow closed, banal and uninspiring (Szakolczai 2015; Thomassen 2015).

The walling in of American Anglos and out of Latino Americans, while perhaps possessing a new determination, vitriol and thoroughness, has deep and extensive origins consistent with modern political structures. Trump's promise of a wall to control migration from Mexico illustrates only the most recent effort to secure a particular identity consistent with an imagined nation, security and prosperity. The walling in of the US and walling out of Mexico at least dates to the 1840s, the US–Mexican War and the implementation of the Treaty of Guadalupe Hidalgo. Until that time, there existed an openness, but also a lawlessness, among the people – indigenous, black, European and Hispanic – of the frontier (Mennell 2015). Prior to the war, the 'border' and identities were amorphous and even fluid. The Treaty, however, required Mexico to 'sell' more than half its territory to the United States. Mexican nationals within the newly ceded territory either abandoned their homes and returned to Mexico, or necessarily became US citizens. Today the descendants of colonial Mexicans in Texas, the Tejanos, view themselves as fully Mexican American. Their identity is a fusion, as understood in the Tex-Mex reference. Consequently, current constructed distinctions between American and Mexican identities cast the Tejanos into a neither-here-nor-there liminal space (Gennep 1960; Szakolczai 2015; Thomassen 2015; Turner 1967). Indeed, significant is the very use and understanding of the term 'American'. Throughout the Western hemisphere, people from all countries identify as American. Yet, US citizens do so in distinction from other peoples of the Americas: North, Central and South. The US's exclusive understanding of the term 'American' highlights the special, imaginary collective identity of the people, and the associated yearning for differentiation from others, who seemingly are less American, less able and less worthy.

From this perspective, it is unsurprising that while the North American Free Trade Accord (NAFTA) aimed to promote development through cooperation and free trade for the people in Mexico and the US, the agreement also heightened concerns within the US regarding Mexican workers, documented and undocumented. The anxiety intensified after the transformative crises of 9/11 and the 2008 recession, eventually leading to exaggerated, unreal fears regarding the numbers of Latinos and their impact on employment, crime and government budgets. Trump's promise to build a wall with Mexican money responds to the human factor of anxiety, and to the appeal of a mythically superior identity, both of which Grišinas analyses. Trump's walling promise ignores, however, not only the existing extensive security measures, but also the recent net flow of Mexicans *out* of the United States and back to Mexico. Migrants, whether attracted to improved economic prospects in Mexico, or frustrated with animosity in the US, are returning to Mexico. From one perspective, these Mexicans might be acknowledging the prevailing social disharmony and pessimism regarding integration, and opting out of the Batesonian schismogenesis (1936) with a break from the US and reintegration into a different environment (Turner 1967).

Nevertheless, Trump's promise to build a 'big, beautiful wall' renews attention to the character of walling and the significance of technologies for state control particularly in times of uncertainty or transformation (Horvath 2015; Thomassen

2015). His election illustrates a victory for an ideology that values metaphorical and concrete walls as a means to an unreal security, while discounting the costs of isolation and lost engagement for the potential development of the autonomous self. This ideology accepts the financial and civilisational price that walling creates for individual emancipation, valuing imitation and even allowing for a type of herd mentality which keeps individuals from realising their own person, values and wonders (Scheler 1973). The decreased horizon, altered natural world and artificial environment constrain the creativity of walled populations, controlling experiences, interactions and communities. State structures thereby limit the autonomy of people to encounter and value the other, denying insights and capping emotional possibilities; inside the walls, people sacrifice the potential of human development to security structures. Instead, political masters and technologies define a particular transformed self in anonymous unanimity within the walls, the identity being primarily a contrast to the outsider (Horvath 2015).

Supporters of the ideology that justifies such technology then risk existence in a permanent liminality (Szakolczai 2017). Liminal people adapt to and mimic the lifestyles of their walled societies, forfeiting the individualised development of the self which values the person and allows them to become distinct beings (Horvath and Thomassen 2008; Szakolczai and Thomassen 2011; Scheler 1973; Tarde 1903). They shelter in the past which has become the present because they fear the future (Szakolczai 2017; Thomassen 2015). They accept an illusory American culture and its myths rather than pursue integration into a new environment. These myths, however, appeal to their emotional senses particularly because the population feels impotent in the face of economic, social and technological changes that accompany crises of modernity (as Horvath discusses), security (as Bowman notes) and liberalism (as Grišinas argues). In the midst of such transformational siege, the population then becomes vulnerable to the trickster and his tactics of scapegoating, excess and violence (Horvath 2007, 2010; Horvath and Thomassen 2008; Szakolczai 2013, 2015).

In the case of the United States, the submission to such a myopic ideology runs counter to the ideals of alternative myths symbolised through Lady Liberty intentionally welcoming the aspiring individual who seeks liberty to form the autonomous self. The parochialism that the wall symbolises diminishes the embrace of the benefits of openness and engagement epitomised in various US principles ranging from the constitutional guarantees to freedom of religion and speech, to traditional preferences for open doors and free trade, to rejection of state ownership or boundaries in outer space. Parochial and myopic ideologies support the liminal condition; these visions prefer to return to mythical American greatness rather than undertake the uncertain grappling with domestic and global transformations. To an extent, candidate Trump, well positioned as blameless for the current political condition, hijacked the situation (Horvath 2007, 2010; Horvath and Thomassen 2008; Szakolczai 2013). His dramatic commitment to walling proved popular, and is now the latest technology to transform the US border with Mexico.

The transformation of the border and Mexican status

Recent controversies surrounding Mexican migration began with the Immigration and Nationality Act of 1965. Ironically, Congress intended the Act to diversify the immigrant pool through the elimination of national origins quotas which preferenced white Anglo-Saxons. This new system did create opportunities for immigrants from Asia, Africa, and Latin America, but deeply cut the migration of Mexicans, terminating their guest worker program. The change stunned Mexicans accustomed to traveling to the US for seasonal work and family visits. Accordingly, these Mexicans entered a particular crisis as the Act interrupted and transformed their pattern of cyclical movement. The shared history and culture of communities in the southwest US and Mexican north seemed ignored. Individual Mexicans, far beyond the quota, possessed reasons to migrate. Thus, the movement of 'undocumented' Mexicans began as they challenged the initial technological efforts to transform the border and control individuals. Nevertheless, the identity of these Mexicans now changed – from the US institutional perspective the Mexicans became 'illegal aliens'. Inherently the migrants were the same people with the same aspirations, but the US deemed them outsiders – outside the community and the law.

In response to the undocumented migration the US then expanded the Border Patrol, prompting Mexicans to turn to coyotes to facilitate border crossing. As the demand for coyotes increased, criminal organisations became active in the trade. Migrating Mexicans then experienced cruelties, not only from the coyotes, but also criminal gangs and border guards (Massey et al. 2016). Spiralling criminality and violence characterised the void, and migration became more chaotic (Massey 2015). Further, given the increasing difficulty of reaching the US, successful migrants stayed and cyclical migration declined. This changed the demographic character of the migrant; whereas prior to 1965 most migrants were young men seeking seasonal work, families now migrated. Single men who migrated remained and started families in the US. These 'illegal aliens' became liminal individuals, trapped like the Tejanos in a neither-here-nor-there-state, with jobs and families in the US, and children and spouses with citizenship (Gennep 1960; Horvath 2015; Szakolczai 2015; Thomassen 2014; Turner 1967, 1969, 1975). These migrants support and raise family members who are Americans, but exist in their shadows without documents. Their status in Mexico is equally liminal – men who come as teenagers do not assimilate easily into the communities they left if they are forcibly deported. Technological structures – borders and laws – which inhibit the natural movement of individuals, now trap people into a liminal void in which they cannot move back to (or even visit) Mexico nor move forward within the US. They can neither obtain drivers' licences nor workers' benefits. If they are victimised, they cannot report crimes. State security structures lock them into a dangerous liminality in which they lack agency.

In 1986 the nature of Mexican migration further changed as the US passed the Immigration Reform and Control Act which enhanced border security. The newly militarised response included dogs, armoured vehicles, surveillance and National

Guard patrols (Dunn 1996). Mexicans more than ever relied upon coyotes to cross at unguarded, but inhospitable areas of desert expanse. The risky journeys ended in death for many migrants. Estimates suggest more than 5600 migrants died in efforts to cross the border. Fifteen hundred families have never heard from relatives, creating a permanent unknowing, and suggesting a fatal outcome (Slack et al. 2016: 16). These deaths highlight the wall as an instrument of both structural and cultural violence (Martinez et al. 2014: 263–5). Yet even in death the migrants retain a type of liminal status given the immigration crisis – are they victims or criminals?

The current combination of high cost and risk creates a situation in which if it still makes sense to migrate, it does not make sense to return to Mexico to visit. Subsequent entry attempts potentially exact too high a price. Whereas prior to 1986, half of all migrants returned to Mexico, the likelihood of a voluntary return now hovers at zero (Massey et al. 2016). Consequently, most Mexican unauthorised immigrants now are long-term residents, with 78 per cent living in the US for ten or more years (Passel 2016). Given the large Latino populations in the southwest, it is unconvincing to conceptualise these Latinos as 'outsiders'. Respective Latino and undocumented immigrant populations of border states are: New Mexico 48 per cent and 4 per cent, California 39 per cent and 6 per cent, Texas 39 per cent and 6 per cent, and Arizona 31 per cent and 5 per cent. In New Mexico and Texas, the Latino population now outnumbers the white population. Yet, the walling rhetoric of Trump designates them as outsiders and threats.

Post 9/11 liminality and walling – enhanced technology

In 2006, The Secure Fence Act passed as a response primarily to 9/11, but also economic concerns. The Act authorised the construction of hundreds of miles of additional fencing, checkpoints, barriers, satellites and drones to protect America (White House 2006). The border region thus changed from interconnected communities and interdependent economies to a militarised region reminiscent of a war zone (Boyce 2015). The walls privileged state security over human security, reinforcing inequalities and hierarchies of 'ins' and 'outs', and justifying violence against people of unacceptable economic and national backgrounds (Weldes et al. 1999). The associated introduction of Operation Streamline, which designated illegal entry as criminal activity, led to en masse trials and deportations of nonviolent migrants, and the construction of the illegal criminal Mexican stereotype. As such, the walls both limit identity and imply the inferiority and danger of outsiders (Campbell 1998).

Meanwhile, the construction and symbol of the wall ignores the reciprocal benefit of openness for investors, students, tourists and workers, denying sociability and inhibiting the possibility of building trust and community. Three hundred and fifty million people legally cross the US–Mexican border each year. Twelve million people live on private land along the border. Tony Estrada, the sheriff of an Arizona border county who himself migrated from Mexico to the US as an infant, misses the 'organic quality' of the old border that allowed communities in the US and Mexico to visit and celebrate events together (Walsh 2016). Residents of the borderlands note 'the bilingual, bicultural, and binational skills that characterize border residents form part of a wider border culture that embraces diversity and engenders creativity' (Heyman 2013: 60). The people of the region possess a critical insight about the enrichment of culture and life which generally is ignored. They perceive the border as imposing an artificial community that divides and excludes aspects of their world. People of the border interact, rejecting the constructed and frozen vision from the US heartland that migrants are terrorists and criminals (Heyman 2013). Yet, more distant US citizens walled from the Latino 'alien' often accept this image of the alien as parasitic or dangerous. Indeed, that is the compelling logic of legal and concrete walls. Inner conviction is displaced as stereotypes and scapegoating replace the ability to make distinctions. While walling fails to address the crises of inequality, job loss, cultural change and personal insecurity in the United States, it codifies certain sacrificial rituals such as racial and ethnic profiling (Girard 1977; Horvath 2015; Szakolczai 2015; Turner 1969).

The physical wall disorients and punishes not only people – who once were part of a single land and culture – but in the modern world indigenous and/or ethnic identities are denied. Already mentioned are the cases of the liminal Tejano and undocumented household heads. Another example concerns the Tohono O'odham people, an indigenous nation whose peoples and lands extend from southern Arizona into northern Mexico. Since the 1850s, the nation has been subject to a variety of transitions beyond its control which have cast them into a liminal status in a modernity not of their choice. The Gadsden Purchase of 1853 divided their land, and denied them the possibility of dual US–Mexican citizenship. The liminality subsequently deepened and froze through the creation of reservations, deprivation of traditional economic sectors, forced attendance in Christian English-language boarding schools and recent damming and flooding of lands. In each case, the imposition of boundaries by external masters disturbed the unity of the people with nature and the harmony of their cosmos.

The nation currently opposes the construction of a wall which again would transform their space. Tribal members desire to move freely across the constructed borders to attend celebrations and ceremonies, worship at sacred shrines, visit relatives and enjoy tribal services. Moreover, a concrete wall would disturb the flow of water to their agricultural lands, excessively flooding some areas. They realise the wall would also divide and disrupt the natural habitats of wildlife within their territory, an environment that they hold sacred. Particularly disturbing to the Tohono O'odham people is the militarisation of the border, and the creation of a foreign climate, a 'culture of fear', leading to 'questioned[s] about who they are' (Schmidt 2016). The poignancy of such liminality is palpable as identity becomes beyond one's control. Other indigenous peoples suffer comparable experiences. Today, walling denies indigenous people their identity, their opportunity to live harmoniously with nature and the freedom to steward their land.

While this walling regime creates controls and confusion for migrants and border communities, it nevertheless responds to the crises and liminality that many

US citizens feel. Current sentiment favouring walling is unfounded based upon the number of migrants, particularly Mexicans, which are declining. In 2015, the Border Patrol stopped 331,313 people – the second lowest since 1972; about half were from Central America, and only 180,000 from Mexico. By comparison, 1.637 million Mexicans were apprehended in 2000 (United States, Immigration and Customs Enforcement 2016). The appeal of walling then arises from a liminoid social drama in reaction to the crisis of loss of status amid societal and global transformations and accompanying disorder. Similar to Bowman's analysis of Israeli walling, the encystation creates a protective environment. The wall serves as a technological symbol of control for people experiencing the chaotic crises of 9/11, the Great Recession, declining mobility and increasing heterogeneity. In demarking Mexican outsiders from American insiders, however, walling nurtures irrationalities such that insecurities, and the very void itself, grow concretised and normalised. Inside the wall the liminality becomes permanent (Szakolczai 2017; Thomassen 2015). Individuals lack the mobility and agency to consider and address the challenges of their environments, and move through disorder to a new identity. The wall which locks individuals into spaces and circumstances also locks out resolution of these crises.

Then how did 'building a wall' become such a rallying cry given the reality of the post 9/11 securitisation and the Obama Administration's own aggressive deportation practices? One element is that Obama's policies attempted to identify and deport only the violent criminal, and this was insufficient for individuals who felt under siege from social transformations. Obama famously called for the deportation of 'felons not families'. Childhood arrivals, the elderly, domestic abuse and trafficking victims, pregnant women and long-time residents were not targeted. In 2016, 92 per cent of deportees were criminals (US Immigration and Customs Enforcement 2015, 2016). Yet, the efforts to welcome childhood arrivals and their parents angered anti-immigration proponents. Indeed, Trump supporters likewise rejected Republican primary candidates who called for immigration reform and/or amnesties. Some of Trump's earliest and most ardent supporters viewed the wall as a crucial issue because it symbolised a strategic goal to reclaim their status. Constructing a wall became a collective identity performance that demarked them from us (Eyerman 2006). The construction creates boundaries, rejects the neutrality of public space and purifies culture (Apter 2006).

In fact, such wall advocates are themselves liminal. They include rural, working-class, high school educated and small businesspeople who embrace the Trump promise of a wall based upon their experience of crises, specifically their uncertain social position (Cramer 2016; Hochschild 2016). Their once elevated status as the workers who built the country with their hands suffered assaults as the service economy, robotisation, globalisation and urbanisation push them towards irrelevance. Multiple transformations now cloud the possibility for upward mobility, middle-class livelihoods, social salience and personal dignity. Their social status as white males slipped to the margins as women outnumbered men at the university level and in professional schools, and as a black son of a Kenyan became president. Threats to their economic, and perhaps more critically social position, are both complex and seemingly intractable, leaving them desperate and bewildered. The crises are multiple, and they believe attributable to others; the confusion and despair captures them in a limbo. With the shuttering of factories and decline of unions, their old identities dissolve, and they become malleable individuals seeking recognition, affirmation and inclusion. Thus, they cling to any promise that offers assurance even if the experience only provides a placebo of emotional relief. In reaction to economic and social transformation and uncertainty, they suffer in a confused, uncomfortable suspension in which any possible relief becomes a worthy antidote.

The stories and concerns of advocates of the wall suggest the wall is a response to an aspect of identity politics that holds their identity as moral and good (Cramer 2016; Hochschild 2016). Trump recognises their vulnerability and loss, and manipulates their desire for efficacy through their inclusion in the theatrical social performances ritualised throughout the primary and continued via Twitter (Szakolczai 2013, 2014). These performances afford them a role and a community as they in unison call to build a wall. Indeed, some of these rallies turned violent, mirroring the violence of both their crises' experiences and the virtual walls (Horvath 2007, 2008, 2010, 2015; Thomassen 2015). Although the social status of Trump supporters primarily relates to forces beyond migration, migration is seized upon because the strong state can more easily control the movement of individuals than job outsourcing and bank transactions. Thus, Trump responds to their personal experiences of chaos and crisis. Unlike Obama who focused upon felon Mexicans, Trump deems all Mexicans as dangers, and therefore justifies the impenetrable, full-length wall. Of course, the claims regarding rapists, felons and job losses are of themselves unreal. Yet the new 'unreal' reflects Trump's imagined nation and its core identity through the exclusion of outsiders. The real reclaiming of America's identity and greatness, however, is not possible through a walling which overlooks inherent weakness, and attributes all crises to scapegoats (Girard 1977, 1989; Szakolczai 2013). Real redressive action necessitates a movement to a new integration (Turner 1974).

Legal and institutional walls

In the United States, legal and institutional 'walls' in the form of visa quotas, refugee status requirements and deportation protocols complement physical border structures, and further emphasise the division of families and communities, the dehumanisation of individuals and the inner impulse for emancipation. Illustrative is the 2011 institution of the Consequence Delivery System intended to punish migrants. The objective was to create an unforgettably miserable deportation process to deter future entry efforts. The associated Operation Streamline's mass trials highlight the type of symbolic violence that now characterises the border control system (Lydgate 2010). The migrant defendants endure Kafkaesque experiences. Mass trials are held in which as many as 80 'criminal' migrants are simultaneously sentenced to deportation without benefit of translation. The outcome labels them as 'criminal' thereby denying them any future possibility of legal migration to the US. Migrants intentionally are returned to areas in Mexico far from their homes so they must seek assistance to survive and reach families. The deterrent aspect of deportation tactics weighs especially hard on women who often travel with children. Men and women apprehended together often are deported to different locales in Mexico. Sometimes deportees are sent to the most violent border areas (Slack et al. 2013: 33). People arrive in Mexico without identity documents, money or cell phones. They fit Turner's concept of liminal – disoriented, alone and in danger (Turner 1967, 1969).

Such border control and deportations inject people into precarious situations under the dubious promise of enhancing security. Indeed, while undocumented migration and border stops have declined, deportations have increased, creating serious strains in relationships because the Mexicans deported often have immediate family in the US, and in some cases no family in Mexico. A 2010–12 research project found that 75 per cent of deportees worked in the US for a median of seven years. At least half have a family member in the US, and 25 per cent leave behind a minor dependant in the US. Most consider the US their home (Slack et al. 2013). In the first three months of the Trump Administration, 67 per cent of deportees' only crime was the lack of documents. Yet, once deported these migrants have criminal records, and therefore can never obtain a legal visa to the US. If few Mexicans can obtain visas, and Mexicans without visas are illegal, that is criminal, so then Mexicans threaten security as criminal. The argument is virtually tautological. Essentially the security threat, the walled-out, the other must be a threat – if not what is the purpose of the border, the security state and national identity?

Additionally, walling creates a schismatic confusion (Bateson 1972) within the US as laws and policies among states, autonomous indigenous regions and cities vary. Certain locales seek to include migrants in society while other jurisdictions favour deportation. The liminal situation is particularly poignant in the borderlands where Fourth Amendment protections often are ignored, and citizens and non-citizens experience frequent checkpoints and administrative stops (Ewing 2014). Arizona passed very restrictive legislation governing migrants, but if a migrant without documents reaches New Mexico, he might qualify for state financial aid for college; in California, he also might qualify for health care and receive a driver's licence. Variation affects opportunities for Deferred Action for Childhood Arrivals (DACAs) the approximately 15 per cent of unauthorised migrants who arrived in the US as children, because only some states offer in-state university tuition. There are sanctuary states, counties, cities and universities across the US, which reject walling, refuse to use local resources to identify and detain migrants, and will not cooperate with federal immigration officials. Here new migrants blend into communities and access social services such that the immigrant and community both feel secure (Suro 2015). The existence of these sanctuaries recalls the possibility of womb-like walls, which both Horvath and Bowman in this volume discuss as a source of protection or exclusion, and Egor Novikov's Chapter 5 on Kalighat highlights as a place of compassion. Yet, legal experts now debate the legality of these sanctuary jurisdictions (Marzorati 2016). One consequence is that

advocates of sanctuary also become alienated; the very disharmony and fragmentation that walling claims to counter actually spirals for sanctuary communities
who experience Batesonian schismogenesis (1936) as they seek to create protective
spaces. The young people to whom DACA applies truly are liminal individuals
who exist in Turner's betwixt and between (1967). Ninety-five per cent are
employed, and almost half speak English well or exclusively (Warren 2016). They
perceive their identity to be American. Their ambiguous status (like that of the
Tejanos and border communities) problematises security technologies because
they ought not to be what they are, that is both temporarily included and permanently
other. Their temporary relief from deportation does not remove their illegal status,
or the stress they feel as liminal. Accepted as DACA, they now have registered their
liminality with the government, and revealed their parents' identities as 'illegal'
migrant. In exchange for a social security number, the right to work, and the right
to receive a driver's licence they have lost certain freedoms. They cannot leave the
country to visit deported family members, they lack an option for citizenship and
they must continue to reregister their liminal status in case DACA is terminated.

Furthermore, while Trump highlights the physical wall and deportation, he also
advocates the termination of birthright citizenship for the US-born children of
migrants. Trump refers to such individuals as 'anchor babies', a derogatory term
that dehumanises the child's existence to a weighted tool for their parents. Rhetoric
that suggests that birthright citizenship threatens US greatness not only scapegoats
migrants' children but also fails to address real challenges. The assumption is that
such legal walling will enhance security, but this arguably is a false assumption
because it neglects other sources of societal division and global and domestic
transformation the potential strength of which Marangudakis highlights in Chapter
8's discussion of Greek politics and economics.

Perhaps the most poignant example of the problem of walling is the case
of *Jesus C. Hernandez v. Jesus Mesa*, which the Supreme Court recently heard.
Sergio Hernandez, a 15-year-old Mexican and son of the petitioner Jesus
Hernandez, was playing with friends in a no-man's land between the territorial
lines of Mexico and Texas, when Mesa, a US border guard, fatally shot him in the
head. The case highlights the liminal perversion of space, identity and rights
associated with walling. Does any law apply in the space between borders, in the
void of the no-man's land? Did both Hernandez and Mesa lose identity in this
space? Mexican aliens in the US possess constitutional rights of due process
and against excessive force, but perhaps not in the in-between space. If Hernandez
was within either US or Mexican territory, he probably would not have died.
Additionally, a US District Court held his father could not sue in US courts because
the effect was felt in Mexico, not the US, and because Mesa was not a government
employee within the in-between space. Thus, a US government employee shoots a
teen in the head and the legal acceptance of walling and the void it creates allows
a judge to conclude there is no effect in the US. The event becomes unreal, as if it
did not occur because it exists in the neither-here-nor-there.

And what of border guard Mesa who, like many border agents involved in
shootings, is also of Latino heritage? Has his personal character succumbed to the

role he must play at the border? Slack et al. highlight the mentality of border guards who view migrants from a war combatant perspective as 'dangerous people and synonymous with terrorists' (Slack et al. 2016: 12). How do notions of citizenship, ethnicity, community and security associated with walling subordinate Mesa's identity and humanity to constructed borders that determine the limits of laws and rights? The violence of the border policy causes individual and communal trauma (Slack et al. 2016).

Walling and the transformation of nature

In between borders, the void overwhelms rights, identity and humanity, leaving space for unregulated violence and chaos. Walls constrain human emancipation, disrupt natural ecosystems and divide wildlife sanctuaries. Walls result in a very visible transformation of linear space with the potential to contribute to the extinction of animals and plants. The harmony of the cosmos is sacrificed, and the intricate beauty of the expanse is corrupted. Transformation via walling creates a disorder with consequences. Animals cross the US–Mexico border in search of food, water and mating habitats; some species seasonally migrate. The habitat range of some species due to the existing fence has decreased as much as 75 per cent, contributing to an increase in animal death caused by disease and dehydration, and the endangerment of more than 1000 species (Lasky et al. 2011). Additionally, animals often carry and distribute seeds throughout the region; obstruction of their migration constrains biodiversity and supports conditions for extinction (Bolstad 2017). Initially conservation groups successfully sued to stop walling of environmentally sensitive areas, but the US Department of Homeland Security then asserted the project's essentiality for security (Schlyer 2012; Felbab-Brown 2017).

The deadly consequence of heavy rains and flooding further demonstrates the potential devastation of efforts to wall nature. Floods in 2008, 2014 and 2016 had severe (including fatal) consequences for people and the environment as recently constructed border walls blocked the natural flow of rainwater. Sierra Club analyses contend even the limited and permeable wall has exacerbated erosion and sedimentation in the San Pedro Riparian National Conservation Area, Organ Pipe Cactus National Park and Otay Mountain Wilderness Area (2017). The problems the current fencing produce are probably minor compared with the environmental damage to which a concrete wall (without any openings) would create. A concrete wall could act like a dam, drowning whole communities during floods (Clarke 2016). The potential chaos due to a supposedly technologically sophisticated wall stands in stark contrast to the harmony of uninterrupted nature.

Moreover, technological questions exist regarding how the wall will be built in the Rio Grande River where the international border is in the middle, and shifting flows regularly alter the boundary. A wall might impede access to navigable river channels as flows shift. Further, the seasonal flooding and ebbing of the Rio Grande and Colorado rivers would affect about 1000 miles of the construction project. An alternative construction of a wall far enough from the flood plain of the Rio Grande would isolate on the Mexican side many US citizens who live between the river and the wall location (Wei-Haas 2017). Questions also concern the construction of a wall the 12-mile length of the US's Pacific Ocean territorial water. As Greek economist Varoufakis states regarding the existing beach barricade: 'Unable to build on sand, the fence builders planted cut-up pieces of railway lines into the white sand. Iron whose purpose was to connect peoples and places was cut up and used as a means of separating the inseparable' (2013). Construction will encounter serious engineering challenges, and if completed real security threats likely will use other technologies such as tunnels, drones and alternative sea routes, to circumvent the wall. Yet Trump and supporters of the wall dismiss such concerns because the wall as a technology has become not only a means to control borders but also an end of itself. If not a real means to American greatness, it nonetheless, as Grišinas discusses, serves as a symbol of such imagined identity.

The wall as an emotional response in a void

Thus, the process of walling and its concomitant creation of liminal space and identities perpetuate a range of negative consequences from which people already suffer. Trump's 'build that wall' is not original as an element of modern US policy, but is new in vehemence and scope. The urge to build an impenetrable full-length wall based upon claims of insufficient border controls and dangerous external environments, despite the reality of declining undocumented Mexican migration, primarily depends upon emotional appeal. Trump's slogans easily manipulate his most stressed supporters as he moves people already confused into a frenzy based upon irrational fears and promises. Indeed, many Americans, even among Trump supporters, appreciate that a wall is not the answer to challenges that confront security and prosperity (Suls 2017). Yet, Trump's election slogan focused upon making America great, regaining prosperity and security, and reclaiming its identity. Therefore, Trump needs a scapegoat, someone or some group that threatens identity, prosperity, security and greatness. The labelling of Mexicans as rapists, gang members, drug traffickers and murderers involves a scapegoating to provide an external explanation for the seeming demise of American mythical exceptionalism (Szakolczai 2013, 2014). While current crises constrain individuals in a liminality, Trump's use of political theatre offers a liminoid experience for ardent advocates of the walling technology. His theatrical drama and proposed technological solutions rely upon dichotomisation which he contends necessarily must precede the reconstruction of identity and return to the utopian America Dream.

Trump's wall conforms to the demands of such an ambitious transformation. The wall must be a transformation of space and relationships that surpasses previous border controls and fences. No one will climb through or over it; no one will tunnel under it. In part, this is symbolic: eliminate the porous character of the current fence and replace it with a solid structure to minimise the openings that allow for negotiated cross-border relations. Yet, the wall's unreality actually portends permanent jeopardy, and therefore permanent liminality and schismogenesis (Horvath and Thomassen 2008; Szakolczai 2017; Thomassen 2015). The promise of greatness exists as a deceptive illusion if it is secured and walled, without basis for comparison or challenge from external experiences and perspectives. Engagement with the world opens one to difficulty and conflict, but without engagement one also forgoes possibilities.

Moreover, walling disregards shared culture, values and history. The borderlands possess a complex history of mixed populations – indigenous, Latinos, blacks and whites – extolling a hardy individualism amidst efforts to balance self-reliance with community (Mennell 2015). The walling process represents a symbolic ritual to create a communal identity among its adherents, but within an unreal vacuum that ignores real overlapping and intersecting experiences. Walling overlooks the fact that iconic American companies such as Sara Lee and Weight Watchers are now Mexican-owned companies. Walling also neglects the fact that 70 per cent of guns seized in Mexico originate with US dealers – security is interdependent.

How, then, do these experiences, transformations and technologies affect US citizens? Do they become more secure if they live near a concrete wall that threatens them with flood water or soil erosion? Do they become great if they make strangers of neighbours who historically lived within the borders? How do indigenous people who also possess US citizenship avoid the liminality and loss of autonomy which walling introduces? What happens to the identity and security of Tejanos and anchor babies? How do members of sanctuary jurisdictions view their relationship to the federal government as the sanctuaries struggle and sue for the benefits and freedom of openness against the federal commitment to restrictive walls?

Walling offers an imagined identity and community as an alternative to other identities: of the United States as a shining light on a hill beckoning the ambitious, as a melting pot for peoples of good will, as the landscape for Horatio Alger, and as a country built through frontier hardy individualism and the manual labour of free workers. Walls, walling rhetoric and walling bureaucracies do not witness to the fortitude these identities embrace, but rather suggest a retreat into fortifications. Walls highlight limits and vulnerability rather than celebrating challenges and liberties. Walls do not transform spirits, but rather transform linear space, isolating people and disrupting ecosystems. Throughout the Trump campaign the embrace of a particular American identity gained momentum in response to real and imagined crises. Yet, the vision is not a vision consistent with exploration, enquiry, opportunity, harmony and liberty. The suspended reality that walling creates reinforces the notion of a sense of permanent impotence and threat which allows structures of state (concrete and legal walls) and their extensive bureaucracies to constrain individual activity. Amidst this liminality, some people believe themselves safer within walls than in an open and free environment. They prefer to secure the borders in reaction to growing challenges to global and cultural hegemony. Walls also necessitate, however, the forfeiture of independence to the police and security apparatuses at the costs of tax dollars and personal opportunities both to go beyond walls and bring others from the beyond. Extraordinary conditions now hold captive individuals confused about their own opportunities and identities. While President Trump might not actually construct a 2000-mile border wall, the acceptance of the need for legal, institutional and material walling freezes people – Mexican and American – into dichotomised communities and bounded spaces, and thereby limits possibilities of personal freedom and natural interaction.

Bibliography

Apter, D. (ed.) (2006) 'Politics as theatre: An alternative view of the rationalities of power', in *Social Performance: Symbolic Action, Cultural Pragmatics, and Ritual*, Cambridge: Cambridge University Press, pp. 218–56.

Baker, S. (2015) 'Effects of immigrant legalization on crime', *American Economic Review* 105(5): 210–13.

Bateson, G. (1936) *Naven: A Survey of the Problems Suggested by a Composite Picture of the Culture of a New Guinea Tribe Drawn from Three Points of View*, Cambridge; Cambridge University Press.

Bateson, G. (1972) *Steps to an Ecology of Mind*, New York: Ballantine Books.

Bolstad, E. (2017) 'The effects of building a massive concrete wall range from increased emissions to blocked wildlife migration routes', *Scientific America*, 26 January. Available at www.scientificamerican.com/article/trumps-wall-could-cause-serious-environmental-damage/. (Accessed on 23 February 2017.)

Boyce, G. (2015) 'The rugged border: Surveillance, policing, and the dynamic mentality of the US/Mexico frontier', *Environment and Planning D: Society and Space*, pp. 1–18. [Online] DOI: 10.1177/0263775815611423.

Campbell, D. (1998) *Writing Security: US Foreign Policy and the Politics of Identity*, Minneapolis, MN: University of Minnesota Press.

Clarke, C. (2016) 'Trump's border wall would be the world's longest concrete dam', *KCET*, 10 May. Available at www.kcet.org/redefine/trumps-border-wall-would-be-the-worlds-longest-concrete-dam. (Accessed on 12 December 2016.)

Cramer, K. (2016) *The Politics of Resentment: Rural Consciousness in Wisconsin and the Rise of Scott Walker*, Chicago: University of Chicago Press.

Customs and Border Patrol (2015) *United States Border Patrol: Sector Profile – Fiscal Year 2014*, Washington, DC: CBP.

Dunn, T. (1996) *The Militarization of the US–Mexican Border, 1978–1992: Low Intensity Conflict Doctrine Comes Home*, Austin: CMAS Books, University of Texas at Austin.

Ewing, W. (2014) 'Enemy territory: Immigration enforcement in the US–Mexico borderlands', *Journal on Migration and Human Security* 2(3): 198–222.

Eyerman, R. (ed.) (2006) 'Performing opposition or, how social movements move', in *Social Performance: Symbolic Action, Cultural Pragmatics, and Ritual*. Cambridge: Cambridge University Press, pp. 193–217.

Felbab-Brown, V. (2017) 'Why the border wall's costs far outweigh its benefits', *Brookings*, 30 January. Available at www.brookings.edu/blog/order-from-chaos/2017/01/30/why-the-border-walls-costs-far-outweigh-its-benefits/. (Accessed 23 February 2017.)

Gennep, A. van (1960) *The Rites of Passage*, London: Routledge.

Girard, R. (1977) *Violence and the Sacred*, Baltimore, MD: Johns Hopkins University Press.

Girard, R. (1989) *The Scapegoat*, Baltimore, MD: Johns Hopkins University Press.

Heyman, J. (2013) 'A voice of the US Southwestern border: The 2012 "We the border: Envisioning a narrative for our future" conference', *Journal on Migration and Human Security* 1(2): 60–75.

Hochschild, A. (2016) *Strangers in Their Own Land: Anger and Mourning on the American Right*, New York: The New York Press.

Horvath, Agnes (2007) 'The trickster motive in Renaissance political thought', *Philosophia* 52: 79–95.

Horvath, Agnes (2010) 'Pulcinella, or the metaphysics of the Nulla: In between politics and theatre', *History of the Human Sciences* 23(2): 47–68.

Horvath, Agnes (2015) 'The genealogy of political alchemy: The technological invention of identity change', in A. Horvath, B. Thomassen and H. Wydra (eds) *Breaking Boundaries: Varieties of Liminality*, New York: Berghahn Books, pp. 72–92.

Horvath, Agnes and Thomassen, Bjorn (2008) 'Mimetic errors in liminal schismogenesis: On the political anthropology of the trickster', *International Political Anthropology* 1(1): 3–24.

Lasky, J., Jetz, W. and Keitt, T. (2011) 'Conservation biogeography of the US–Mexico border: A transcontinental risk assessment of barriers to animal dispersal', *Diversity and Distributions*, 17: 673–87.

Lydgate, J. (2010) 'Assembly line justice: A review of Operation Streamline', *California Law Review*, 98(2): 481–544.

Martinez, D., Reineke, R., Rubio-Goldsmith, R. and Parks, B. (2014) 'Structural violence and migrant deaths in Southern Arizona: Data from the Pima County Office of the medical examiner, 1990–2013', *Journal on Migration and Human Security*, 2(4): 257–86.

Marzorati, L. (2016) 'Sanctuary cities under a Trump Administration', *Lawfare*, 23 February. Available at www.lawfareblog.com/sanctuary-cities-under-trump-administration. (Accessed 23 February 2017.)

Massey, D. (2015) 'How a 1965 immigration reform created illegal immigration', *The Washington Post*, 25 September. Available at: www.washingtonpost.com/posteverything/wp/2015/09/25/how-a-1965-immigration-reform-created-illegal-immigration/?utm_term=.6a161d242945. (Accessed 2 February 2017.)

Massey, D., Durand, J. and Pren, K. (2016) 'Why border enforcement backfired', *American Journal of Sociology*, 121(5): 1557–600.

Mennell, S. (2015) 'Liminality and the frontier myth in the building of the American Empire', in A. Horvath, B. Thomassen and H. Wydra (eds) *Breaking Boundaries: Varieties of Liminality*, New York: Berghahn, 112–29.

Passel, J. (2016) 'Overall number of US unauthorized immigrants holds steady since 2009', *Pew Research Center*, 26 September. Available at www.pewhispanic.org/2016/09/20/overall-number-of-u-s-unauthorized-immigrants-holds-steady-since-2009/. (Accessed on 2 January 2017.)

Petraeus, D. and Zoellick, R. (2014) *North America: Time for a New Focus*, New York: Council on Foreign Relations.

Schlyer, K. (2012) *Continental Divide: Wildlife, People and the Border Wall*, College Station, Texas: Texas A&M University Press.

Schmidt, S. (2016) 'A 75-mile-wide gap in Trump's wall? A tribe says it won't let it divide its land', *The Washington Post*, 15 November. Available at www.washingtonpost.com/news/morning-mix/wp/2016/11/15/a-75-mile-wide-gap-in-trumps-wall-a-tribe-says-it-wont-let-the-wall-divide-its-land/?utm_term=.dbd3d3c7d5fe. (Accessed on 22 February 2017.)

Scheler, M. (1973) *Formalism in Ethics and Non-Formal Ethics of Values: A New Attempt Toward the Foundation of an Ethical Personalism*, Evanston, IL: Northwestern University Press.

Sierra Club (2017) 'Damage caused by the border wall', *Borderlands*. Available at www. sierraclub.org/borderlands. (Accessed on 23 February 2017.)

Slack, J., Martinez, D., Lee, A. and Whiteford, S. (2016) 'The geography of border militarization: Violence, death and health in Mexico and the United States', *Journal of Latin American Geography* 15(1): 7–32.

Slack, J., Martinez, D., Whiteford, S. and Peiffer, E. (2013) *In the Shadow of the Wall: Family Separation, Immigration, Enforcement and Security: Preliminary Data from the Migrant Border Crossing Study*, Tucson, AZ: University of Arizona.

Slack, J., Martinez, D., Whiteford, S. and Peiffer, E. (2015) 'In harm's way: Family separation, immigration enforcement programs and security on the US–Mexico border', *Journal on Migration and Human Security* 3(2): 109–28.

Suls, R. (2017) 'Less than half the public views border wall as an important goal for US immigration policy', *Pew Research Center*, 6 January. Available at www.pewresearch. org/fact-tank/2017/01/06/less-than-half-the-public-views-border-wall-as-an-important-goal-for-u-s-immigration-policy/. (Accessed on 23 February 2017.)

Suro, R (2015) 'California dreaming: The new dynamism in immigration federalism and opportunities for inclusion on a variegated landscape', *Journal on Migration and Human Security* 3(1): 1–25.

Szakolczai, Arpad (2013) *Comedy and the Public Sphere: The Rebirth of Theatre as Comedy and the Genealogy of the Modern Public Arena*, New York: Routledge.

Szakolczai, Arpad (2014) 'Theatricalized reality and novels of truth: Respecting tradition and promoting imagination in social research', in M.H. Jacobsen, K. Keohane, A. Petersen and M.S. Drake (eds) *Imaginative Methodologies in the Social Sciences: Creativity, Poetics and Rhetoric in Social Research*. Farnham: Ashgate, 158–9.

Szakolczai, Arpad (2015) 'Liminality and experience: Structuring transitory situations and transformative events', in A. Horvath, B. Thomassen and H. Wydra (eds) *Breaking Boundaries: Varieties of Liminality*, New York: Berghahn, pp. 11–38.

Szakolczai, Arpad (2017) *Permanent Liminality and Modernity*, London: Routledge.

Szakolczai, Arpad and Bjorn Thomassen (2011) 'Gabriel Tarde as political anthropologist', *International Political Anthropology* 4(1): 43–62.

Tarde, Gabriel (1903) *The Laws of Imitation*, New York: H. Holt & Company.

Thomassen, Bjorn (2014) *Liminality and the Modern: Living Through the In-Between*, Farnham Surrey: Ashgate.

Thomassen, Bjorn (2015) 'Thinking with liminality: To the boundaries of an anthropological concept', in A. Horvath, B. Thomassen and H. Wydra (eds) *Breaking Boundaries: Varieties of Liminality*, New York: Berghahn, pp. 39–58.

Turner, Victor (1967) 'Betwixt and between: The liminal period in *rites de passage*', in *The Forest of Symbols*, New York: Cornell University Press.

Turner, Victor (1969) *The Ritual Process: Structure and Anti-Structure*, Chicago: Aldine.

Turner, Victor (1974) *Dramas, Fields, and Metaphors: Symbolic Action in Human Society*, Ithaca, NY: Cornell University Press.

Turner, Victor (1975) *Revelation and Divination in Ndembu Ritual*, Ithaca, NY: Cornell University Press.

Turner, Victor (1982) *From Ritual to Theatre: The Human Seriousness of Play*, New York: Performing Arts Journal Publications.

Turner, Victor and Turner, Edith (1978) *Image and Pilgrimage in Christian Culture*, New York: Columbia University Press.

United States, Immigration and Customs Enforcement (2015) 'DHS releases end of fiscal year 2015 statistics', *Official Website of the Department of Homeland Security,*

22 December. Available at www.ice.gov/news/releases/dhs-releases-end-fiscal-year-2015-statistics. (Accessed on 23 February 2017.)

United States, Immigration and Customs Enforcement (2016) 'DHS releases end of fiscal year 2016 statistics', *Official Website of the Department of Homeland Security*, 30 December. Available at www.ice.gov/news/releases/dhs-releases-end-fiscal-year-2016-statistics. (Accessed on 23 February 2017.)

Varoufakis, Y. (2013) 'US–Mexico border', *The Globalising Wall*, Chapter 8, Vital Spaces. Available at www.vitalspace.org/chapter-8-us-mexico-border. (Accessed on 23 February 2017.)

Walsh, D. (2016) 'The wall is a fantasy', *The New York Times*, 14 October. Available at www.nytimes.com/2016/10/16/opinion/sunday/the-wall-is-a-fantasy.html. (Accessed on 1 November 2016.)

Warren, R. (2016) 'US undocumented population drops below 11 million in 2014, with continued decline in the Mexican undocumented population', *Journal on Migration and Human Security* 4(1): 115.

Wei-Haas, M. (2017) 'What geology has to say about building a 1000 mile border wall', Smithsonian.com, 7 February. Available at www.smithsonianmag.com/science-nature/vast-geological-challenges-building-border-wall-180962072/. (Accessed on 23 February 2017.)

Weldes, J., Laffey, M., Gusterson, H. and Duvall, R. (1999) *Cultures of Insecurity: States, Communities, and the Production of Danger*, Minneapolis, MN: University of Minnesota Press.

White House (2006) *Fact Sheet: The Secure Fence Act of 2006*, 26 October. Available at: https://georgewbush-whitehouse.archives.gov/news/releases/2006/10/20061026-1.html. (Accessed 2 February 2017.)

Conclusion

Agnes Horvath, Marius Ion Benţa
and Joan Davison

The first thing about walling we noticed was its puzzling uniqueness: it was invented at a certain point in history and under particular circumstances. This uniqueness incorporates both the fact that walling was unique, in terms of its structure, and the manner of this uniqueness: it set in motion a moulding process. Walling as destiny served primarily as a form of protection, but mainly by intersecting hopes, desires and beliefs into the texture of a solid substance. The architectural complex that constituted the Great Wall of China was meant to control and limit foreign incursions, the Palestinian wall was meant to protect the Jewish communities by containing Palestinians, whereas the Berlin Wall was meant to separate Germans from other Germans, and the Mexican wall against the migrants appear to curve around the protected. This led us to the problems of walling itself. But was the intention behind constructing walls merely defensive? What is the relationship between the external and internal impacts of walls? Were walls built to exclude or, quite on the contrary, to enclose? These were some of the questions that needed to be approached from the perspective of political anthropology, as the more one looks closely at the phenomenon of walling, the more certainties dissipate and question marks multiply.

The theme of walling includes a multiplicity of forms of social experience and political usage, not limited to the case of concrete physical walls, but including walling in a metaphorical sense, such as the lightweight and modular Chinese painted screens, empty spaces, such as ditches, finger fluting or the ancient *pomerium*; physical or symbolic barriers that separate wealthy residential areas from the poor neighbourhoods in some cities; or even walls that have no physical or symbolic appearance at all and existed only in the minds or the behaviour of people, such as religious or magical conceptions related to impure or sacred areas that must be avoided by ordinary people, or could be done artificially, as for example in Mother Teresa's hospice. At the same time, walling needs not be limited to our experience of space, as it could include barriers that were at work at the level of sociality or political identity. The caste system in India, the ban on intermarriages in Ezra's time in ancient Israel, or the barriers of language or culture between two communities that share the same area also could have been be seen as forms of the transcendental meaning of walling as destiny.

Since the moment they are being built, walls are enshrined in enormous, truly mind-boggling paradoxes – only intensifying in our own times, literally with every day. Walls are supposedly built in order to defend those enclosed, yet at the same time they might serve to imprison the people they are supposed to serve – a switch-over that might happen suddenly, almost any minute. They are supposed to keep away intruders, yet their very existence calls attention to whatever is contained behind them, thus, far from discouraging invaders, only incites their appetite. Movements that supposedly came into being to liberate the people from all kinds of yoke, like communism, soon after gaining power transmogrify all kinds of walls and borderlines into tools to keep the people under their control enslaved. Self-proclaimed liberals promote the ideal inside by trying to keep, at any cost, everyone outside from entering. The more borders are eliminated in some places in the name of universal ideals, the more they are mushrooming, and being policed, elsewhere. And the list, from the chapters of this volume and from outside, can be continued, practically without end.

The paradox can be explained with the help of the term 'liminality'. Walls, borders and boundaries are limits that try to separate two or more areas, dividing up the space, eliminating the very possibility of undesirable movements; but by their very construction, physically or in mentality, they generate liminal places that call for increasingly strict and rigid but also increasingly impractical and impossible separations. Walls do not offer a solution, least of all for a liminal problem, as they instead inaugurate and/or escalate a play with liminality by re-inserting the cause of the problem/disease as the purported solution. Once walling emerged in history, and especially once the escalating movement of linear transformation was set in motion, decent existence could only be preserved, or restored, by keeping the practice limited by holding the sizes of enclosed entities relatively small, and having certain background coherence that offered stability, rendering dignified life possible, and assuring that internal cohesion was not assured by the mere fact of walling, or technical and institutional mechanisms to secure internal cohesion, but generally valued cultural practices shared by community members who personally were acquainted and familiar with each other. Yet, in liminal crises, especially if the cultural unity underlying cohesion became threatened or even undermined, there was always the danger of a new escalation of walling and the dysfunctional linear transformation produced by it.

Walling never offered a stable, lasting solution to any crisis, yet it becomes again and again re-proposed as the way out of almost any liminal crisis situation and never more than in the modern world, especially intensifying in our own days. We moderns fancy ourselves as having built the most advanced, purportedly most 'rational' world that ever existed on this planet, and yet in the case of a crisis – which, to begin with, in our 'enlightened' and rational world should not even exist, as modern economic and political theories argue that in a 'rational', free economy and a 'rational', democratic political system crises simply cannot emerge – the only idea we can come up with is to use a quarantine-type system set up in the Middle Ages to deal with plague. Thus, modernity clearly has a certain knowledge deficit, and this is connected to the knowledge of liminality; a knowledge connected to the flux. Such knowledge is indeed paradoxical, as it is a kind of non-knowledge, or at least a knowledge that should not be divulged or named. In another terminology, developed in contemporary social and cultural anthropology, such knowledge is possessed and mobilised by tricksters, can be deployed under liminal conditions, and carries the ultimate danger of transforming liminality into a permanent condition.

The essays in the volume, as least most of them, converge around the idea that this is indeed the case of our contemporary modern global world; that our existence is indeed being transformed into a paradoxical situation of perverted liminal transformation; and the idea of constructing walls, whether in physical reality or mentally, is a central aspect of this process. Rational thinking, as it is understood in the footsteps of Kant, and institutional arrangements cannot deal with this problem, as they rather are parts of this very, dysfunctional linear transformation logic. This is particularly evident in the case of the European Union, fully trapped inside rational institutional Kantianism, but in this respect the situation is by no means different in North America.

Of crucial importance is the problem of the relationship between walling and liminality. As we noted, walling is essentially a spatial experience, given that a wall is first of all a physical object with a definite spatial location. If one raises a wall in the middle of an area, one automatically transforms that zone into a liminal, in-between space, as was shown by Göbekli Tepe in southern Turkey, through Eastern and Southern European examples, the US–Mexican wall, and others. However, the notion of liminality in anthropology refers mainly to temporal experiences, as it originated in the rites of passage in traditional societies. A liminal experience is one that can bring about, in the course of a linear transformation, a change in the condition of an individual or a community; it is not only transitional, it effectively transforms. Thus, one could speak of three forms of liminality: spatial liminality (such as the areas in the proximity of a wall or a frontier), temporal liminality (such as the periods of transition in the life cycle, or the sacred time as opposed to profane time in traditional societies) and social liminality (such liminal figures as the foreigner, the trickster, the Samaritan, etc.). Yet, this distinction is just an apparent one, because most often spatial, temporal and social liminalities in their intersecting purpose go hand in hand and cannot be dissociated.

To understand the place of walling in the transforming of the individual, we needed to cast a glance at the modern conception of the state, which was largely influenced by the individualism of Thomas Hobbes and other thinkers, who sought to disconnect governance and sovereignty from character and root them in the 'people'. Hobbes's individualism stemmed from his separation of 'inward' and 'external', and led him to the idea of separating political and religious institutions. For him, humans are evil beasts driven by egoistic and passional desires, intolerance, power struggles and fear, and for this reason the world finds itself in a perpetual civil war (*bellum omnium contra omnes*), a war that was deeply rooted in human nature, as it was said. For this reason, it must be the exclusive duty of the state to govern people through proper laws and to reach the desideratum of peace, which otherwise cannot be attained. The state was seen as a transformative machine, and no transformation can take place without a process of divine interference; thus, Hobbes smuggled back inside the state what he previously excluded. This view paradoxically came in line with other philosophical conceptions that are part of a larger 'project of autonomy' of the human being, as Castoriadis called it, where one could add Pascal's conception of the solitude of man in the universe, Descartes' *cogito*, which later inspired the Husserlian project of founding intersubjectivity upon subjectivity, the whole project of mechanicist physics that saw to find laws that permit us to determine the behaviour of complex systems based upon the rules of behaviour and interaction that regulates elementary particles, and so on. This culminated in Durkheim's idea of society itself being divine.

Modernity has moved roughly along the path of this linear transformativity, which can be summarised in the following points: (1) the self (either individual or collective) was an entity disconnected from its previous character and propelled in its movement by its own attitude and desires; (2) the present was in constant progress, which manifests itself as a perpetual inflationary movement: the present constantly devalues its past (Horvath and Szakolczai 2018); (3) the whole was determined by its parts in an alchemical manner, and complexity emanates from, and was being founded upon, the elementary bricks of nature which themselves emanate or were founded upon the divine. Epistemologically, this perspective has invited scientists and philosophers to look everywhere for the foundational bricks of reality, to identify those elementary bits that, multiplied and combined together against the background of a 'tabula rasa', can help them re-create and reconstruct the image of the world. In this view, evolution and order could occur 'spontaneously' (see Wydra 2015: 62), the inferior precedes the superior (i.e. the complex) and the self's main political drive was to master or to conquer its environing world. Thus, the essence of the self was best described using the abstract image of Leibniz's monad, the thinking ego who meditated on his/her own existence and the existence of the world. In this way, slowly, an entire unreal, synthetic world was built around us.

The problem with this view of the self resided in its self-sufficiency. It saw community as based upon individuals who take precedence over plurality and saw discourse as emanating from identity poles and being absorbed and reflected by other monads. In other words, community lived in the Girardian logic of desire and the Hobbesian logic of appetite, which are reflective and mimetic.

Walling like every matrix is first and foremost the emission of a new structure; an encystation. It renders a new form-structure physically visible, so every walling starts by an interruptive phase that emerges out of the climax of liminality. An interruption breaks, intersects and thus multiplies. However, each multiplicity could cross over into another given multiplicity, constituting a transformation without a genealogy, operating instead by assimilation, union or occupation. It is a mechanism, where things are not moving themselves, but rather in an automatic dynamism are moved by the previous and move the next thing; a sensual unifier, yet a devilishly productive institution.

Visibly, something went wrong with walling, because since its first application an infinite sequence of deep and ever deeper crises occurred, with the enormous anomalies of disastrous developments that ruled over man, who was losing the strength of *agon*. The term *agon* – combat, struggle or contest in Greek – implies a force, a power, an effort, a contest for the good, for which Plato used the metaphor of wrestling (*Laws* 796A–B), and which was also central for Huizinga's foundational anthropology of play in *Homo Ludens*, as playful con-testing. It was also described by Foucault (1982: 222): 'Rather than speaking of an essential freedom, it would be better to speak of an "agonism" – of a relationship which is at the same time reciprocal incitation and struggle.' But this walling and moulding mechanism was built on the weakness of man, who fails to have trust in his own and others' properties, following solely the appetite. Walling is a confiscation, but confiscating others eventually grew into a utilitarian universalism, where enclosure within walls jointly stimulated a spirit of entrepreneurship and conquests, strengthening an insular community spirit (at the expense of other communities), and the satisfaction of sensuals. As a result of the walls, energy was entrapped, accumulated, and thus eventually had to be oriented in an aggressive manner towards the outside.

A situation of breakdown produces feelings and experiences that are easily intelligible. Whoever became walled will be the next wall-builder in the linear transformation process, which they now spread across borders, as a disease, replacing gift-giving, wealth, health and the good (*res* in Latin), the very orbit of reality. If such emotional appeal of contentment in our life is lost, we also lose our sense of reality, because reality cannot be anything else than itself – perfect in its completeness, forming this same substance ever and again in all beings who do not differ in their contest for goodness. Natural order is real in that it continuously gives without needing to receive. Something is either real or false, there are no other alternatives 'in between' the two.

The building of walls only ever produces illusory, ostensible, virtual results. The wall closes off, blocks and obstructs, making one blind to whatever is left outside and ignores what these others intend to reciprocate. The concrete as the token of reality evaporates, fading away, as a purportedly universal solution is offered to any delicate question. The wall blocks our abilities that are necessary for a proper living: to look around, to perceive, to comprehend, to investigate, to search for understanding and explanation; instead, it is a caving in. It produces a paranoid vision of the world, in which whatever falls outside the wall is transmogrified and demonised into something threatening and terrifying, justifying the ever renewed and necessarily failing efforts to annihilate it.

Bibliography

Foucault, Michel (1982) 'The Subject and Power', in H. Dreyfus and P. Rabinow, *Michel Foucault: Beyond Structuralism and Hermeneutics*, Chicago: University of Chicago Press.

Horvath, Agnes and Arpad Szakolczai (2018) *Walking into the Void: A Historical Sociology and Political Anthropology of Walking*, London: Routledge.

Wydra, Harald (2015) *Politics and the Sacred*, Cambridge: Cambridge University Press.

Index

nomadic people 45, 122, 124–6, 132–3; threat 45, 122, 124–6, 132–3
normativity 161
Novikov, Egor 4, 16, 33, 140, 179

oikodoméō 60–1
Old Testament 37–8, 50, 64, 69; *see also* Bible
ombilicus mundi 64
omphalos 56, 58–61, 63–6
'open female' image 29
Orbán, Viktor 158–9, 168
Orbetello 44
Oslo accords 81, 86
Otranto 44
outsiders 2, 66, 171, 173–5, 177–8; *see also* identities, limbo
Oxbridge 48

pain 4, 17, 19, 28–30, 102–3, 137, 142, 149
Palaeolithic 23, 28, 35, 43, 45–6, 58; caves 14, 17, 22–3, 38; finger fluting 8; homology 25
Palestine 7, 38, 41, 76, 80, 82, 88; communities 76–7, 79–80, 82–3, 85–6, 161
Palestinian National Authority (PNA) 81–3
Palestrina 43
Panopticon 12
paralysis xv, 17, 68, 162
Pascal, Blaise 191
passage 21, 23, 54, 64, 67, 86, 90–1, 95, 110, 190; *see also* rite of passage
passionate interests 18
Patočka, Jan 70
Paul (Saint) 60
Pech-Merle 29, 33
Pelasgians 43–4
Pelasgiotis 44
Pentateuch 55
Pergouset cave 33, 51
perversion xvii, 7, 13, 15–16, 22, 27, 30, 32, 42, 66
Phaedrus (Plato) 8
Philebus (Plato) 15
philosophy 54; neo-Kantian 47; political 153; postmodern 93
Phoenicia 42
Physics (Aristotle) 5, 12–13, 25
pilgrimage 46, 58, 97, 138
pilgrims 43, 98
pillars 37, 40, 58, 81; megalithic 37–8
Pizzorno, Alessandro 47, 52
plague 108, 128, 189

plan(ning) 1, 31, 33, 39, 41, 44, 46–8
Plato 8, 11–13, 15–17, 19, 22–3, 27, 32, 34, 44, 63
police 47–8, 77, 82, 142, 147–8, 183
Polignac, François de 43, 45, 52
political imagination 107, 112, 119, 162
politicide 83
politics 1, 3, 8, 47, 118, 121, 161, 163, 165; contemporary 156, 166; international 119
politics of death 80–1
pomerium 3, 92
populist(s) 146–7, 163
Portoghesi, Paolo 52
power: authoritative 151; controlling 16; divine 60; foreign 115; individual 18; inner 11; matrixing 3; political 59, 61–2, 65, 129, 139, 150, 157, 161; protective 79; transformative 104, 130
prehistory 122
primordial 37, 57, 139
prison(er) 2, 36, 38, 40, 46, 48, 68, 75, 78–9, 113
profit 19, 21, 130
progress 11, 13, 45, 49, 65, 120, 123, 132, 156; industrial 65; technological 113; transformative 16
Prometheus 61
promised land 144, 149
propaganda 111
prostitution, sacred 43
protection, walls 85, 129
Prussia 47–8, 119
public sphere 62, 137, 140, 146, 149, 161
pulsation 6, 104
Pygmies 2

racialised profiling 79
ratio 164; *see also* rational(ity)
rational 164–5
rational(ity) 7, 50, 127, 162
rational choice 97
rational individual 20–1
rationalism 91, 103
reality 29, 32, 39, 48, 56, 59, 90–1, 113–14, 116, 118; political 164; second 112, 115; virtual 161; *see also* unreality
rebel 144; *see also* rebellion, ritualised
rebellion, ritualised 59
recognition 60, 63, 78, 86, 112, 116, 128, 148, 155, 164
Reformation 47, 102
refugees 7, 77, 83, 109, 137–47, 149, 152, 158–9, 168, 170; settlement quotas 159